The Power Platform Playbook for Digital Transformation

Implement strategy, automation, and AI for scalable digital transformation

Victor Dantas

Chris Huntingford

The Power Platform Playbook for Digital Transformation

Portfolio Director: Pavan Ramchandani

Relationship Lead: Uzma Sheerin, Larissa Pinto

Program Manager: Divij Kotian

Content Engineer: Gowri Rekha, Esha Banerjee

Technical Editor: Vidhisha Patidar

Proofreader: Esha Banerjee

Indexer: Manju Arasan

Production Designer: Prashant Ghare

Growth Lead: Priya Bhanushali

Production reference: 2121125

Published by Packt Publishing Ltd.

Grosvenor House

11 St Paul's Square

Birmingham

B3 1RB, UK.

ISBN 978-1-80512-139-8

www.packtpub.com

To my family – Edlene, Bea, Laura, and Lily. Edlene, your love and patience keep me going, through every late night and crazy idea. Bea, Laura, and Lily, you fill my days with laughter, curiosity, and the kind of wonder that reminds me why I do what I do. I love you, Dantas crew!

To Chris Huntingford and every contributor who made this book possible:

Chris, your energy and brilliance made this journey unforgettable. To everyone who shared their time, insights, and support – I am eternally grateful.

Thank you!

To the Power Platform community, my fellow MVPs, colleagues, and the incredible mentees of Zero To Hero: This book is as much yours as it is mine. Your passion, curiosity, and drive to push boundaries make this journey worth it. Thank you for the inspiration, the collaboration, and for proving time and time again that technology is most powerful when shared.
Keep building. Keep learning. Keep transforming.

- Victor Dantas

To my family – Nicolle, Lexi, Adam, and Lulu: Thank you for being so patient with me and for allowing me to do this. I love you very much! None of the things I do would be possible without you.

A huge shout out to Jason Earnshaw (my sense-maker) and the low-code mob (both past and present) at ANS Group. We came up with so many of these concepts together, we worked late, and then delivered them as a team! It has been an honor working with you.

To my incredible friends Dona, Will, Mark, Andrew, and Ana – thank you for helping me with this and for being hugely impactful in my tech career and life in general. I can't thank you all enough!

To my friend and absolute legend, Victor Dantas, its been incredible putting this book together with you and I'm so grateful for your insights and friendshhip! Thank you!

- Chris Huntingford

Contributors

About the authors

Victor Dantas

With over 25 years of experience, Victor Dantas is a pioneering force in digital transformation, blending deep technical expertise with a passion for empowering others. A five-time Microsoft MVP, he stands among a global community of experts shaping the future of Microsoft technologies. As the founder of Eyedeas Inc., Victor helps businesses navigate the digital age with Power Platform solutions that drive efficiency, innovation, and real-world impact.

Beyond his work in the tech world, Victor is an international thought leader and speaker, sharing insights on digital transformation with audiences across the globe. His influence extends beyond the stage – he's a dedicated mentor, guiding professionals and aspiring technologists through initiatives such as *Zero to Hero*, where he helps individuals unlock their full potential.

At his core, Victor is driven by a simple but powerful mission: to empower people – whether through technology, mentorship, or storytelling. When he's not shaping the future of digital transformation, he's a devoted husband and a proud father of three amazing girls, finding inspiration in family, community, and the pursuit of meaningful impact.

Chris Huntingford

Chris is an accomplished expert and proud self-proclaimed geek in the Microsoft ecosystem, with more than 15 years of experience in Dynamics 365 and the Power Platform. He is also a Microsoft Most Valuable Professional (MVP), Microsoft Certified Trainer, and one of a small group of Microsoft FastTrack Recognized Solution Architects. He is a seasoned global speaker and has made significant contributions to the tech community by regularly sharing his knowledge at major events. Chris has a deep love for technology and enjoys delving into how technology can help people in their day-to-day lives.

Beyond work, he is known for his love of art, guitar, exercise, drumming, flamboyant shirts, global travel, and passion for social gatherings. He believes in the power of community and collaboration to achieve great things.

About the reviewer

Keith Atherton is a Power Platform Solution Architect, Microsoft MVP for Business Applications, Microsoft Certified Trainer (MCT), published LinkedIn Learning instructor, Power Platform Community Super User, public speaker, Power Platform Community High Five user group founder, *On Air in the Cloud* podcast host, blogger, and mentor.

Keith has over 25 years international experience of leading and developing software solutions in permanent and contract roles for sectors including finance, legal, manufacturing, construction, game development, retail, healthcare, travel, and charity.

Keith is based in Scotland, enjoys illustration and painting, and can be contacted at `https://linktr.ee/keithatherton`.

Join our community on Discord

Join our community's Discord space for discussions with the authors and other readers:

`https://packt.link/powerusers`

Table of Contents

6

Orchestrating Success: Key Considerations for a Digital Transformation Strategy Using Power Platform   109

7

Collaboration and Change in Digital Transformation   135

8

Power Platform Solutions for Digital Transformation   159

9

Streamlining Operations: Automating Processes with Solutions Built with Power Platform 183

10

Fortifying the Foundation: Integrating Systems, Ensuring Governance, and Security 207

14

Tracking Success Measures: Monitoring Progress and Achieving Objectives   277

15

Embracing AI-Powered Copilots and Agents in Digital Transformation   293

16

Preface

Welcome to a transformative journey with *The Power Platform Playbook for Digital Transformation*!

If you're eager to recognize Power Platform as a strategic ally in your business's digital transformation, you're in the right place. Imagine empowering everyone in your organization to quickly solve problems using technology, driving innovation and efficiency across the board. This book is your guide to enabling that exciting transformation in a safe and reliable way.

Today's organizations are on the lookout for innovative ways to harness technology for growth, and we believe that Microsoft's Power Platform is the key. Whether you're an IT professional, a business analyst, a manager, a consultant, or an aspiring developer, this book offers valuable insights tailored just for you.

Before we dive in, it's helpful to have a basic understanding of business processes and technology concepts, particularly around Power Platform components such as Power Apps, Power Automate, and Power BI. Don't worry if you're not already an expert in cloud-based services; our journey together will guide you every step of the way!

What sets this book apart is its holistic approach. Rather than focusing solely on individual components, we'll explore how Power Apps, Power Pages, Power Automate, Copilot Studio, and Power BI work in harmony. You'll discover a unified framework for digital transformation that shows you how to streamline processes, automate workflows, and extract meaningful insights.

Our approach here is pragmatic, practical, and action-oriented. We blend theoretical concepts with real-world scenarios, offering you step-by-step guidance along with useful tips, best practices, and hands-on exercises. You'll find a treasure trove of practical examples and use cases designed to help you effectively leverage Power Platform for your digital initiatives.

We don't just skim the technical surface. We delve deeply into critical areas essential for successful implementation, including business process analysis, change management, governance, and security. By addressing these important aspects, we'll equip you with the skills needed to navigate the challenges that come with digital transformation.

By the time you finish this book, you will have a solid understanding of how to harness the Power Platform to drive valuable change in your organization. You'll walk away with practical tools, strategies, and insights to tackle complex business challenges and propel your organization into a successful digital future.

So, whether you're looking to enhance your IT skills, streamline processes as a business analyst, or lead digital initiatives as a manager, *The Power Platform Playbook for Digital Transformation* is here to empower you with the knowledge and resources you need to thrive in the digital age.

Let's embark on this exciting adventure together!

What this book covers

Chapter 1, Unleashing Transformation: Power Platform's Role in Digital Evolution, discusses Power Platform's key role in digital transformation and Microsoft's leadership in the low-code app and automation market. It highlights the co-pilot features developed with OpenAI, which simplify low-code development through AI, enabling easier application creation and process automation. The chapter provides insights for organizations looking to leverage Power Platform for innovation and growth.

Chapter 2, Gauging Growth: Assessing Digital Maturity for Strategic Advancement, discusses how assessing digital maturity is crucial for organizations using Microsoft's Power Platform. Organizations can be categorized into foundational, developing, advanced, and leading levels based on their proficiency. The Center of Excellence (CoE) evaluates maturity and sets best practices, while the Center for Enablement (C4E) improves user skills through training. Together, these resources help organizations enhance their digital capabilities and drive innovation within the Power Platform ecosystem.

Chapter 3, Unlocking Potential: Enhancing Operations with the Power Platform, looks at how Microsoft's Power Platform provides low-code/no-code tools that empower organizations to transform their operations. It enables both professional and citizen developers to create applications, automate processes, and analyze data quickly. Key tools include Power Apps for custom applications, Power Automate for task automation, and Power BI for data insights; all designed to enhance productivity and agility in a competitive digital landscape.

Chapter 4, Creating Your Center for Enablement, looks at the Center for Enablement (C4E) empowers individuals and teams in their digital transformation with the Power Platform by providing a supportive environment for innovation and exploration. Through training and resources, users enhance their skills in creating applications and automating processes. The C4E also fosters collaboration among diverse teams to tackle challenges, ultimately enabling organizations to drive meaningful change and thrive in the digital landscape.

Chapter 5, Executing and Scaling Transformation Initiatives, discusses how with an intuitive design, business users can easily prototype and deploy applications, while the platform allows for seamless scaling from small initiatives to enterprise-wide solutions. By integrating with Microsoft Azure, organizations can adapt and grow their solutions alongside evolving needs, driving meaningful change and innovation in their digital transformation efforts.

Chapter 6, Orchestrating Success: Key Considerations for a Digital Transformation Strategy Using Power Platform, looks at the three key stages when embarking on a digital transformation with Power Platform involves three key stages: Envision, Onboard, and Scale. In the envision phase, organizations should define clear goals, secure executive sponsorship, and develop an adoption strategy aligned with business objectives. It's vital to manage resistance, assess readiness, and implement training to empower employees. Addressing these aspects lays a strong foundation for a successful transformation journey.

Chapter 7, Collaboration and Change in Digital Transformation, highlights the importance of stakeholder analysis and change management in adopting Power Platform for digital transformation. It underscores the need for executive and managerial buy-in to empower citizen developers and discusses the roles of various stakeholders and the Microsoft Power Platform admin team. By fostering a culture of collaboration and learning, organizations can effectively leverage citizen developers to drive innovation.

Chapter 8, Power Platform Solutions for Digital Transformation, discusses how embracing the Power Platform is key for digital transformation, requiring an understanding of an organization's maturity level through the Capability Maturity Model Integration (CMMI). Organizations start at the initial level with limited success, then move to "Repeatable" with some controls, followed by "Defined" for standardized practices. At the "Capable" stage, they refine practices for critical applications, and finally, at "Efficient," they demonstrate the platform's transformative potential with expert support. Assessing maturity helps prioritize initiatives for early success and stronger leadership engagement.

Chapter 9, Streamlining Operations: Automating Processes with Solutions Built with Power Platform, discusses how in today's business landscape, automating processes is crucial for efficiency. Power Platform offers tools for task automation, with organizations focusing on repetitive tasks when choosing proof of concept candidates. Understanding Application Lifecycle Management (ALM) is important, and Microsoft's ALM Accelerator helps manage solutions effectively. New users can start with the Creator Kit for practical tutorials. Establishing key performance indicators will help measure success and optimize the benefits of Power Platform in enhancing operations.

Chapter 10, Fortifying the Foundation: Integrating Systems, Ensuring Governance, and Security, looks at the four stages of the CoE journey that organizations use to strengthen their technological foundation through a Center of Excellence (CoE) journey involving four stages: Secure (establishing a security framework), Evangelize (promoting security awareness), Monitor (detecting threats), and Evolve (continuous improvement). This approach ensures robust governance and protection of valuable assets in a dynamic tech landscape.

Chapter 11, Establishing Strong Foundations: Governance and Security in Power Platform Solutions, explains how governance and security in the Power Platform ecosystem are essential. Microsoft addresses these concerns with Data Loss Prevention (DLP) policies that protect data, tenant isolation that secures data flow, and specialized security roles such as the Power Platform admin for user control. By prioritizing these measures, organizations can effectively leverage Power Platform while safeguarding their data.

Chapter 12, Navigating Compliance: Meeting Industry Regulations in Power Platform Deployments, discusses how navigating compliance for Power Platform applications is crucial, and Microsoft's Trust Center offers key resources on security and privacy, with a focus on Power Apps. The platform features global data centers, allowing geo-specific environments and secure data transmission via encryption and TLS protocols. It provides tools for GDPR compliance and the Microsoft Purview Compliance Manager to streamline compliance management across Microsoft cloud services.

Chapter 13, From Metrics to Milestones: Measuring Success in Power Platform Initiatives, discusses how the Microsoft Power Platform transforms organizations with its low-code approach, enhancing productivity. Success relies on identifying relevant KPIs, establishing SMART benchmarks, and maintaining documentation for tracking progress, ultimately enabling transformative change.

Chapter 14, Tracking Success Measures: Monitoring Progress and Achieving Objectives, looks at how, to measure measure progress with the Power Platform, organizations should define KPIs and use surveys to assess user knowledge and satisfaction. Initial surveys identify starting points, while follow-ups after six months evaluate experiences and highlight improvement areas. Quarterly surveys can track user adoption and productivity, guiding informed decisions for optimization.

Chapter 15, Embracing AI-Powered Copilots and Agents in Digital Transformation, discusses how AI-powered copilots are transforming digital processes by enhancing user interactions and automating tasks. They boost productivity and improve organizational efficiency, enabling better collaboration. This accessibility empowers organizations to optimize operations and drive innovation.

Download the color images

We also provide a PDF file that has color images of the screenshots and diagrams used in this book. Please note that some images in this book are presented for contextual purposes, and the readability of the graphic is not crucial to the discussion. You can download the PDF here: `https://packt.link/gbp/9781805121398`.

Conventions used

The following text conventions have been used throughout this book.

Bold: Indicates a new term, an important word, or words that you see onscreen. For instance, words in menus or dialog boxes appear in **bold**. Here is an example: "**Power Automate** is a service that enables users to create workflows and automate tasks across different applications and services".

> **Tips or important notes**
> Appear like this.

Get in touch

Feedback from our readers is always welcome.

General feedback: If you have questions about any aspect of this book, email us at customercare@packtpub.com and mention the book title in the subject of your message.

Errata: Although we have taken every care to ensure the accuracy of our content, mistakes do happen. If you have found a mistake in this book, we would be grateful if you would report this to us. Please visit www.packtpub.com/support/errata and fill in the form.

Piracy: If you come across any illegal copies of our works in any form on the internet, we would be grateful if you would provide us with the location address or website name. Please contact us at copyright@packtpub.com with a link to the material.

If you are interested in becoming an author: If there is a topic that you have expertise in and you are interested in either writing or contributing to a book, please visit authors.packtpub.com.

Share Your Thoughts

Once you've read *The Power Platform Playbook for Digital Transformation*, we'd love to hear your thoughts! Scan the QR code below to go straight to the Amazon review page for this book and share your feedback.

https://packt.link/r/1-805-12139-1

Your review is important to us and the tech community and will help us make sure we're delivering excellent quality content.

Free Benefits with Your Book

This book comes with free benefits to support your learning. Activate them now for instant access (see the "*How to Unlock*" section for instructions).

Here's a quick overview of what you can instantly unlock with your purchase:

PDF and ePub Copies

Next-Gen Web-Based Reader

Access a DRM-free PDF copy of this book to read anywhere, on any device.

Use a DRM-free ePub version with your favorite e-reader.

Multi-device progress sync: Pick up where you left off, on any device.

Highlighting and notetaking: Capture ideas and turn reading into lasting knowledge.

Bookmarking: Save and revisit key sections whenever you need them.

Dark mode: Reduce eye strain by switching to dark or sepia themes

How to Unlock

UNLOCK NOW

Scan the QR code (or go to packtpub.com/unlock). Search for this book by name, confirm the edition, and then follow the steps on the page.

Note: Keep your invoice handy. Purchases made directly from Packt don't require one.

1

Unleashing Transformation: Power Platform's Role in Digital Evolution

In this chapter, we delve into the profound impact of Microsoft Power Platform in driving digital evolution and its role as a catalyst for transformative change. We explore the economic dynamics surrounding digital transformation and shed light on its far-reaching implications for organizations across industries. Specifically, we examine Microsoft's significant market share in the low-code app and automation development market, highlighting how Power Platform has emerged as a leading force in empowering businesses to navigate the digital landscape with agility and efficiency.

Moreover, we explore the latest advancements in Power Platform, particularly the copilot features developed in collaboration with OpenAI. These cutting-edge capabilities use the power of AI to revolutionize the low-code development experience, enabling users to create applications and automate processes with remarkable ease and speed.

By delving into economics, Microsoft's market position, and the innovative copilot features, this chapter provides valuable insights and guidance for organizations seeking to tap into the potential of Power Platform. It equips you with a comprehensive understanding of how Power Platform can be harnessed as a strategic tool to unleash transformation, drive digital innovation, and achieve sustainable growth in the evolving digital landscape. We will cover the following topics:

- Driving digital change with Power Platform
- Understanding economic forces in digital transformation
- Leading the low-code market with Microsoft
- Revolutionizing low-code development with AI Copilot
- Harnessing strategic growth with Power Platform

Driving digital change with Power Platform

Over a vast number of years, technology has gone through significant changes, which have transformed how society perceives it and its impact on our work and home lives.

Ultimately, innovation is going to happen regardless of what your perspective is on it or what you think. We have seen it in many, many different forms throughout history: cars, bicycles, food, drinks, medical advancements. Humans are naturally curious and want to optimize the way we do things, sometimes regardless of the impact, which could be either good or bad. To understand the digital evolution and transformative change of low code in general, and specifically, Power Platform, we need to explore what "innovation" really means and why it is important.

An example of innovation

One of my favorite analogies to help understand the shift in innovation as we see it today is the simple concept of farming. We all eat food, we all need food… farming is one of our primary sources of food, so it's extremely important.

Many years ago, and in some places still today, farmers would plant crops and then walk to a water source to collect water in buckets, then walk to where their crops were planted and manually water the crops.

This worked perfectly for a long time. However, further innovation was applied, and a less labor-intensive method for crop watering was applied. Horse-drawn carts were used to carry more loads of water to the fields. Crop plantations got larger because more water could be dispersed.

As progression continued, farmers realized that they could bring the water to the crops in an even more innovative manner by digging channels for the water to simply run through the fields. Instead of people carrying buckets or loading the horse and cart, they planned the flow of water and dug channels.

As time passed, the concept of water diversion became even more sophisticated, with farmers finding even better mechanisms to direct water. The planning took more time and irrigation experts were required to lay pipes, understand pressure, and equally disperse water.

Even larger fields of crops were planted because of this method of crop maintenance, and more people with many different skill sets needed to be employed to maintain and manage these fields.

The more we learn, the more we innovate, the faster we find smarter ways of making our more manual jobs a lot easier. In the future, there will be even more ingenious methods where farmers can maintain and manage their crops to feed the world.

The fact of AI-managed matter is that innovation is happening whether we like it or not. People will always find ways to do things smarter to save time and avoid manual work.

In this scenario, as time progressed, the people doing the work here: carrying buckets of water, leading a horse-drawn cart, watering crops, digging channels in fields, laying pipes, figuring out the pressure, programming computers to manage the flow of water; they all needed to learn. We aren't born with the understanding of how to carry a bucket or write code, we learn!

As time progressed, we learned how to innovate.

"Hey, maybe instead of carrying one big bucket, I could carry two medium-sized ones, which actually allows me to carry more water without spilling any." This has been happening for centuries and, of course, in the digital world as well.

Shift up to digital – the start

digital transformation is a young concept that has morphed rapidly over time. If we dial back the clocks to around 1990, when the first web browser was released, and around 1998, when Google was released to the public, there was a fundamental shift in the way people thought about developing easy-to-use solutions.

There was panic because many people thought that the concept of the World Wide Web search would ultimately take their jobs. Imagine what was going on in the minds of people who collated dictionaries and encyclopedias.

Another interesting example is that of when Excel was first released. There is a fantastic video that Microsoft released in 1990 that shows a few people in an elevator. One chap is holding what appears to be a large doorstop-sized laptop and is prepping his spreadsheet for a business presentation as the elevator reaches the top floor of a building. He seamlessly uses basic drag-and-drop functionality to generate a budget that looks "great."

You can watch the advert here: `https://www.youtube.com/watch?v=Ckr2mLXDw3A`.

Fine, I understand the advert is slightly tongue-in-cheek; however, imagine what would have been going through accountants' minds at this point.

The main thing to understand here is that encyclopedias still exist in hard, soft, and digital copies. People use search every day to help them, and Excel is still the world's most widely used accountancy tool. All we did was find ways to adapt to the technical changes that were happening.

In fact, 1990 to 2000 was a really important time, so much so that there was a lot of insecurity and fearmongering about job loss and technical revolution. The greatest example of this is the *"fear of the clock"*. What would happen if clocks ticked over from 1999 to 2000? Would all the computers break? What about our data? Ultimately, we were all fine, the computers didn't break, and we are still progressing perfectly up the innovation ladder.

Enter digital transformation

In around 1990, a person by the name of Mark McDonald, group vice president at Gartner, coined the term digital transformation. This was incredibly timely considering all the changes taking place in the 1990s. As the clocks ticked over, digital transformation started to solidify itself as one of the most widely used buzz phrases of the 20th century. Hundreds of organizations established digital transformation practices, rightly advising others to transform their operations by moving from manual practices to more streamlined digital processes.

This involved many facets, ranging from movement to cloud-based computing to process optimization and away from file and paper-based processes. The movement was and is huge and has become increasingly important as the era of enablement takes hold, and AI becomes more prominent in organizations.

Over a period of around 15 years, between 2000 and 2015, many solutions were created, a huge number of processes were optimized, and an extraordinary number of organizations understood that keeping up with technical and digital innovation was hugely important to their strategy and their growth, so much so, that the demands on IT became even more excessive. Organizations' IT teams were and still are not able to keep up with the demands made by the organizations themselves. In a nutshell, the challenges faced far outweighed the number of people who could solve them. This is known as **The Great Developer Shortage**.

Some organizations had and still have years and years of archaic processes to unpick, papers and files to digitize, and attitudes to change. There just aren't enough people and organizations around to help with this in such a short time. There are cases where nearly 100 years of history need to be unpicked, and this does not and cannot happen overnight. Cloud-based computing was already a huge cliff to climb, but completely digitizing an organization's landscape is an entirely new problem to solve. The reason for this is it's not just about technology; it requires the ability to redesign processes, understand people, and map these processes and people to a set of technologies that best addresses the challenge.

Enter low code

In around 2014, many of the leading research and development organizations started to spot the trend of there being a skills gap and a supply and demand challenge based on the number of organizations needing to transform. It is speculated that Forrester coined the term **low code** around 2014.

Essentially, the concept exists where vendors such as Microsoft, Google, Salesforce, and many others made changes to their platforms that allowed people to build and extend solutions without needing to write code. Previously to this, if you faced a business challenge and wished to solve it using technology, you could do the following:

- Buy an off-the-shelf solution
- Build a solution from scratch
- Extend these solutions through basic configuration and/or custom development

Now there are hundreds of software development and low-code platforms to speak of which allow people to create solutions rapidly. *Figure 1.1* shows a brief summary of some of the platforms available.

Figure 1.1: A collection of low-code platforms

Turnkey solutions

Turnkey solutions, such as **out-of-the-box customer relationship management solutions**, were a great start but didn't always fit the organization's requirements. Not every company in the world is the same. These solutions need to be extended and configured to cater to a specific requirement. Not every business requirement has a turnkey solution. The skills required to build and extend became hugely in demand and hard to find.

The vendors started working more and more on their base products, making them far easier to extend than before. The ability to configure or customize solutions without writing code became more commonplace. Tools such as Dynamics CRM and SalesForce allow field, table view, form, and dashboard configuration without the need to write any complex logic. This allowed many businesses the ability to configure base vendor-based solutions for their needs and ONLY extend through custom code where necessary.

Essentially, the more widely the vendor-based product could be configured without complex logic, the better. In fact, these products became so configurable that the term **xRM** was coined by several organizations that were delivering configured solutions, with the X representative of the X in algebra, where X could be anything. So, instead of **Customer Relationship Management**, organizations embraced **Anything Relationship Management** and, effectively, were extending and configuring their various tool sets a lot more than originally anticipated.

Solutions built from scratch

There are many other low-code development platforms to speak of; however, the most notable are as follows:

- **Mendix**
- **OutSystems**

Both organizations recognized the need for **Rapid Application Development** (**RAD**) based on the lack of development skills in the market, so both focused on providing tools to developers so that software solutions could be created and placed into production at a rapid pace.

Gartner releases a report each year talking about the trends and strategies companies who provide low-code platforms are employing. This report contains a growth indicator called the Gartner Magic Quadrant, which splits the platform providers into four categories: Niche Players, Challengers, Visionaries and Leaders. The Leaders quadrant being the top right and representative of the leading vendors. Both providers are found in the top-right quadrant of the Gartner reports, and both are extremely popular within organizations. It is very common to find a mixture of about three low-code platforms within an organization, and even more common that Mendix or Outsystems will be one of them.

Power Platform

Microsoft Power Platform is a set of low-code tools that enables makers of varying technical skill levels to create useful solutions that answer business challenges of varying complexity. Power Platform is Microsoft's ever-growing answer to RAD.

Power Platform was not created from the ground up. It was born from the Microsoft cloud and is a combination of various technologies that have been democratized in a manner that makes rapid application development available to anyone willing to learn.

Makers can manipulate, automate, analyze, and visualize data through multiple tools in the platform. As Microsoft evolves, so does Power Platform. There is a constant drive for innovation at Microsoft, and the more innovation takes place, the better the tools in Power Platform become. This makes it much easier to achieve results and reach the desired outcome with fewer clicks. The more instantly gratified we are, the better. *Figure 1.2* shows a summary of Power Platform components and how they relate to one another.

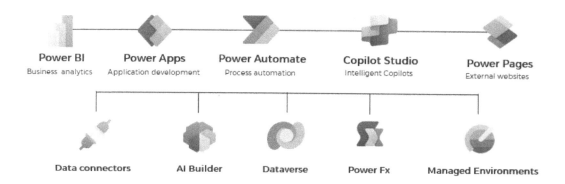

Figure 1.2: Summary overview of the Microsoft Power Platform

Often, when looking at the Microsoft Cloud stack, we can identify where various Power Platform products originated from and then have been expanded and grown to work with many of the other areas and products. *Figure 1.3* shows how Power Platform components actually have come from existing areas in the Microsoft stack.

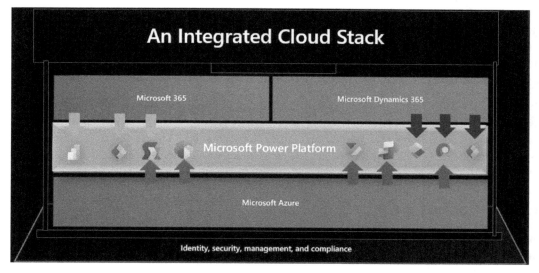

Figure 1.3: A summary overview of the Microsoft Cloud and how Power Platform fits in

As an example, Power BI originated from Microsoft Excel and from a product called **Power Pivot**. Excel had the ability to generate visualizations on top of data for several years. In order to drive a centralization of data into the cloud, this functionality was democratized into a cloud based visualization tool – Power BI.

Dataverse is a democratized data storage and governance facility and acts as the base for many of the Dynamics 365 products. Previously, this layer was known as xRM within the customer and partner community.

Ultimately, Power Platform works within Microsoft's integrated cloud and product stack, which is one of the main reasons it has such high adoption rates.

The world around us is changing rapidly, and this is evident in the technology trends we have seen in the past and the trends we are currently seeing. We need to learn to change with these trends and to learn. We now understand that there is a huge opportunity for all of us to learn and change the way we do things and start using low code as a mechanism to work faster. We have all been using low-code tools a lot longer than we probably realize. In the past, having the ability to use Microsoft tools such as Office, Azure, and Dynamics 365 has equipped many people with the tools to build useful solutions with Microsoft Power Platform. In the next section, we will take a look at the economic dynamics of digital transformation and how they have influenced various aspects of society.

Understanding economic forces in digital transformation

There are hundreds of economic dynamics of digital transformation and with the introduction of low-code platforms and AI, the drive towards transforming digitally even more quickly has become a real focus across all organizations. Organizations that established a digital transformation strategy early on and actually allocated budgets to changing the way they work are forging ahead of many others and establishing a more dominant position in the market. Organizations that have not seen digital transformation as a priority may suffer from a productivity and growth perspective.

The output is relatively simple; organizations that are digitally equipped will serve their customers faster and more accurately with less need for process and manual work. The classic example is that instead of manually building a document, have your CRM system do it for you and auto-share it with your customer. That may eliminate 30 minutes of work from a specific individual each time. If we took it to the metric of money, how much money do we save by doing X? It is possible to work this out.

But what about my job?

The hyper progression of technology and its place in society can be quite tough to consume because the person building the documents may be at risk as they will be outperformed by the person who understands the CRM system that is making the documents.

This is going to be similar for people using AI. AI will not take someone's job; the person who understands AI might take someone's job.

Companies at the forefront of innovation will have more time to transform their ways of working and train their teams to use the tools, be more productive, and quite simply outperform other organizations.

As mentioned in the analogy of the person watering the crops, there will need to be a lot of learning that takes place and, most importantly, space for learning. Organizations will need to assign learning time to people and ensure that there are metrics in place that cater to this. Reskilling and upskilling are important.

Digital inequality

The fact of the matter is that the more the organizations who are in front spend time in front, the worse off it will be for people in other organizations. They will ultimately earn less money, spend more time doing things they don't want to do, and will feel the effect of digital inequality.

This happens when there is no clear visibility of the future and disengagement at a leadership level from a technology and business perspective. It will lead to things such as **Silent Quitting** and **The Great Resignation**, where people ultimately shift gear to move roles to places where they will be more effective and ultimately get paid more.

This mass shift is not good for organizations that are less innovative as they will struggle to hire and provide their services.

Who fixes the machines?

In any scenario where there is innovation, there is not always job loss, but often there is job creation. In a world of innovation, new skills need to be acquired. The analogy of a toothpaste factory comes to mind.

Person X works at the toothpaste factory screwing on toothpaste caps. A machine is implemented to screw on toothpaste caps at double the speed of the humans. The machine breaks. Who fixes the machine?

Well, of course, the human who was screwing on the toothpaste caps understands how the caps need to be screwed on and what the machine needs to do; they just need to learn how the machine works.

The concept is common across society and is a primary focus on the economic dynamics of digital transformation. Growth in transformation requirements across organizations will require new skills, transferable skills, and upskilling.

In the world of low code, we see the likes of bus drivers, windscreen repairers, safety administrators, and pro developers learning how to use Power Platform to upskill and help their businesses by building business solutions to solve problems that previously were managed manually and were not optimized.

The rules

This is a fundamental shift in thinking because there is absolute surety that as the digital landscape changes, so do the rules and laws around the security of data and how we govern this data. Data is the digital footprint of ourselves and our company and processes. If data is disrespected, it can be used for nefarious purposes.

Organizations will need to take a new approach to how security and governance are perceived and, again, think of how to drive their current workforce into a more well-structured compliance machine. This will become far more relevant as AI starts moving into organizations and acts as a loud hailer for terrible data and security. Compliance managers will need to become digital compliance managers. Health and safety managers will now have a significant digital tone to their roles. When laws are made, they will require some level of digital literacy.

Look at the **General Data Protection Regulation (GDPR)**, a law that took effect in around 2018 that legislated how data needs to be treated when any organization is dealing with data from an organization within the European Union.

There was a lot of preparation done by organizations and many organizations employed a Chief Data Officer and a data team to ensure that the rules were respected. This led to an entirely new set of transformative offerings and processes that organizations needed to implement.

It's the right time all the time

It's important to understand that, often, innovation and transformation happen to us rather than for us. We are shifting tones now into an era of enablement, where we are far more in control of how we innovate and transform! It is very important to understand that waiting is not an option in this scenario! The waves between changes in the digital world are getting smaller and smaller and more rapidly, so if you are thinking about the right time to do anything, it's now, so just do it and get on board.

Those that prioritize digital transformation allocate budgets, and establish a strategy will have a competitive advantage. digital transformation allows organizations to serve their customers faster and more accurately, with less manual work. However, those who do not prioritize will suffer from a productivity and growth perspective. The importance of upskilling and reskilling employees to keep up with the digital changes needs to become an area of investment for all companies. Organizations must take a new approach to security and governance and prioritize compliance and digital literacy. We cannot ignore innovation and growth, and this must become a significant area of focus within businesses that want to grow and succeed. In the next section, we will take a look at how Microsoft helps us drive transformation and innovation forward in an inclusive manner.

Leading the low-code market with Microsoft

What has become incredibly clear is that Microsoft has become one of the primary leaders within the low-code space. Typically, they can be seen in the Gartner top-right quadrant with the following:

- Mendix
- Outsystems
- ServiceNow
- Salesforce
- Appian

The six leading vendors typically shuffle around a fair amount, depending on their ability to execute the creation and implementation of solutions and their completeness of vision.

There are a few things that make Microsoft a clear leader, but one of the main things that makes Microsoft a front-runner is how Power Platform has been positioned alongside the rest of its products. When many of the Microsoft Cloud products are purchased, such as M365, Dynamics 365, and Azure Services, Power Platform comes as part of the package as a seeded license.

When Dynamics 365 is purchased, it is effectively a collection of complex Power Apps (Model-Driven App), which includes Power Automate Cloud Flows as the workflow and process automation engine.

When an organization purchases Office 365 E5, there are levels of Power Apps and Power Automate that are included with the license, so makers could make Power Apps and Power Automate Flows part of their day-to-day business productivity processes.

There are 1.2 billion users of Microsoft Office around the globe, and that implies there are 1.2 billion Power Apps and Automate users of varying levels. Power Platform products are extremely popular with the Microsoft Office community because they add to the business and personal productivity landscape of products.

Ultimately, in a lot of scenarios, when talking to an organization about Power Platform, the toolset already exists in varying ways and, because of its deep integration within the Microsoft Cloud stack, there is no need to do additional reviews or security analysis as it has already been taken through the relevant process as part of the existing Microsoft products.

This approach does not exist for most of the other low-code vendors because the choice to use the product needs to be a conscious decision, rather than a natural evolution of what's already in place.

Maker types

Since the inception of RAD across the world, many organizations have adopted varying sets of low-code tools. Some organizations simply keep low-code tools within their IT departments and deliver as a central unit, and others open these tools up to their wider business communities and allow them to build as needed. Power Platform products are extremely broad from a maker (developer) adoption perspective. There is a lot of tools and content for people to adopt, and what is evident is that makers of varying skill levels and from various walks of life have used tools within Power Platform to resolve varying challenges.

In the low-code community, there are typically two types of developers:

- **Citizen developers**: People outside of the IT department making solutions
- **Professional developers**: People within the IT department making solutions

There are varying levels of agreement regarding the terminology here; however, not all makers (developers) can be treated the same way. Typically, citizen developers require more training and guidance than professional developers when creating a solution.

To drive utilization of the Power Platform, it's important to understand that not everyone early on in their career as a maker is going to be proficient and, therefore, the tools need to feel familiar and easy to use. However, this is a double-edged sword; the tools also need to allow for highly complex scenarios and extremely experienced professional developers. This is a very tough tightrope to walk as there is a propensity to lean too much on one side and, therefore, lose one very important element of the maker community.

Ease of adoption

In any organization, when exploring new technologies and ultimately adopting them, the adoption process can be relatively complicated. It is important to understand that driving adoption is mostly reliant on people, rather than technology. The manner in which a wider set of people are communicated with and the manner in which knowledge is shared is incredibly important.

Getting started

The tools in Power Platform allow developers of all types to create useful solutions, and the barrier to entry for people who know how to use regular Microsoft Office tools such as Excel and PowerPoint is not high. As an example, the Power Apps Canvas App maker experience is very similar to that of PowerPoint and Excel.

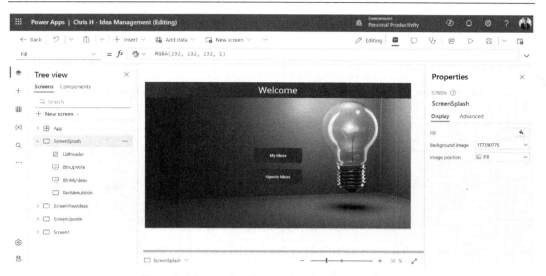

Figure 1.4: Power App Canvas App maker experience

This barrier to entry is similar across the toolset, where makers can easily access the set of tools they require (providing they have the relevant licensing and security access) and start creating useful solutions.

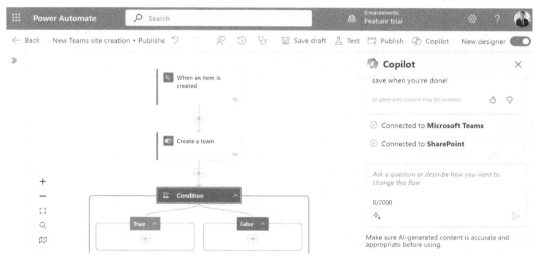

Figure 1.5: Power Automate Cloud Flow maker experience

The Power Automate Cloud Flow designer is incredibly simple to follow and drives a high level of adoption for all maker types.

For those already equipped

For those makers who are already in the know and already understand how areas within the Power Platform function, there are layers they may dig into to start interacting with the platform at a deeper level. Tools such as Visual Studio Code and Power Platform Tools, shown in *Figure 1.6,* can be used to drive professional development within Power Platform.

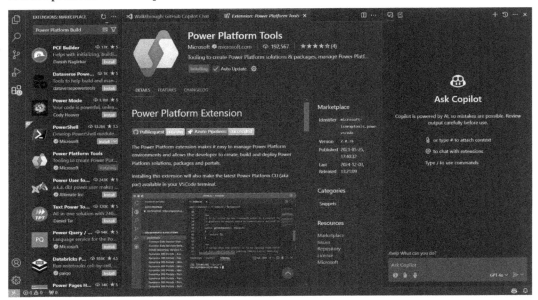

Figure 1.6: Visual Studio Code with Power Platform Tools

Tools such as **Power Platform Tools** for Visual Studio Code may be added and used to dive a lot deeper into the solutions and extend and build more complex layers of functionality, should this be required. As makers progress through their learning, the wider toolset becomes more and more important from an adoption perspective.

Solution sizing

There can be a perception that Power Platform is only for solving simple problems by creating simple solutions. The ultimate response to this is that it is untrue. There are many organizations out there that run extremely important and critical parts of their businesses on Power Platform.

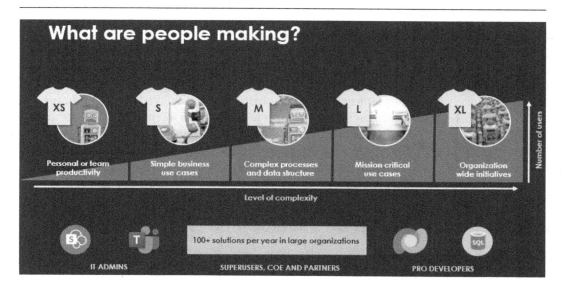

Figure 1.7: Overview of the types of solutions that are regularly created with Power Platform technologies

The fact of the matter is the solution size and type will completely depend on the type of problem the maker is trying to solve. Solutions that are of high criticality often require very stringent rules around data, security, and uptime and, therefore, will be built on very reliable structures such as Dataverse and will therefore come at a different cost to solutions that are not as critical and can be built on top of less governed structures.

Low code does not mean low complexity! The solutions that can and are built using the tools in Power Platform are often intensely complicated and highly integrated.

As an example, the Dynamics 365 Sales, Service, and Marketing suite of products is built on top of Dataverse and is a set of extremely well-thought-out, robust model-driven applications using multiple custom components and plugins. Model-driven apps are digital building blocks of Power Platform.

In review, Power Platform allows makers of varying skill types to build solutions of varying complexity in a secure and robust manner, within a framework that is highly flexible and, often, already approved within an organization. The fact that Power Platform is one of the most widely adopted technologies within the low-code space can be credited to these points.

We've taken a look at Microsoft's dominance in the low-code app and automation development market. Microsoft is one of the leaders in the low-code space and is positioned alongside other leading vendors, such as Mendix, Outsystems, and Salesforce. Power Platform has been positioned alongside its other products, making it a clear leader in the market. Power Platform products are extremely popular with the Microsoft Office community as they add to the business and personal productivity landscape of products. Power Platform allows developers of all types to create useful solutions, and the barrier to entry for people who know how to use regular Microsoft Office tools such as Excel and PowerPoint is not high. It is also highly flexible and often already approved within an organization, making it one of the most widely adopted technologies within the low-code space. In the next section, we will see how Microsoft has super-charged these products with generative AI in the form of AI copilot features.

Revolutionizing low-code development with AI copilot

Over the last few years, it has been necessary to increase the drive for the adoption of low-code platforms due to an increased demand for business productivity solutions. In the last couple of years, **Large Language Models (LLMs)** have appeared on the scene, especially through companies such as OpenAI and within products such as ChatGPT. LLMs are a subset of AI that perform natural language processing. Essentially, they harness natural language to perform tasks.

Microsoft announced a partnership with OpenAI and has been embedding the LLM functionality into various products, such as Dynamics 365, Microsoft 365, and, importantly for this area of focus, Power Platform products. These are called **copilots**. Specific products from Microsoft will have this embedded copilot functionality to enable the creation and extension of solutions using natural language.

This is significant for Power Platform for several reasons; the main one is that it lowers the barrier of entry to creating even lower solutions. People who can simply write in their natural language can now ask the copilot to create an app, automation, or bot in seconds.

A live example

Let's look at an organization that needs to create a basic vehicle inspection application that is responsive and allows users to undertake swift vehicle inspections that will be used in a report at a later point. To get started, simply ask the Power Apps copilot in natural language to create the app for you.

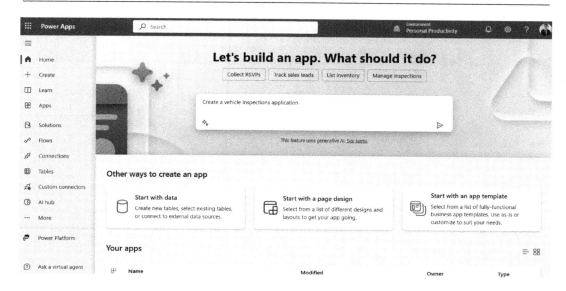

Figure 1.8: Power Apps copilot user interface

The Power Apps copilot interprets the natural language to generate a data table in Dataverse.

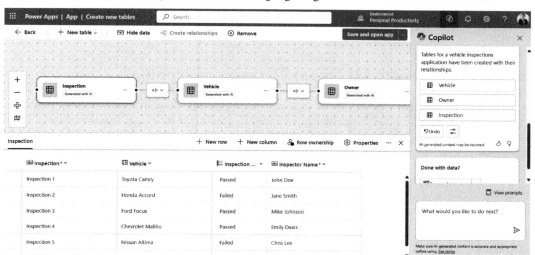

Figure 1.9: Power Apps copilot user interface with data

The data is then reviewed, and a responsive Canvas App can be created directly from this data.

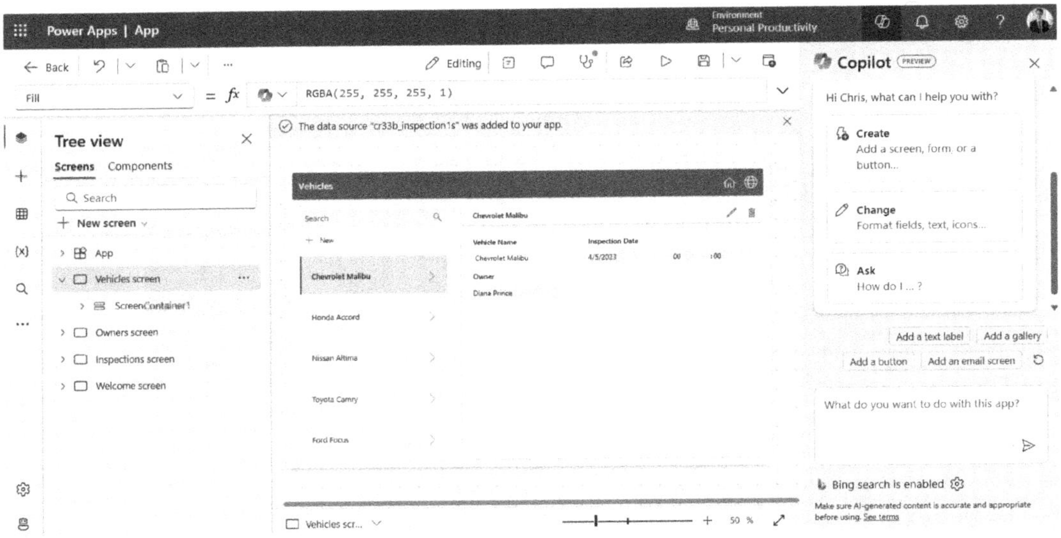

Figure 1.10: Power Apps Canvas App maker experience with copilot

This simple three-step process would normally have taken a maker of mid-level experience around half a day.

What does this mean for Power Platform as a whole?

There are multiple benefits of using the embedded copilot functionality within the Power Platform tools. The level of productivity this drives when creating certain sizes of solutions is amazing. The ability to build and extend solutions using natural language can and will drive a monumental shift in how makers create and manage the things that they make.

As people use the immersive natural language experience in copilot, and as feedback is shared with Microsoft, these tools will only get better and faster. We have seen this pattern already with the current product stack within Power Platform. The products have grown significantly in the last few years, and now that they are supercharged with AI, there is an expectancy that their technical foundations and functionality will skyrocket.

We can also expect rebrands of tools to map to the copilot functionality the same way we see that Power Virtual Agents has been rebranded to Copilot Studio, and the functionality within Copilot Studio has been so heavily infused with deeply embedded AI that it has taken on a life of its own. Copilot Studio is the go-to product for creating low-code custom copilots from scratch, as well as for extending Microsoft 365 Copilot.

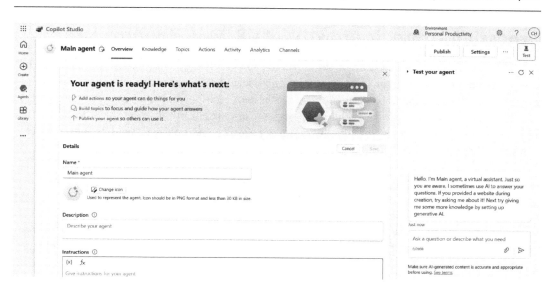

Figure 1.11: Copilot Studio user interface

There is a high expectancy that generative AI will be further integrated into Microsoft products and into the Power Platform in varying forms. We can expect our maker's experience to become more reliant on prompting the AI engine and configuring it in natural language rather than writing hundreds of lines of Power Fx and plugin code.

These are extremely exciting times.

We have taken a look at the recent partnership between Microsoft and OpenAI to embed LLM functionality into various Microsoft products, including Power Platform. This allows users to create solutions using natural language and lowers the barrier of entry for creating apps, automations, and bots. A live example has been provided of how Copilot can be used to create a basic vehicle inspection application in just three steps. The benefits of using Copilot and how it can drive productivity and revolutionize the way makers create and manage solutions have been discussed. We can expect further integration of generative AI into Microsoft products and Power Platform, making it more reliant on natural language input. We understand that the future is now, so in the next section, we will delve into how organizations can harness Power Platform to create strategic growth.

Harnessing strategic growth with Power Platform

Power Platform is exactly what the name says… it is a platform! It is not an app. This is a continuous perspective that needs to be repositioned as many people and organizations make the assumption that the Power Platform only solves one problem rather than multiple problems. Many organizations think that buying Power Platform is about making one app or one automation. This is really and truly not the case. This perspective is the same as buying Office, but only ever sending one email or making one Excel document.

Enabling strategic transformation vision

The first step in this process is to change the perspective and culture around how Power Platform is viewed. It cannot be simply a tactical solution to solve one or two problems. Viewing this from the lens of a wider organization, the platform should be strategic and should be viewed as a way of solving many business problems.

To achieve this, a decision must be made at the very top level to invest both time and money in this approach and enable a wider ecosystem of people, processes, and technology. This needs to be a decision that has full support at all levels.

When reviewing the adoption of tools such as Microsoft Office by 1.2 billion people, most senior and exec types didn't truly understand what was being invested in, only that the tools were important for business productivity and that most of their competitive friends were using it as well.

The dreaded ROI

Realizing Power Platform's capabilities in the same way that Office's capabilities are realized is important. An ROI is not generated for every email you send or each spreadsheet you create. You send these emails and create these spreadsheets because, ultimately, it is understood that they are important and a requirement.

Sure, some solutions will require an ROI calculation, but only those requiring significant time and investment. If you review the solution sizing approach again, many solutions will never take a significant amount of time to create, and the maker of the solution can ultimately own the solution.

Mechanisms and an agreement on how the platform is measured will need to be defined and agreed upon. Quantitative and qualitative metrics normally form the combination of how ROI is measured for the solutions that require it.

Who can make things?

Many organizations do not allow all people in business to create solutions, and some organizations don't have any idea that people are already making things. There have been examples where the IT department has installed and reviewed the Microsoft Center of Excellence starter kit and found thousands and thousands of assets that makers have created.

It's important to define who can build things in your ecosystem. You may not want citizen developers building things up front until the governance layers and data strategy have been defined correctly. If the ecosystem is overrun with assets and there is no support and operational structure in place, the platform may get a bad name as it doesn't have the correct governance setup.

If you know who you would like to open the platform up to, you can control this by using Azure Entra ID security structures and many of the governance features in Power Platform.

What are people allowed to do?

Not all people will build complicated solutions. For the most part, citizen developers will be creating solutions that are not as complex as the ones professional developers will be creating, or they may be working with professional developers to create complicated solutions. It is extremely rare that a citizen developer will build something highly complex.

Not all solutions are deemed equal either. Not all solutions need to be placed into a state of production! Not all solutions need to be supported by IT! Not all solutions are permanent! In many organizations, there is a culture of productionizing everything; however, this is not the case with Power Platform. Solutions obey different rules depending on their size and criticality.

If you can define what each maker type will build, then the platform can be managed and governed in a manner that best drives capacity to the more critical solutions.

Where will people build things?

Once you understand what people will make and who is allowed to make it, you will be able to set up a place for them to create things. These environments are managed differently and have different rules and regulations depending on what is being built in them.

Only certain environments will receive support and guidance from IT. Not everything requires support. As an organization, you wouldn't support every spreadsheet that gets created. Power Platform works in a similar manner. By setting up the rules up front, the governance layer can be defined.

Dare to do

There is a certain group of people within an organization who are outside of the IT department but are relatively technical. We refer to this specific group of people as Business Technologists. These employees are more experienced than just citizen developers and use technology actively to solve business problems. It is highly likely that you will find many people in your business who are already using tech to solve problems. These people should be embraced and have Power Platform shared with them as an approved set of tools for them to build. The idea is that in this scenario, at least there is a level of governance that can be applied to this digital ecosystem, and the right help can be given to people who need it.

Power Platform cannot be viewed as tactical. It must be considered as strategic for it to be widely adopted and for your business to truly harness the full value of the platform.

> **Note**
> Power Platform is not just an app, but a strategic platform for solving multiple business problems. To fully realize its capabilities, organizations need to change the perspective and culture around the platform and invest time and money in it. ROI should not be the only metric used to measure the success of the platform, and organizations need to define who can build solutions, what they can build, and where they can build them. By embracing Business Technologists and treating the platform as a strategic investment, businesses can fully harness its potential.

Summary

As we conclude this chapter, we are left with a profound understanding of Power Platform's impact on digital evolution. Power Platform has emerged as a powerful catalyst for transformative change, enabling businesses to navigate the digital landscape with agility and efficiency. We have explored the economics surrounding digital transformation and Microsoft's market share in the low-code app and automation development market, highlighting Power Platform's leading role in empowering organizations.

Furthermore, we have examined the latest advancements in Power Platform, including the copilot features developed in collaboration with OpenAI. These cutting-edge capabilities use the power of AI to revolutionize the low-code development experience, enabling users to create applications and automate processes with remarkable ease and speed.

This chapter has equipped you with valuable insights and guidance for harnessing Power Platform as a strategic tool to drive digital innovation, unleash transformation, and achieve sustainable growth. Power Platform has truly transformed the digital landscape, and its potential for transformative change is only just beginning to be realized.

Get This Book's PDF Version and Exclusive Extras

UNLOCK NOW

Scan the QR code (or go to `packtpub.com/unlock`). Search for this book by name, confirm the edition, and then follow the steps on the page.

Note: Keep your invoice handy. Purchases made directly from Packt don't require one.

2

Gauging Growth: Assessing Digital Maturity for Strategic Advancement

Gauging growth and assessing digital maturity is crucial for organizations seeking strategic advancement within Power Platform—a comprehensive suite of tools by Microsoft for low-code app development and process automation. To evaluate digital maturity, organizations often employ a framework that categorizes different levels of maturity across various dimensions.

One common framework for digital maturity assessment includes levels such as foundational, developing, advanced, and leading. At the foundational level, organizations are in the early stages of adopting Power Platform, with limited awareness and utilization. In the developing stage, organizations start to expand their usage and gain proficiency in leveraging the platform's capabilities. Advanced maturity indicates a higher level of proficiency, where organizations have well-established processes, governance, and successful adoption across departments. Finally, at the leading level, organizations are at the forefront of innovation, driving continuous improvement and demonstrating exceptional results through Power Platform.

The **Center of Excellence (CoE)** and the **Center for Enablement (C4E)** play integral roles in assessing and advancing digital maturity within Power Platform. The CoE takes the lead in evaluating the organization's current maturity level, identifying gaps, and defining a strategic roadmap for advancement. It establishes best practices, governance frameworks, and standards for Power Platform adoption, ensuring a structured approach to Digital Transformation. The C4E focuses on building capabilities and enabling users to unlock the full potential of Power Platform. It offers training, resources, and support to enhance skills and proficiency, empowering employees to contribute effectively to the organization's digital maturity journey.

By employing a maturity framework and leveraging the expertise of the CoE and C4E within Power Platform, organizations can systematically assess their digital maturity across various dimensions and strategically advance their capabilities. This holistic approach ensures a clear understanding of the current state, identifies areas for improvement, and guides the organization toward higher levels of digital maturity. As organizations progress through the maturity levels, they gain the ability to drive innovation, streamline processes, and achieve sustainable growth within the Power Platform ecosystem.

We will cover the following topics in this chapter:

- Understanding digital maturity in Power Platform
- Navigating maturity levels in Power Platform adoption
- Driving digital maturity with the CoE
- Empowering digital maturity in Power Platform

Understanding digital maturity in Power Platform

Various mechanisms allow organizations to measure the maturity of their Power Platform ecosystem centrally or within various departments or communities of practice. Often, the term *maturity* can be relatively negative depending on the organizations or departments we may find ourselves working with, so the term *readiness* is leveraged within the industry to drive the process forward. It's important to ensure that whichever body of the organization, or the entire organization itself, is *ready* to take on the responsibility of embracing, adopting, and managing a low-code ecosystem.

There are many different interpretations of the concept of *ready*. Sometimes, the actual definition of the concept of *ready* needs to be clearly defined. Does *ready* mean you have your technical infrastructure set up and your environment strategy defined, or does *ready* mean you have installed the Microsoft CoE Starter Kit and decided that that's that? There are many defined states of readiness and actually, even most Microsoft Power Platform partners will have a differing opinion of what *good readiness* looks like. Often, this opinion or perspective may differ somewhat from what Microsoft may even say. Ultimately, there are going to be several versions of this *readiness* model. Depending on the size and complexity of your organization, the need for varying depths of the readiness assessment will differ.

As an example, if you are a five-person organization that is just starting out and you want to use Power Platform to build and run business productivity solutions that help you in your day-to-day, you probably don't need to go down the route of a 500-question assessment focusing on all the aspects of low-code technical guardrails, user adoption, maker enablement, and process automation. This just does not fit the bill for what you really need and will ultimately be far too much. You want to get going fast and get the basics in place as soon as possible.

If you are a half-a-million-person organization that has a global presence, with multiple departments, communities of practice, and varying subsidiaries, then depending on the layer of the business being assessed, you definitely want to think about a more in-depth assessment. This will be important because there will be far more processes that exist and many different teams of people who will be affected by the release of a wide range of tools that will drive productivity.

Ultimately, one size does not fit all, so what is the best approach?

People, processes, platforms (technology)

Let's rewind a bit before we decide to start assessing everything. It's important to find a common point (or common *points*) where at least most organizations have commonalities. This makes it easier to be more focused. In around the 1960s, a person by the name of Harold Leavitt generated a model called *Leavitt's Diamond*. The diamond's four corners represented **people**, **structure**, **technology**, and **tasks**. This was later changed in the 1990s; the structure and tasks corners were rolled into one single corner representing Processes. In recent adaptions, technology has been updated to **platforms**. This is indicated in *Figure 2.1*:

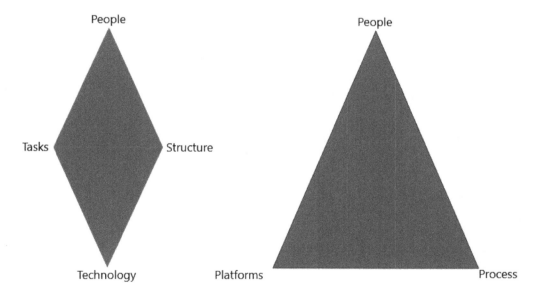

Figure 2.1: Leavitt's Diamond and a recent adaptation in the form of a triangle

When looking at the core majority, most organizations consist of people. People are the core of most businesses and will drive growth. Making people more productive is the key to ensuring that more can be done, as accurately, in a shorter amount of time. In fact, *many* businesses boast the fact that people are the core of their business and are most important to them.

In order to ensure things are done correctly, a set of rules is put in place. These rules are known as processes. The processes define *"how we do things here."* The better the processes are thought out and laid out, the easier it becomes for people to do their work.

Good processes are repetitive. People and processes require tools to work efficiently. In this modern world, some refer to these tools as *apps* or *automations*, but of course, the scope is *much* wider than just these two things. The tools ultimately do their best to make the person's life easier, allowing them to work more efficiently and thus saving time. In fact, some of these processes can be completely automated to the point where they do not even need a human in the loop. Platforms typically supply these tools that allow people to follow these processes more efficiently.

If the readiness assessment can be focused on these core areas, it becomes way easier to set a baseline readiness score that can be common among many organizations. This is because most companies will have these three core areas as a focus in some way, shape, or form.

The importance of baselining

One of the most important aspects of undertaking a readiness assessment is the ability to set a baseline. This process is known as *baselining* and is extremely common in *many* change and project management methodologies. Essentially, the act of baselining sets the bar of the level of the organization with regard to the perceived level of what is "good" or a "best practice". In order to baseline, there needs to be a set of levels, rules, and metrics that are deemed relevant to what "good" looks like. Typically, a type of framework is followed to ensure that everyone who is implementing a certain product follows the same process and is ultimately successful.

The process of baselining is incredibly important when implementing Power Platform. That's because it sets the bar and then enables the organization to *re-baseline* as the project is undertaken and then ultimately is completed, in order to show a level of progression. The key question here is: *"Where were we and where are we now?"*

The process of baselining is one that should happen periodically as the platform is implemented and adopted. This is because it will provide a great mechanism of reporting and structure to anyone following the delivery and adoption. It's important to ensure that *all* updates and metrics are constantly tracked. As an example, the report in *Figure 2.2* shows a custom baseline report with current readiness metrics focusing on people, process, and platform as the primary categories around several core sub-categories.

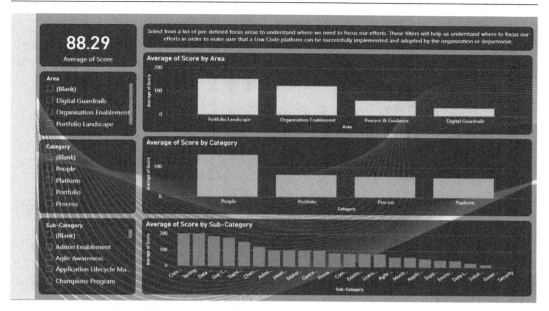

Figure 2.2: An example of a baseline report that shows the current
scoring for various categories and sub-categories

The score here is a total out of 500, which will be aggregated from the various sub-categories per category. In the example, Microsoft's Power BI was leveraged as the reporting mechanism as it is interactive and a great way for the people involved in the project to understand exactly where the points of growth are. In this report, these points are highlighted by the areas with the lowest scores. These areas will become points to focus on when implementing governance.

Another reason why baselining and tracking these scores against a framework is extremely important is that often, *governance* (or, as we term it here, *ecosystem enablement*) can be considered *non-tangible* where a lot of the work is done on a strategy and operational level. There is often not a tangible *app* that gets released. The core output is the ability to derisk an ecosystem and make it safer for makers to create solutions in a more compliant manner. There will need to be a tangible output of metrics and goals achieved.

Readiness categories and sub-categories

Power Platform is extremely diverse, and there is a lot to consider because the technical ecosystem is extremely vast and reaches into so many other areas of the Microsoft stack. When talking about concepts such as *security*, it's important to realize that this is not just localized to Power Platform but to Microsoft 365, as well as many other areas within Microsoft Azure. Power Platform is one of the most interlinked Microsoft product sets in the stack, and this seems to be by design.

This can often be difficult when undertaking readiness assessments as there are many aspects to consider, which are not necessarily technology-focused. Just because an organization understands the core security areas within Power Platform environments does not necessarily give them a high readiness score in the category of security. There will be other aspects to consider, such as the following:

- The relationship between the Power Platform team and the security team
- The processes involved in requesting a new Entra Security Group
- The process to get users added to that group
- The way in which new connectors are reviewed and passed through the security team

These are just examples of questions that need to be asked when understanding the readiness of an organization, department, or community of practice when looking to adopt Power Platform. Again, as mentioned before, this level of depth may not be required, but it is important to know that it absolutely can be.

Essentially, when looking at the example mentioned, there is a combination of the categories of people, processes, and platforms, with a focus on the subcategory of security.

If you were to explore the wider subcategories of Power Platform, you would find that there are many. Several white papers, websites, and even Microsoft Learn will go into varying levels of detail regarding these subcategories. The list of aspects includes, and is definitely not limited to, the following:

- Environment management
- Data policies
- Security
- Support
- Operations
- Communities of practice
- Champions programs
- Ideation
- Project intake
- Landing zones
- Copilot/AI
- Rings of release
- Communications and collaboration

It's important to note that not all of these aspects mentioned will be specific to your business, and therefore, the readiness assessment will need to be flexible to an extent. Not all organizations can or should be treated as a complex, large business.

In conclusion, the readiness assessment for a Power Platform ecosystem should be tailored to an organization's size and complexity. The assessment should be focused on people, processes, and platforms, and a baseline readiness score should be set and periodically tracked. The process of baselining is important as it enables an organization to show progress and identify areas of growth. The Power Platform is diverse, and there are many aspects to consider, including security, which requires a holistic approach. The level of depth required in the assessment may vary depending on the organization's perception. Overall, the assessment should focus on the categories of people, processes, and platforms, with a focus on subcategories such as security. In the next section, we will discuss the pathway to readiness with the assessment frameworks.

Navigating maturity levels in Power Platform adoption

Driving growth and progression with Power Platform in your organization can seem like a difficult task with many moving parts. Thankfully, there are defined pathways to help organizations on this journey. It's not just haphazard guesswork. Many partners, as well as Microsoft themselves, have developed assessments based on detailed experience. As the platform has matured, many experts and organizations have fed back to Microsoft with fantastic detail and experiences that have ultimately helped the wider community understand the best practices. Understanding and setting levels of maturity is important when undertaking these readiness assessments. The better and more well-defined the levels are, the more each organization can understand its level of readiness and the steps needed to progress.

The Microsoft Power Platform adoption maturity model

After implementations of Power Platform at multiple organizations, and with the world's largest low-code adoption of tools such as Power Apps, Microsoft was able to generate a great mechanism for organizations to baseline their readiness levels and get a great idea of where they are in their Power Platform journey.

The way in which the framework is created leverages several primary categories, which are broken down into five levels of maturity. Typically, this is a great way to get an initial idea of where your organization is in its Power Platform journey. However, you may find that you will want to conduct a deeper assessment should your organization be of a more complex nature. Normally, the Microsoft Partner Network is a great place to leverage expertise to conduct such assessments.

Primary categories and levels

Microsoft's model is broken up into seven levels, which have an all-round focus on multiple areas within an organization. It's not just a technology-focused model, as suggested in the first section of this chapter. These categories are as follows:

- Strategy and vision
- Business value
- Admin and governance
- Support
- Nurture and citizen makers
- Automation
- Fusion teams

The primary aim here is to think about the wider plan for adoption and not just the creation of apps and flows. This is important because Power Platform is a business productivity set of tools and is not designed to solve only one single problem. To compare this set of tools to Microsoft Office, you almost certainly did not buy Office to send only one email or make a single Excel spreadsheet. Chances are, you bought Office to be more productive. This is why this approach to Power Platform and low-code, in general, is massively crucial to realizing a true return on investment.

Each of these key categories is broken down into five levels, which are summarized as follows:

- **Level 100**: Initial
- **Level 200**: Repeatable
- **Level 300**: Defined
- **Level 400**: Capable
- **Level 500**: Efficient

An interesting point to make here is that the concept of leveling in this manner is not actually different from other low-code vendors such as Mendix, who have a similar way of understanding maturity.

Microsoft adoption assessment

Microsoft has worked hard to create a relatively generic adoption assessment that will give an organization a first baseline of where they are in their journey, as well as some suggestions of things that need to be done to reach their preferred baseline. The adoption assessment leverages elements of the model mentioned previously and walks the user through a set of relatively open questions. You can access the assessment through the Microsoft Learn site. From the **Discover** menu, select **Assessments**.

Simply search for **Power Platform** and you will see **Power Platform Adoption Assessment** appear in the list.

You will notice an assessment summary where you can simply select **Start Assessment**, provided you are logged in. All your past assessments will be saved so you can reference them at a later point for baselining purposes. As you can see in *Figure 2.3*, there are past assessments available from past dates in this user profile. If you are unable to complete the assessment, that's perfectly fine because it saves your progress and lets you continue in your own time.

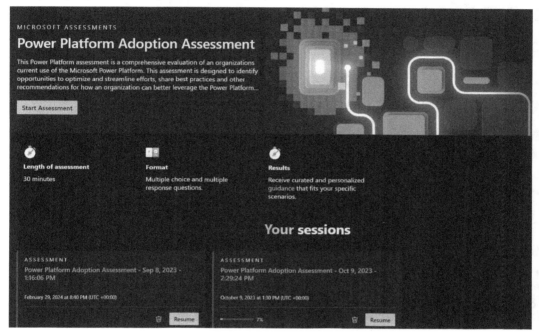

Figure 2.3: A user profile with past Power Platform assessments

To progress the assessment, you are able to select your specific interests from a list of three options. As you select interests, more questions will be added to the list under each interest category, so you can focus your efforts as you need and even have specific assessments focusing on specific interests. In *Figure 2.3*, two of the three interests have been captured in order to focus this assessment on these two primary interests. As you select your interests from the list shown in *Figure 2.4*, you will see the number of questions building on the left.

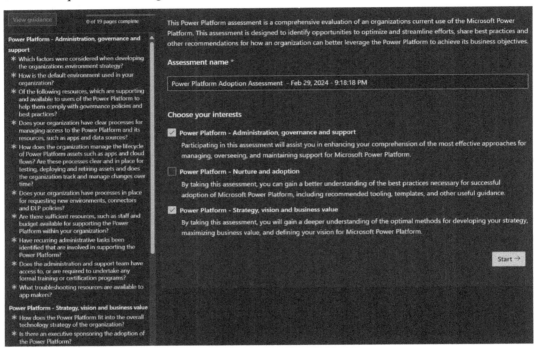

Figure 2.4: Power Platform adoption assessment focused on administration, governance, support, strategy, vision, and business value

As you track through the assessment, you can see your progress on the left, as well as what still needs to be answered. This is visible in *Figure 2.5*.

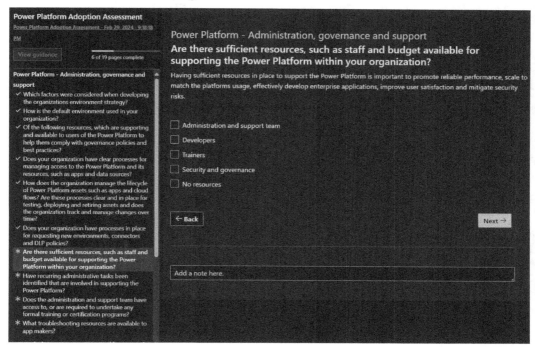

Figure 2.5: Power Platform assessment progression visibility

Tracking through the assessment is relatively straightforward, with complete visibility of where you are, where you have been, and how to answer questions. You can see in *Figure 2.6* that the user is about to complete this assessment and get guidance on what to do next.

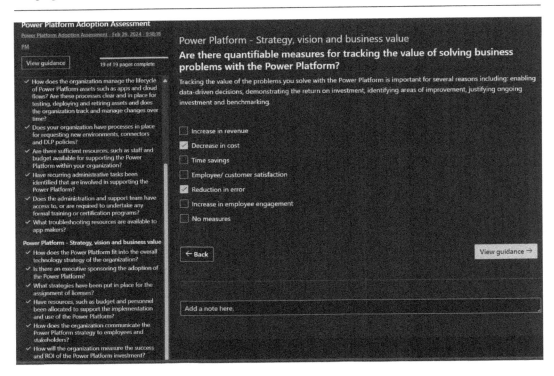

Figure 2.6: A user wrapping up an assessment, about to get guidance

Once the assessment is complete, you will notice that there are three levels as opposed to the five mentioned in the initial model. This is just an initial assessment and only uses three of the five mentioned categories. As you can see in the model in *Figure 2.7*, this assessment suggests that there is a fair bit of work to be done to reach efficiency.

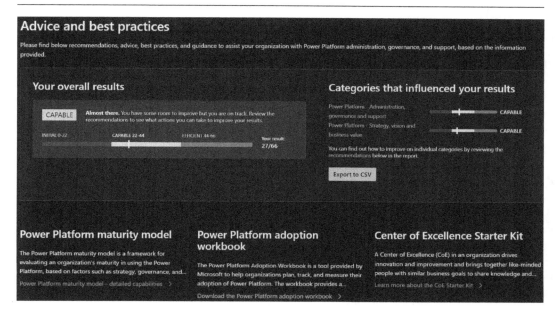

Figure 2.7: The final assessment result with guidance for the organization

This is a great way to get started and to understand immediate gaps. However, as you may have noticed, a more thorough assessment may need to be undertaken in order to establish a more detailed view of an organization's readiness to adopt Power Platform.

The concept of setting levels of maturity or readiness across an organization, department, or community of practice is enormously helpful to enable both governance and adoption within a business. The idea is that people can create solutions safely in a space that is well-governed but also provides users with the freedom to be productive. These assessments are meant to set a clearer path for the organization to truly adopt Power Platform in a manner that best suits them and their people.

This section discusses how to drive growth and progression with Power Platform in an organization. It starts by highlighting the defined pathways available to help organizations on this journey. These pathways are based on detailed experiences and assessments developed by Microsoft and its partners. The section then introduces the Microsoft Power Platform adoption maturity model, which is a readiness model that leverages several primary categories broken down into five levels of maturity. The primary categories are not just technology-focused but encompass a wider plan for adoption. The section explores the Microsoft adoption assessment, which is relatively generic and gives an organization a baseline of where they are in their journey, as well as suggestions for things that need to be done to reach their preferred baseline. The aim of setting levels of maturity or readiness across an organization is to enable both governance and adoption within a business. Next, we will explore the ways in which an organization can drive this process forward to encourage wider adoption.

Driving digital maturity with the CoE

The concept of a CoE has existed for a long time in the world of solution and platform adoption. In the world of Power Platform, the CoE concept started out as being completely associated with a technical toolkit built by one of the teams at Microsoft. The Center of Excellence Starter Kit is an exceptional tool that helps organizations manage and monitor a large amount of user and maker engagement within the Power Platform ecosystem. This tool is extremely technically focused and a great start in setting up a full CoE. However, there is a *lot* more to it than just a technical toolset.

Center of enablement

As we have progressed our thinking around low-code tools, especially Power Platform, we have realized that we need to focus our efforts on more than the technology. Once again, people and processes become equally important. As organizations started to adopt Power Platform more widely, it was soon realized that without the trio of people, process, and technology, a proper CoE was nearly impossible to create. Also, it was not at all possible to drive proper adoption across an organization to provide value to the wider user and maker communities without that trio.

Thought patterns started to change somewhat over the years. The focus on change management and adoption become much more prominent than originally anticipated. Switching to Power Platform was not just a technical thing that people did; it was so much more than that. Organizations started to become well-known for having thriving maker communities. A classic example is a UK-based rail organization with the center of enablement being organically generated and managed. At the time of writing this, Power Platform has organically grown to almost 28,000 assets; this was mainly organic growth. Maker communities organically appeared and people started naturally collaborating.

Now, this is a rare case, as most organizations have to work for this level of adoption. Ultimately, the community plays a huge part in the adoption of the platform, and this is classic word of mouth based on proven technology that solves problems. This is one example of *many* companies that have thriving maker communities that leverage Power Platform as their preferred technical platform to solve issues.

Something that has become extremely apparent is the fact that people form the center of the Power Platform ecosystem. The more we enable people to solve problems with technology and processes, the more widely the platform will be utilized. This means that people will have better tools to optimize the way they work.

Look at the tools in the Microsoft Office suite. There aren't many "Excel Centers of Excellence"; people just naturally use spreadsheets because they seem to make sense for the use cases that people experience. This is similar to other Office products, and therefore, the adoption has been huge. So, why can't the Power Platform tools be treated the same way as the Microsoft Office tools? They are both built for business productivity and to optimize the way people do their jobs!

This exact scenario is what is happening more and more as people realize that they can better perform their job roles with low code tools, but they require guidance and help. This is where the center of enablement comes in. The center of enablement is a great centralized mechanism to help people engage with Power Platform to solve business problems. It's not just technically focused; it is *much* wider than that and includes the people and process aspects while having a strong focus on *enablement and adoption*.

You will notice that the original readiness assessment suggests that there needs to be a focus on people, processes, and platforms. The reason for this is to drive a wider enablement program throughout an organization. This is otherwise known as ecosystem enablement.

How to get going

The toughest part is starting out! Power Platform is just so expansive and starting out on your enablement journey can be tough. There is so much content out there and so many differing opinions that all of this information can become convoluted and not really make sense, which then can become difficult to manage. There is a recipe for success in this scenario and it's not as difficult to get going as it may seem.

Stakeholder mapping

The first action is to find your people! Who are the people in the organization who are likely to support an enablement program such as this and who will most likely benefit? There are always people in organizations looking to optimize processes, work smarter, and just be more productive. This is great! However, someone will need to provide resources to do all of this and this is typically in the form of time from people, as well as money. What you need to find and establish is a group of stakeholders to sponsor the program of work. This may be you, or it may be a group of people in your business, but ultimately, someone needs to be responsible for the overall input and output of the work done.

In order to achieve this, a stakeholder mapping exercise needs to be undertaken. This is the very start of the process whereby you will look for people with the budget and appetite to be willing to participate in this program.

Assemble the team

This step sometimes happens before stakeholder mapping and sometimes after it! It's very dependent on the scenario; however, it is still important. These programs of work cannot all be completed by one person, as there are many areas to focus on and many types of roles that need to be filled. It's important to also understand that these roles are *not* all technical and that many of the roles are people-focused. There are a number of skills that you will need and not each skill is related to one person. Also, if you are a smaller organization, some of these skills may not be at all relevant as you will not need the same level of governance, administration, and enablement.

The typical roles you would be looking for in implementing a C4E in an organization are as follows:

- **Program sponsor**: This person is responsible for the sponsorship of the program of work and the overall CoE. Typically, this person controls the budget.

- **Head of CoE**: Overall, the Power Platform CoE owner plays a critical role in ensuring the successful adoption and effective use of Power Platform within an organization, driving business value, and enabling digital transformation initiatives.

- **Change management and adoption**: The role of a change manager within the Power Platform CoE is to plan, manage, and implement change initiatives related to the adoption and utilization of Power Platform within an organization. The change manager is responsible for driving successful change management practices and ensuring that the changes are well received and effectively integrated within the organization.

- **Power Platform admin**: The role of the Power Platform admin is responsible for operationally maintaining and managing the Power Platform ecosystem. This role focuses on many of the technical aspects of Power Platform, including environments, DLP, security, and monitoring. This person will work closely with the head of the CoE.

- **Solution architect**: A solution architect designs and implements solutions using the tools available in the Power Platform. They translate business requirements into technical specifications, ensuring solutions are secure, scalable, and aligned with organizational goals. Their role is essential in integrating platform components to create efficient workflows and valuable data insights. Solution architects are technical experts who will own the design of a solution.

- **Support lead**: The head of support in a Power Platform CoE is responsible for overseeing the application and platform support function within the CoE. This role involves managing a team of platform and application support professionals. It also involves ensuring that the applications built using Power Platform are functioning correctly and meeting the needs of the business, as well as ensuring that the platform support team is working with the operations team.

Your team will grow over time as your enablement program grows. You can expect to add more and more people, or to split these roles out into other areas such as capability management, operations, technical architecture, and many more.

Setting your purpose

The most important aspect of starting is simply to start communicating with your peers. We call this *setting a purpose*. What exactly are you looking to achieve? The answer can't simply be "making apps and flows." There is way more to it than that. It's important to ensure that the relevant stakeholders in the organization are on the same page and that everyone agrees on the purpose of initiating a Power Platform ecosystem enablement program.

Typically, the focus should be on driving organization-wide productivity through a centralized enablement and governance framework, which protects data and allows people to use and create Power Platform assets safely. We will explore this process in more detail in *Chapter 5*.

Defining success and ROI

When stakeholders are all on the same page and it is apparent and agreed that some level of a center of enablement is important to drive productivity, it's time to start that baselining process again. This time, think about **Return on Investment (ROI)**. What will make this project a success? What does "good" look like? How do you ensure that actual results are achieved?

In any sort of implementation of Power Platform, it's important to have these types of goals, especially because someone is likely to be spending some money and time on this. Agreement is crucial here, even if the data is captured manually and not automatically generated through the information generated in the CoE starter kit. This data will only get you so far. You will need to get people to report back through feedback loops when interacting with the products.

It's important to bear in mind that ROI is not always money or time. It's essential to break down your metrics and success criteria into both qualitative and quantitative metrics.

Qualitative metrics

The term *qualitative* refers to a type of information that describes traits or characteristics. Qualitative metrics focus on the subjective aspects of performance evaluation. They are gathered through surveys, interviews, or observation, and are usually presented as a story. Qualitative metrics provide an in-depth understanding of various factors that contribute to overall performance. They can be particularly helpful in understanding how a phenomenon or action affects individuals and groups. While gathering and analyzing data through qualitative measurements can be challenging, the insights you get at the end of the project are often well worth the effort. They provide insights that aren't necessarily numerical, such as customer feedback or product reviews. Qualitative metrics help you see patterns and trends so you can make actionable changes. They can also answer questions posed by your project so you can provide company stakeholders with helpful information and insights.

Quantitative metrics

The term *quantitative metrics* refers to measurable impacts that are related to certain business choices and actions. They are represented numerically, which experts may analyze to provide meaning and support for their business assessments. These metrics are often communicated using visual tools like charts and graphs, which may assist professionals in comprehending their significance and how measurements may connect to one another. They are commonly used for assessing, comparing, and tracking performance or production. They provide numerical data that can be used to make better data-driven decisions.

Focus areas for your plan

You are now ready to define a plan for your ecosystem enablement program. This is absolutely essential for success. It is important to ensure that your plan takes your baselining and success measures into account and includes your team at the correct times. This seems obvious, but actually, it can be difficult to map the process to an overall timeline.

There are also multiple aspects to the plan that need to be taken into consideration. However, using the maturity assessment and understanding the people, process, and platform mapping, a certain strategy can be employed when designing your plan.

This specific breakdown is something that is relatively common across *many* customer and partner organizations. It is a great way to get started when defining exactly what it is you need to do first.

Digital guardrails

The best way to get started is by securing Power Platform and ensuring the actual technology is secured so that people can build safely. There are several workstreams or categories in the ecosystem enablement program that need to be reviewed within the digital guardrails pillar. These areas include, but are not limited to, the following:

- Environment strategy
- Data policies
- Security
- Monitoring

There may be areas you would like to focus more on in the guardrails section, such as tenant isolation, licensing, and more. However, this is the core you will require to get started. These will be further explored in *Chapter 5*, in the *What is your plan?* section.

Processes

The processes that you put in place are inherently reliant on the technical areas that have been configured. The guardrails need to be completed before any processes can be defined. You may notice a blurred line between the guardrails and some of the processes. However, this is by design. Initial areas to focus on as a start are as follows:

- **Application Life Cycle Management (ALM)**
- Support
- Change management
- Governance
- Ideation

There are many other areas that can be reviewed here, such as process and automation, feedback, project intake, operations, and more. It's important to get going in these primary areas and then grow outward. As you mature in your program of work, so will the processes you put in place. The better the processes and the more automated they are, the easier it will be for the team to manage the CoE. Further process-related areas will be focused on in *Chapter 5*, in the *What is your plan?* section.

People – organization enablement

The people element of this is often referred to as *organization enablement*. This essentially means that we find ways to enable people in the organization to be more productive through the CoE, as well as set up structures to manage the program. There are several workstreams that can be focused on. However, it is suggested that initially, the following workstreams are a great place to start:

- Community
- Training
- Communications
- Community champions

As you grow your CoE, your team will grow, and so will the roles of people. The more people engage in the platform, the more people will need to make sure things run smoothly. There are many organizations out there with thousands of makers. Therefore, these people will need support when building out their solutions and supporting their creations. Further process-related areas will be focused on in *Chapter 5*, in the *What is your plan?* section.

Defining your plan

Once you have established the workstreams and/or categories you would like to focus on, you can start establishing the order in which you will do them. It is highly suggested that you start by securing the platform with digital guardrails, as this is going to help you set off in the correct direction. After that, focus on the processes and people elements as you ensure that your platform is considered safe.

Once your key workstreams are selected, it is advised to set up a timeline or Gantt chart, as you would in a regular project, where tasks and timelines can be accurately managed. This means that each workstream selected will have sub-actions and tasks. A great way to manage this is within Azure DevOps or even Microsoft Planner, as you can see in the example shared in *Figure 2.8*. The program of work is meant to be collaborative. Therefore, you will need to ensure that people are constantly sharing and communicating.

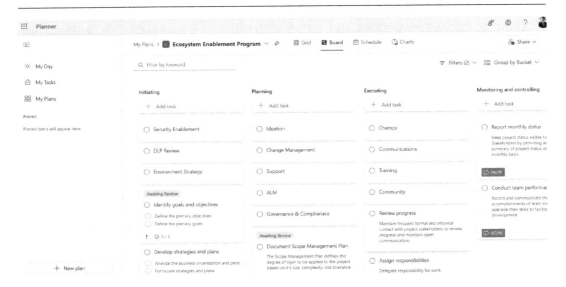

Figure 2.8: A basic example of a simple project plan in Microsoft Planner relating to ecosystem enablement

In conclusion, the concept of a CoE for the Power Platform ecosystem has evolved to focus on more than just technical tools. It has evolved into a center of enablement. People and processes have become equally important for a proper CoE to be created and for driving adoption across an organization. Setting up a CoE requires finding stakeholders who will sponsor the enablement program, assembling a team with various roles, and defining success measures with both qualitative and quantitative metrics. The plan should include digital guardrails to secure the platform, processes to manage the platform effectively, and people enablement to increase productivity. It is important to establish a timeline and manage tasks collaboratively to ensure the success of the program.

Empowering digital maturity in Power Platform

We have spoken about the concept of ecosystem enablement throughout this chapter. It is one of the most important aspects of driving a center of enablement in an organization; it is a new way of thinking. This is by design because, in the past, we have been completely focused on technology as the main part of any implementation or program of work.

As we progress through understanding the mechanisms to mature from a readiness perspective, we cannot simply look at one area. We have also mentioned the trifecta of people, processes, and platforms, which inherently give us more than one angle to observe the areas, categories, and subcategories that make up a center of enablement.

A key focus for any organization right now is to ensure that Power Platform is adopted more widely across the organization and that people find it a useful tool for optimizing their day-to-day tasks and processes. This doesn't just happen; actually, this can be rather complicated as all people are different. Everyone has different ways of interacting with the Power Platform ecosystem, so we need to think widely about how we support the various parts of our organizations to ensure that there is a wider adoption.

The difference between enablement and adoption

This comes up constantly in organizations as there can be a very fine line between the two areas. It is important to understand both concepts in order to ensure that Power Platform is leveraged to its full potential in an organization.

Enablement

Enablement is the methods taken to ensure that the right tools, processes, and people are available across the center of enablement so that makers have the ability to learn freely and create solutions in a safe, supported space and so that people can access and use these solutions in a safe and supported space. This means the following:

- Guardrails need to be set up to provide safety
- Processes need to be set up and automated in a refined manner
- Organizational enablement needs to be executed such that people can access the information they need to create freely, safely, and productively

There are *many* fine lines in this scenario as there is a difficult tightrope to walk. You do not want to "over-govern" so people cannot do what they need to, but you absolutely cannot make it free for all and risk compliance issues. It's important to provide just the right amount of room for people to be creative and safe. Enablement is about helping people do their jobs more productively.

Adoption

Adoption is normally a result of well-planned and placed enablement. The better the enablement, the more widely Power Platform will be adopted. After defining your ecosystem enablement program, it's important to define an adoption program.

We need to ask a critical question. What is the best process we can implement in order to help our staff be more productive?

Power Platform is an amazing set of tools. When leveraged in a well-governed, safe space, those tools are extremely effective. Great governance is when people don't know it's happening, and they feel comfortable using the tools without worrying about breaking something or disobeying the rules.

Driving enablement

In order to drive wider enablement across the organization, it's key to ensure that you're ready for wide uptake because people will use things if you let them. Once you go out with your Power Platform launch communications, make sure that the guardrails are already set up, your processes are in place, and your enablement infrastructure is set up and ready, typically in that order.

In order to achieve this, it's important to build capabilities to grow your readiness maturity. This can only come from actively growing the wider enablement team and program of work. There are some key areas you can focus on when driving this level of enablement.

Community

Community is one of the most important aspects of driving enablement and will form one of the core, essential areas of focus as you grow your Power Platform adoption in your business. The community is the central location where people can congregate to share experiences. A great community will consist of extremely strong community champions and a highly collaborative network of people who follow the same message and are intent on helping one another.

If the community is set up and managed correctly, it will act as your epicenter for problem-solving, support, feedback, collaboration, and centralized communications.

Training

A well-thought-out training plan is important for both users and makers. People learn in many ways, so it's important to take that into account. People will assume that training and enablement content will be made available through the centralized community portal. This is correct, as this should act as a central hub for people to communicate and learn. A well-laid-out training plan with the right array of materials and content will really get people engaged. It's essential to spend time on this and get feedback from your audience as often as possible.

Community champions

These people are the heart and soul of the community! These people are your key advocates and will often be passionate about problem-solving and engaging others. It's really important to make sure that these people are recognized for their work and are attributed change agents. This is all about visibility and visibly rewarding those who grow your Power Platform community. The more the change agents are recognized, the more widely they will be able to drive growth and passion for problem-solving. This type of hero network is essential to adoption and enablement.

Communications

Communications are your center of enablement voice into the community and into your entire hero, maker, and user base. Often in larger organizations, the CoE team will have one shot at getting the communications correct. Therefore, the enablement infrastructure needs to be ready for people to visit and engage in a safe and governed way.

Driving these types of enablement processes will ultimately increase adoption and capability across your organization and therefore increase your readiness maturity within your Power Platform ecosystem.

In conclusion, ecosystem enablement is a crucial aspect of driving a center of enablement in an organization. It involves the right tools, processes, and people being available to ensure makers have the ability to learn and create solutions in a safe and supported space. Adoption of Power Platform is a result of well-planned and placed enablement, and it's important to build capabilities to grow your readiness maturity. This can be achieved through community training, community champions, and effective communications. By driving these types of enablement processes, organizations can increase adoption and capability across the board, leading to an increase in readiness maturity within the Power Platform ecosystem.

Summary

In this chapter, we explored various aspects of the digital readiness of an organization wanting to adopt Power Platform and build a thriving ecosystem focused on enablement and adoption. We learned that adopting Power Platform requires more than just technical skills and tools. It also requires a holistic approach that considers people, processes, and platforms.

This chapter introduces a framework for assessing the readiness and maturity of an organization in adopting Power Platform. It also provides guidance on how to set up a center of enablement that can drive adoption and governance across the organization.

The concept of readiness and how it can be measured using various categories and levels was a central topic in this chapter. We learned that it is an important area of impact when setting up a center of enablement. We also covered the Microsoft Power Platform adoption maturity model and the adoption assessment.

There was a focus on how to drive growth and progression with Power Platform in an organization. We explored the defined pathways available to help organizations on this journey, based on detailed experiences and assessments developed by Microsoft and its partners.

The Center of Enablement is a central topic for the Power Platform ecosystem and how it has evolved to focus on more than just technical tools. It outlines the steps and roles involved in setting up a CoE, such as finding stakeholders, assembling a team, defining success measures, and planning the program. We covered this topic in this chapter as well.

We focused on the importance of ecosystem enablement and how it involves the right tools, processes, and people being available to ensure makers have the ability to learn and create solutions in a safe and supported space. We also highlighted the key areas to focus on when driving enablement, such as community training, community champions, and communications.

In the next chapter, we will focus on the possibilities of enhancing operations leveraging the tools in Power Platform and how to further optimize processes that are specific to your organization.

Further reading

The further reading sources shared below will be useful when doing research and developing your center of enablement.

You will be able to find more information at the following locations:

- Microsoft Learn: `https://learn.microsoft.com/en-us/power-platform/guidance/adoption/maturity-model-details`
- Power Platform adoption framework: `https://github.com/PowerPlatformAF/PowerPlatformAF`
- An example of a readiness (maturity) model that is available for public use right now, published by Microsoft: `https://learn.microsoft.com/en-us/power-platform/guidance/adoption/maturity-model-details`

Join our community on Discord

Join our community's Discord space for discussions with the authors and other readers:

`https://packt.link/powerusers`

3
Unlocking Potential: Enhancing Operations with the Power Platform

The Power Platform, a suite of low-code/no-code tools by Microsoft, offers organizations the opportunity to revolutionize their operations and unlock untapped potential. With its user-friendly interface and intuitive design, the Power Platform empowers both professional developers and citizen developers to create applications, automate processes, and drive digital transformation without extensive coding expertise. This low-code/no-code approach brings numerous advantages, such as accelerated development cycles, increased agility, and reduced reliance on traditional software development methods.

One of the key roles played by citizen developers within the Power Platform is their ability to bridge the gap between business requirements and technical implementation. Citizen developers, who possess deep knowledge of business processes but may not have formal coding backgrounds, can leverage the Power Platform's tools to rapidly build and deploy applications tailored to specific operational needs. This democratization of app development allows for quick iterations, frequent feedback loops, and greater collaboration between business users and IT teams.

Within the Power Platform, various tools are available to enhance operations and drive efficiency. Power Apps enable the creation of custom applications, empowering users to design intuitive interfaces and connect with data sources seamlessly. Power Automate offers a visual interface for automating repetitive tasks and streamlining workflows, reducing manual efforts and enabling efficient processes. Power BI enables organizations to visualize and analyze data, gaining valuable insights to drive informed decision-making. Together, these tools within the Power Platform empower organizations to optimize operations, improve productivity, and unlock their full potential in a rapidly changing digital landscape.

In summary, the Power Platform unlocks the potential for organizations to enhance their operations by leveraging its low-code/no-code advantages, empowering citizen developers, and utilizing the range of tools available. With the ability to rapidly develop applications, automate processes, and gain insights from data, organizations can drive digital transformation and achieve operational excellence. By harnessing the Power Platform, businesses can transform their operations, increase agility, and stay ahead in an increasingly competitive marketplace.

We will cover the following topics in this chapter:

- Reimagining operations with Power Platform
- Enabling developers: the low-code/no-code edge of Power Platform
- Connecting citizen developers: aligning business needs and tech solutions
- Leveraging Power Apps, Power Automate, and Power BI for operational gains
- Advancing transformation: elevating operations with Power Platform

Reimagining operations with Power Platform

The Power Platform is a suite of tools developed by Microsoft that enables users to build and deploy applications, automate workflows, analyze data, and create copilots without writing code. The Power Platform consists of several primary components: Power Apps, Power Automate, Power BI, Power Pages, and Custom Copilots, previously known as Power Virtual agents.

The Power platform is designed for rapid application development and is designed as a business productivity tool that enables makers to build solutions to business problems fast. Power platform can be described as set of prebuilt digital building bricks that snap into one another to allow makers the ability to architect and build software solutions so solve business problems without having much coding or software development experience. In the market Power Platform is referred to as a Low Code software development platform.

The platform is typically split into 2 layers; The "Interaction Layer" and the "Data and managment layer", which then ultimately integrate to the wider Microsoft product stack.

The interaction layer

The first layer being the interaction layer, where people will interact with data through some sort of user experience. The experience may or may not be directly visible, however it is normally initiated by a user-based action. It's important to state that this is the layer that most makers will have their first interaction with and will essentially drive the creation of assets in the Power Platform.

The interaction layer consists of Power Apps, Power Automate, Power BI, Power Pages and Copilot studio, formally known as Power Virtual Agents. Some of the components have several sub-components which will be explored in more detail later in this chapter.

To drive true efficiency and to truly revolutionize the way in which the Power Platform is leveraged within an organization, its absolutely key to focus on the data and governance first. Retro fitting this later will become a difficult task.

The data and management layer

The data and management layer is the most powerful aspect of the Power Platform and is the part that matters the most. There can be multitudes of applications, automations and copilots, however, if the data and the governance isn't managed correctly, these assets will never be productionised. This layer consists of several components which we will look into detail.

Dataverse

Dataverse is a low-code data platform that allows users to store and manage data for their Power Platform solutions. Dataverse provides a secure and scalable cloud relational and secure data storage facility that can integrate with various data sources, such as SharePoint, Excel, or external systems. Dataverse also enables users to define business rules, logic, and workflows for their data, as well as to create rich data models with relationships, validations, and metadata. Dataverse is important because it simplifies the data management process and ensures data quality, consistency, and compliance across the Power Platform. A person with a basic knowledge of data modeling can design sophisticated data structures with relative ease.

Managed environments

Managed environments are containers that host the Power Platform resources, such as apps, flows, connectors, and data, for a specific solution or project. Managed environments allow users to control the security, access, and deployment of their Power Platform solutions, as well as to monitor and manage their performance and usage. Managed environments are important because they enable users to create and test their solutions in isolation, without affecting other environments or users. They also provide users with the flexibility to choose the type and size of environment that best suits their needs, from trial environments for experimentation to production environments for live deployment. Managed environments help users to ensure the quality, reliability, and governance of their Power Platform solutions.

AI Builder

AI Builder is a feature of the Power Platform that allows users to create and use artificial intelligence models without writing any code. AI Builder enables users to automate processes, analyze data, extract insights, and enhance their Power Platform solutions with the power of AI. Users can choose from a range of pre-built AI models, such as sentiment analysis, object detection, and form processing, or build their own custom models using a guided, no-code interface. AI Builder integrates seamlessly with other Power Platform components, such as Power Apps, Power Automate, and Power BI, allowing users to easily add AI capabilities to their apps, flows, and reports. AI Builder is a powerful tool for democratizing AI and empowering users to solve complex problems with ease. *Figure 3.1* shows the prebuilt AI builder models available:

Figure 3.1: AI Builder options

Connectors

Connectors are a key feature of the Power Platform that allow users to connect their solutions to various data sources and services, both within and outside the Microsoft ecosystem. Connectors enable users to access and manipulate data, trigger actions, and automate workflows across different applications and platforms. For example, users can use connectors to send an email from Outlook, create a record in Salesforce, or analyze data in Power BI, all from within their Power Platform solution. Connectors provide users with a wide range of possibilities and functionalities, without requiring them to write any code or deal with complex integration issues. Connectors are essential for creating powerful and flexible solutions that can leverage the best of what the cloud has to offer. Connectors are THE MOST important part of the platform as they super charge all power platform assets with the data, they need to be useable.

Power FX

Power FX is the low-code programming language of the Power Platform that allows users to create formulas and expressions to define the logic and behavior of their solutions. Power FX is based on Microsoft Excel, which makes it familiar and easy to use for millions of users around the world. Power FX is also an open-source language that can be extended and customized by developers and community members.

Power FX is important in the Power Platform ecosystem because it enables users to build solutions that are dynamic, interactive, and responsive, without requiring them to write complex code or learn a new syntax. Power FX is the common language that connects the various components of the Power Platform, such as Power Apps, Power Automate, Copilot Studio and Power BI, and allows users to create seamless and integrated experiences across them. Power FX is the language of the citizen developer, as well as the professional developer, who can use it to accelerate and enhance their development process. Power FX is the key to unlocking the power of the Power Platform and creating solutions that can solve real-world problems and challenges.

Power Platform has deep roots into Microsoft Products

Figure 3.2 shows us a consolidated view of the Power Platform and how it has deep roots in the Microsoft Azure Platform. The fact of the matter is, if you are using any Microsoft products, there is a strong chance that you are already using Microsoft Power Platform in some way, within your organization.

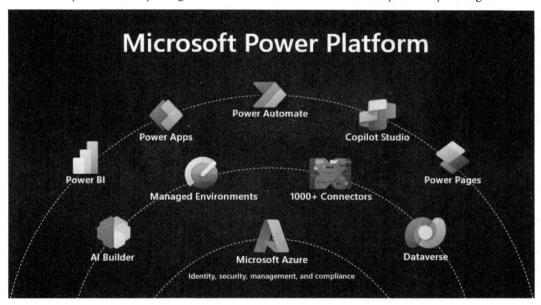

Figure 3.2: Breakdown of the various Power Platform components

By using the Power Platform, users can leverage the power of Microsoft's cloud services, such as Azure, Dynamics 365, and Office 365, to create innovative and scalable solutions that can transform their operations and unlock their potential. The Power Platform also empowers users of all types within an organization, from developers to business users, to collaborate and innovate without relying on IT or external vendors. The Power Platform is a game-changer for driving digital transformation and achieving operational excellence.

How has Power Platform revolutionized operations?

One of the ways that the Power Platform has revolutionized operations within organizations is by enabling people of all types, from developers to business users, to create and use applications, workflows, reports, and Copilots (chatbots) that suit their needs and goals. The components in the platform allow users to build and deploy solutions using scalable methods, from high code to no code at all, meaning that they can use High code interfaces like Visual Studio, graphical interfaces, drag-and-drop features, pre-built templates, and connectors to access various data sources and services which suite their preferred method of creating solutions.

By using low-code or no-code tools, users can benefit from several advantages, such as:

- Faster development and deployment: Users can create and launch solutions in a matter of hours or days, instead of weeks or months, saving time and resources.

- Reduced dependency on IT or vendors: Users can solve their own problems and challenges without waiting for IT support or external help, increasing their autonomy and agility.

- Enhanced innovation and creativity: Users can experiment with different ideas and features, test and iterate quickly, and customize their solutions to fit their specific needs and preferences, fostering a culture of innovation and creativity.

- Improved collaboration and communication: Users can share and co-create solutions with other users across the organization, as well as with external partners and customers, enhancing collaboration and communication.

- Empowering makers of all types: the barrier to entry of using digital tools to solve business problems has significantly dropped and this means that people of multimple technical literacy levels can create solutions. While the Power Platform is designed to be accessible and user-friendly for non-technical users, it also offers many benefits and opportunities for developers who want to leverage its capabilities and extend its functionality.

Developers can use the Power Platform to:

- Accelerate and simplify development: Developers can use the low-code or no-code tools of the Power Platform to build the core functionality and user interface of their solutions, and then use code to add custom logic, integrations, or advanced features. This way, they can reduce the amount of code they need to write and maintain and focus on the most complex and valuable aspects of their solutions.

- Enhance and optimize performance: Developers can use the Power Platform to monitor and analyze the performance, usage, and quality of their solutions, and identify and resolve any issues or bottlenecks. They can also use the Power Platform to optimize their solutions for different devices, platforms, and environments, and ensure they meet the security and compliance standards of their organization and industry.

- Expand and scale up their solutions: Developers can use the Power Platform to connect their solutions to various data sources and services, both within and outside of Microsoft's cloud ecosystem, such as Azure, Dynamics 365, Office 365, SharePoint, SQL Server, and more. They can also use the Power Platform to leverage the power of artificial intelligence, machine learning, and natural language processing to add intelligence and automation to their solutions. Moreover, they can use the Power Platform to distribute and share their solutions with other users and organizations, and scale them up as needed.

There are many more versions of these points mentioned. It's important to remember that every organization will find its methods to improve the way they do things and achieve results. The key here is to be open to changing the ways that people work and be ready to adopt a different approach to problem solving. The more people who can solve problems in a safe space, the more problems will be solved and the more likely the organization is to be successful and enabled digitally.

Enabling developers: the low-code/no-code edge of Power Platform

Developers have existed in digital ecosystems for many years and under many titles and roles. Software Engineer, Professional Developer or "pro-dev", Coder, Full Stack Developer, Front End Developer, Back End Developer, Software Development Engineer. Ultimately, the concept of development is synonymous with the concepts of being a creator or a maker.

The typical role of a developer

Typically, developers are the people who CREATE most of the parts of a digital solution that solves a problem. The concept of *"Please make me an app for…"* is VERY common in all organizations and a lot of the time is performed by developers. It's extremely prolific in larger organizations to have teams of developers working off a backlog of requirements shared by the business and then building to those requirements. The stream of "Things" is normally never ending. If business challenges exist in organizations, developers will be needed to solve those problems using technology.

Developers are often the ones who maintain and improve the software solutions that power organizations and enable them to achieve their goals. They have the skills and expertise to write code, use various technologies and frameworks, and follow best practices and standards.

However, developers also face many challenges and constraints in their work, such as limited resources, tight deadlines, complex requirements, changing needs, security risks, and technical debt. Moreover, they may not always have access to the data and systems they need, or they may have to rely on third-party services and APIs that are not fully compatible or reliable. As time has progressed, it has become more and more difficult for developers to create solutions rapidly as the ever-changing ecosystem constantly presents newer and more complex challenges. This is because the way in which we perceive and realize business problems and challenges has changed and become more advanced.

How Power Platform can help enable developers

The Power Platform can help developers overcome MANY challenges and enhance their productivity and creativity. Developer may not necessarily be the person creating the app or the automation, but they could be the person building the custom components or integrations required by these assets. Developers can also leverage the existing data and services in the Microsoft ecosystem, such as Azure, Office 365, Dynamics 365, and SharePoint, and integrate them with other sources and platforms. Furthermore, they can customize and extend the functionality of the Power Platform using pro-code tools and languages, such as Visual Studio, C#, JavaScript, and Power Fx. They can also use the platform's governance and administration features to ensure security, compliance, and performance of their solutions. These developers may leave the front-end app user experience or simple flow processes to other people within the organization.

The Power Platform enables developers to deliver value faster and more efficiently, while also allowing them to innovate and experiment with new ideas and solutions. It empowers them to solve problems at scale, collaborate with other makers and users, and provide better experiences and outcomes for their customers and stakeholders.

Ultimately, developers in the typical "Code Writing" sense, can spend less time on the parts of the solution they deem less complex, or even outsource these to other makers within the organization, and they can focus on the parts they are more comfortable with and are more complex.

Drive Time to Value at pace

Fail fast! Maybe not the words everyone is expecting to hear, but ultimately the concept is true for many scenarios when needing to come to an outcome for a solution.

One of the advantages of using the Power Platform is that it enables developers to deliver solutions faster and more efficiently than traditional methods. By leveraging the low-code or no-code capabilities of the platform, developers can build apps, workflows, chatbots, dashboards, and other components without writing much code or relying on complex infrastructure. This allows developers to focus on building the solution out at a rapid pace, or even as a working prototype and then bolt on the pieces they need as they go. Essentially, it's as if the development team were clipping a set of digital building bricks together to generate a working solution. This type of approach is extremely common in the realms of Power Platform and Low Code.

The Power Platform also supports a collaborative and iterative approach to solution development, where developers can work with other makers, such as business analysts, domain experts, or end users, to co-create and validate solutions. The platform provides tools for testing, debugging, deploying, and monitoring solutions across different environments and devices, ensuring quality and performance. This is a great way to drive the concept of Fusion Team development with help from people who are closest to understanding the problem.

By using the Power Platform, developers can provide time to value at a rapid pace, delivering solutions that meet the needs and expectations of their customers and stakeholders. The platform empowers developers to innovate and solve problems with agility and flexibility, while reducing costs and risks.

Using the rest of the stack

Power Platform is one of the rare platforms that branches through MANY of the Microsoft tools in the ecosystem. If you are using Dynamics 365, Office 365 or Azure tools, you will encounter the Power Platform in some way, shape or form. This is great for makers of all types but even more fundamentally important for people who consider themselves developers who work with complex cloud products and write code.

When looking at the cross-stack integrations and interfaces that are available within Power Platform, we soon realize that the platform was designed to be a tool used for extending other solutions BUT ALSO, to be extended with the complex Microsoft platforms that it is built directly on top of.

One of the key advantages of Power Platform is its ability to leverage the power of Microsoft Azure, the cloud computing platform that provides a wide range of services and capabilities for building, deploying, and managing applications. Azure offers many tools that can enhance and extend the functionality of Power Platform, such as Azure Functions and Logic Apps.

Azure Functions are serverless computer services that allow developers to run code on demand without having to provision or manage servers. Azure Functions can be triggered by various events, such as HTTP requests, timers, queues, or messages. Azure Functions can be used to perform custom logic, integrate with other systems, or manipulate data in response to Power Platform events. For example, an Azure Function can be triggered by a Power App button click, a Power Automate flow, or a Power BI report refresh, and execute some code that performs a complex calculation, calls an external API, or sends an email notification.

Logic Apps are another serverless service that enables developers to create workflows that orchestrate and automate business processes and tasks across multiple systems and services. Logic Apps provide a graphical designer that allows users to drag and drop connectors and actions to build their workflows. Logic Apps can also be triggered by various events, such as HTTP requests, schedules, or messages. Logic Apps can be used to connect Power Platform with hundreds of other services, such as Office 365, Salesforce, X (formerly Twitter), or Dropbox. For example, a Logic App can be triggered by a Power Automate flow, a Power App form submission, or a Custom Copilot chatbot conversation, and perform actions such as creating a document, updating a record, or posting a tweet.

By using Azure Functions and Logic Apps, Power Platform developers can extend the functionality of their solutions and integrate them with other systems and services. Azure Functions and Logic Apps can also help developers overcome some of the limitations of Power Platform, such as the delegation limits, the connector limits, or the licensing costs. Additionally, Azure Functions and Logic Apps can enable developers to reuse existing code and workflows or create reusable components that can be shared across multiple Power Platform solutions. Azure Functions and Logic Apps can also benefit from the security, scalability, and reliability of the Azure platform, as well as the monitoring and debugging tools that Azure provides.

There are many more tools that can be used to extend the way in which Power Platform can augment solutions or build custom solutions from the ground up. The preceding examples are a small flavor of what can be done.

Developers play a crucial role in digital ecosystems, creating and maintaining software solutions to solve problems. However, they face challenges such as limited resources, tight deadlines, and evolving business needs. The Power Platform offers solutions to these challenges by empowering developers to enhance productivity and creativity. It provides low-code or no-code capabilities for building apps and workflows and integrates with Microsoft Azure to expand its capabilities. This allows developers to deliver solutions faster, innovate with agility, and provide better experiences for customers and stakeholders. In the next section we will look at how citizen developers work within the wider Power Platform and maker community to build solutions to solve business problems.

Connecting citizen developers: aligning business needs and tech solutions

One of the key benefits of the Power Platform is that it enables a new category of makers: citizen developers. Citizen developers are non-professional developers who can create apps and workflows without writing code, or with minimal coding. They are often business users or domain experts who understand the problems and needs of their organization and can leverage the Power Platform to create solutions that address them. Citizen developers can also work collaboratively with professional developers, who can provide guidance, support, and governance for their projects. By empowering citizen developers, the Power Platform can bridge the gap between business requirements and technical implementation and accelerate digital transformation.

Talk about the different types of makers – Maker archetypes

We often talk about Citizen Developers but there are MANY more types of "Developers" or "Makers" that will leverage the Power Platform in an organization. A maker is someone who uses the Power Platform to build solutions and not all makers can be classified as the same. A person who deeply understands the way custom code works cannot be interacted with in the same way as a person who is still learning about technology and can make a 3-screen canvas app. These people need to be given their own rules and interaction journeys to grow and build useful solutions, hence the concept of "Maker Archetypes.

The maker archetypes will typically dictate the maker pathway and the tools that people will be enabled to use to create solutions to problems. It's important to ensure that people at the correct levels have access to the tools that match their skillset. As an example, we probably would not give makers who are early on in their journey access to Visual Studio Code however, we would want new makers to access Canvas apps and Power Automate.

Essentially, the easiest way to classify makers is by setting up a set of criteria that define what a maker is and what they need to do to get to the next level. This may be that they pass certain exams, like the PL-900 or the PL-200 for Power platform, or that they have produced a certain number of usable solutions. Typical maker archetypes may include:

- Beginner Makers: Typically, at the start of the journey and need to learn how to build solutions with Power Platform.

- Intermediate Makers: Relatively technical with know-how in base elements of the platform. Can solve problems with Low code and could be self-sufficient. These makers are known as Citizen Developers.

- Advanced Makers: Proficient in most of the components in the Power Platform and can build relatively complicated solutions to solve business problems. These makers are not part of the IT team but have very high technical skills. They are known as Business Technologists.

- Professional Developers: Employed as developers as part of the IT team in a business. Can write code and leverage all areas of the Power platform. These people are known as "ProDevs".

Barrier to entry

One of the main benefits of the Power Platform is that it lowers the barrier to entry for people who want to create solutions for their business needs. The tools in the Power Platform are designed to be used by different types of makers, from citizen developers to professional developers, depending on their skill level and requirements. The Power Platform enables makers to build applications, automate processes, analyze data, and create chatbots without writing code or relying on IT. This empowers the people closest to the problem to solve it themselves, using their domain knowledge and creativity.

The Power Platform also provides a copilot feature that guides the makers through the steps of creating a solution and provides tips and best practices along the way. Copilot is gaining more and more traction within the Power Platform toolset and allowing people to use natural language prompts to develop solutions really makes it extremely easy to create solutions. By lowering the barrier to entry, the Power Platform democratizes innovation and helps businesses achieve their goals faster and more efficiently. *Figure 3.3* shows copilot embedded directly within canvas apps:

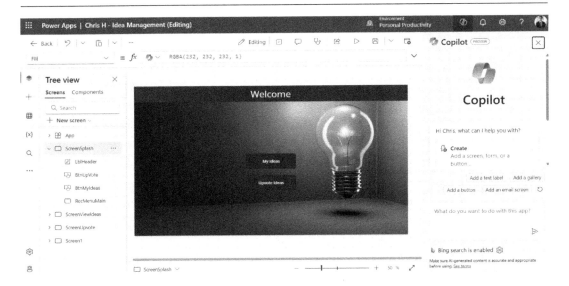

Figure 3.3: Copilot enabled within Canvas apps

People closest to the problem

The individuals who are closest to the problem are the ones who truly understand its intricacies and impact. They are the end users, customers, or business stakeholders who are deeply invested in finding a solution that effectively addresses their needs. Their firsthand experience provides them with an in-depth understanding of the causes and consequences of the problem, making them uniquely positioned to spearhead the development of a suitable solution.

When leveraging the Power Platform, these individuals can transform into solution creators. With the intuitive and user-friendly tools provided by the Power Platform, such as Power Apps, Power Automate, and Power BI, they can develop and deploy applications, workflows, dashboards, and chatbots tailored to their specific challenges and requirements. These tools enable them to design, build, test, and deploy solutions without the need for extensive coding knowledge, putting the power of solution creation directly into their hands. Furthermore, they can collaborate with other makers, including citizen developers, professional developers, or IT professionals, to exchange expertise and feedback. This collaboration enhances the quality and functionality of the solution, drawing on the diverse perspectives and skills of different stakeholders.

By empowering those closest to the problem to take charge of the solution, the Power Platform enables them to create customized and efficient solutions more quickly and effectively than traditional development methods. This approach not only results in solutions that are tailored to their specific needs and expectations but also fosters a sense of ownership and empowerment among the solution creators.

Achieving goals

Achieving success with the Power Platform can be done rapidly! It's important to remember the Fail Fast approach when building solutions. Another concept is that not everything needs to be perfect. Often when building a solution, the scope will grow, and your creation will need to have things added to it and may be larger than anticipated. That's okay, if correct tools are used for the desired outcome. Think a bit about an excel document, where you add new rows, new data and even build pivot tables on the fly. Building Power Platform solutions has a similar approach, and it is perfectly okay to change things as needed, if the documentation and the plan supports the change.

Building things in Power Platform is best done as a team sport. Many different people with different skills can work on a Power Platform solution and complete a build while working together. In fact, even people who don't focus on technology can contribute as part of a project. This makes it increasingly more likely for a solution to be produced as the people closest to the problem can have actual hands-on time in building the outcome.

Solutions also come in all shapes and sizes. Not everything is complex and permanent. Sometimes much smaller solutions are generated with the Power platform, and they are generated rapidly, making it extremely easy to achieve an outcome. A lot of these smaller solutions do not even require any sort of **Application Lifecycle Management** (**ALM**) and can be left where they are created and can be managed and supported by their maker communities.

Ultimately, the goal here is to build something useful as fast as possible and the Power Platform really allows makers of all types to achieve this.

Developers play a crucial role in digital ecosystems, creating and maintaining software solutions to solve problems. The Power Platform aims to assist developers in overcoming challenges by enhancing their productivity and creativity. Additionally, it enables a new category of makers known as citizen developers, who can create apps and workflows without writing code or with minimal coding. The platform lowers the barrier to entry for these makers, empowering them to solve business problems using their domain knowledge and creativity. Ultimately, the goal is to build useful solutions as quickly as possible, and the Power Platform facilitates this for makers of all types. In the next section, we will talk about how to drive operational enhancements with the tools in the Power Platform.

Leveraging Power Apps, Power Automate, and Power BI for operational gains

As we explore the various components within the Power Platform, we need to dive deeper into the interaction layer and lift the veil on what is available for people to create solutions with. Each tool integrates with the other tools in varying ways, which makes the Power Platform increasingly highly adopted with various maker archetypes widely across organizations.

Power Apps overview

Power Apps is a low-code/no-code platform that allows users to create custom apps for web and mobile devices using pre-built templates, drag-and-drop features, and a user-friendly interface. Users can connect their apps to various data sources, such as Dataverse, Dynamics 365, SharePoint, Excel, or Salesforce, and use AI Builder to add artificial intelligence capabilities to their apps.

Power Apps are broken up into two types of applications, these are:

Canvas apps

Canvas apps are a type of Power Apps that allow users to create custom user interfaces from scratch or by using pre-built components, such as buttons, galleries, forms, or charts. Users can design the layout and appearance of their apps by dragging and dropping elements on a canvas and add logic and interactivity by using formulas and expressions like Excel. Canvas apps are meant for scenarios where users need full control over the app design and functionality and want to create personalized and engaging experiences for their target audience. Canvas apps can run on web browsers, mobile devices, or desktops, and can access device capabilities, such as camera, microphone, or location.

Model-Driven apps

Model-driven apps are another type of Power Apps that allow users to create data-driven applications that follow a predefined model and structure. Users can define the data sources, entities, relationships, forms, views, and business logic of their apps by using tools such as Power Apps Studio or the Dataverse. Model-driven apps are meant for scenarios where users need to work with large amounts of data and complex processes and want to create consistent and standardized experiences across devices. Model-driven apps can run on web browsers, mobile devices, or desktops, and can leverage the capabilities of the Power Platform, such as Power Automate, Power BI, or Copilot Studio. Dynamics 365 Customer Engagement or **Customer Relationship Management** (**CRM**) first party applications are extremely complex, business process focused Model-Driven apps. *Figure 3.4* shows a relatively simple model-driven app that has been built to manage claims. This was designed and written by an intermediate maker and a claims agent as the subject matter expert.

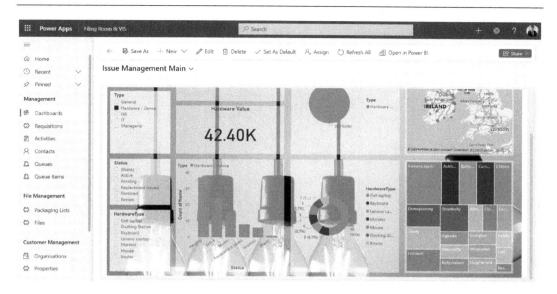

Figure 3.4: A Power BI report embedded within a Model-Driven app

Power Automate overview

Power Automate is a tool that helps users automate repetitive and time-consuming tasks across different applications and services. Users can create workflows, or flows, that trigger actions based on certain conditions, events, or schedules. For example, a user can create a flow that sends an email notification when a new file is added to a Dropbox folder, or a flow that posts a message to a Teams channel when a new tweet is published with a specific hashtag. Power Automate is a bit like the wind, it operates all around us without us necessarily seeing it operating. You may not physically see Power Automate running, but you may see the results of Power Automate. There are two types of automation that can be built within the Power Automate framework. These are:

Power Automate Cloud Flows

Power Automate Cloud Flows are workflows that run on the cloud and can connect to different online services, such as Office 365, SharePoint, Dynamics 365, X (formerly Twitter), Dropbox, and more. Users can create cloud flows from scratch, using a graphical interface or a code-based editor, or choose from hundreds of templates available in the Power Automate gallery. Cloud flows can be triggered manually, by a schedule, by an event, or by a button. Cloud flows can perform various actions, such as sending emails, creating tasks, updating records, posting messages, and more. Cloud flows are useful for automating common business processes, streamlining workflows, and enhancing productivity. *Figure 3.5* shows the Power Automate user experience where flows can be built.

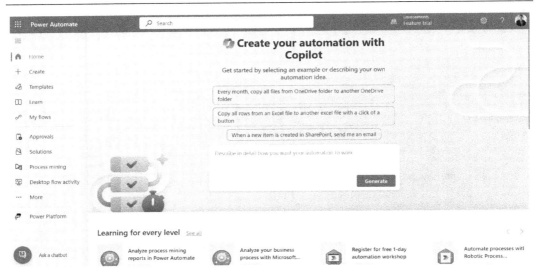

Figure 3.5: Power Automate user interface

Power Automate Robotic Process Automation (RPA)

Power Automate Robotic Process Automation (RPA) is a tool that allows users to automate repetitive and manual tasks that involve interacting with legacy systems, desktop applications, or web browsers. Users can record their actions using a desktop recorder, or create scripts using a code-based editor, and then run them as UI flows. UI flows can be integrated with cloud flows to create end-to-end automation solutions that span across different environments and platforms. RPA is useful for improving efficiency, accuracy, and compliance in various business scenarios, such as data entry, form filling, invoice processing, or report generation.

Power BI overview

Power BI is a versatile and robust business intelligence platform designed to empower users to seamlessly connect, visualize, and analyze data from a wide array of sources, including but not limited to Excel, SQL Server, and Azure. Through its user-friendly interface, individuals can harness the power of data to craft interactive reports and dynamic dashboards that not only present key insights and trends but also facilitate sharing within their organization or online. Furthermore, Power BI equips users with the capability to construct intricate data models, conduct advanced analytics, and seamlessly embed visualizations into other applications, thereby enhancing the overall accessibility and utility of the platform.

An important point to make with regards to Power Bi is that Power BI does NOT use the same connectors as the rest of the Power Platform and does not obey the same set of rules. It FUNCTIONALLY integrates with the wider platform but the way it interacts with data is slightly different. *Figure 3.6* shows a Power BI report with copilot stats.

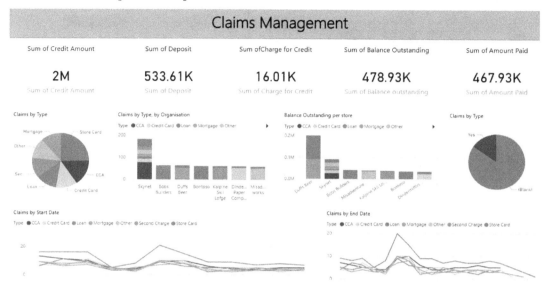

Figure 3.6: Copilot Report in power BI

Copilot Studio

Copilot Studio, previously known as Power Virtual Agents, is a tool that allows users to create custom natural language experiences (chatbots, now known as copilots) that can interact with customers, employees, or partners through natural language. Users can design conversations, or topics, that guide the chatbot to answer questions, provide information, or perform actions. Users can also integrate their chatbots with other services, such as Power Automate, to enable more complex scenarios.

For example, a user can create a chatbot that can book a flight, check the weather, or send an email confirmation. *Figure 3.7* shows Power Virtual Agents user experience rebranded to Copilot Studio.

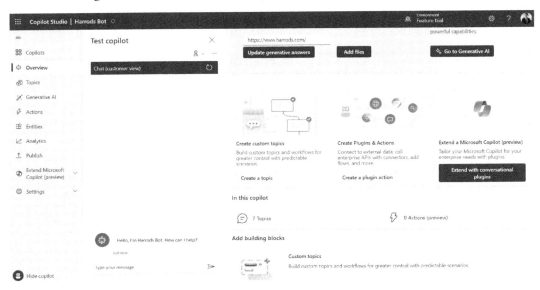

Figure 3.7: Copilot studio

Power Pages

Power Pages allows Makers to create and publish web pages with dynamic content and interactive elements. Power Pages leverage the power of Microsoft Dataverse, the common data service that stores and manages data across the Power Platform. Users can use Power Pages to create websites, blogs, landing pages, newsletters, and more, without coding or hosting. With Power Pages, users can easily create and share web content that drives business outcomes and digital transformation. *Figure 3.8* shows the Power Pages build experience.

Figure 3.8: Power Pages build Experience

Advancing transformation: elevating operations with Power Platform

Achieving operational excellence with the power platform requires that the organization does not only focus on the tools in the platform but includes the people and the processes as well. This approach of People, Platform and Process is vitally important as ultimately, it will be the people who drive the success.

Talk about the era of enablement

Society is currently in a phase called the *"Era of Enablement"*, where organizations no longer need to hire costly partners and contractors to build their solutions, they can do this themselves. This is not to say that CAN'T use contractors and partners. Some organizations just don't have the capacity at hand and in their own teams to build solutions. The point is, The Power Platform provides tools that are easily adopted by makers of all types and therefore people within the organization can simply build their own solutions. It's similar to when Microsoft Office was released. We used to pay people to make us spreadsheets, and now we simply do it ourselves as we have digitally evolved.

Essentially the era of enablement is a period where vendors such as Microsoft are driving people to be self sufficient and are releasing platforms that allow us to do this. It's a wonderful time to be in technology as we can see people within companies driving operational excellence leveraging these very platforms.

This very approach does come with some flaws or risks and ultimately, there needs to be a cultural shift in the way organizations view technology and how it is used.

Allowing people to optimize the way they work

The biggest cultural shift we have had to face in organizations is persuading IT departments to allow people to build solutions to their problems themselves! Typically, IT departments have been stringent and locked down their ecosystems in fear of data leaks and breaches form malevolent agents, which is the right thing to do, however, it is possible in Power Platform to secure the ecosystem AND allow people the freedom to build the things they need to.

Think ABOUT Microsoft Office. People across the world use the Office stack to create all sorts of things and many organizations do not stop or block this as Office is what drives productivity. Why should this be any different with power Platform? People store huge amounts of data in Excel and most organizations have no idea what's out there, at least with Power Platform, there are ways to get visibility across the ecosystem and into the assets that have been created.

It's about treading a fine line between allowing people to be creative and stifling creativity. More mature organizations understand this and allow people the ability to create things, but ALSO respect their data and drive people to leverage the correct data storage facilities for their data all while managing the connectors people have access to by leveraging the Power Platform data policies. Its important people feel empowered to build, but also feel safe.

Driving operational excellence by enabling people to do more with their time

The concept of leveraging technology to drive efficiency and be more productive is not new. In fact, you could say that that is one of the core goals of technology. In this day and age, people are constantly looking for smarter ways of doing things and in fact we have gotten so focused on efficiency, we even have tools such as Microsoft 365 Copilot, which can write our emails for us.

People in all roles and in all circumstances have parts of their jobs that are manual or are cumbersome. The more we advance as society, the less manual tasks we want to do, so we will ALWAYS search for ways to work smarter. One day in the future, the automations and apps we perceive to be time saving right now, will be considered archaic and "Old News". Right now, many organizations are trying to remove the proliferation of micro databases and spreadsheets from their organizations and centralize data. At the time, these tools were considered hugely innovative. We simply have moved on.

Currently, the tools in the Power Platform provide amazing functionality to allow people to automate and digitize their tasks, processes and even some interactions. Manual data capture, file movements, swivel chair integrations and many more scenarios are considered mundane, manual tasks that can be digitized and automated by leveraging tools such as the Power Platform. The more time we can give back to people to do things that matter, the better, even if it's 1 minute at a time. Ultimately, this drives efficiency gains and increases productivity, IF that is the goal of course.

Governance is key when managing these operations

Optimizing an entire ecosystem is a great idea and can absolutely be achieved. However, with great power comes great responsibility. Governance is an absolute need. Governance will protect your ecosystem (people, processes and platforms) from harm or misuse. Essentially, governance provides the rules for "how we do things here". We don't always call it "Governance" as the best governance is applied when people do not know they are being governed. The idea is to create a safe and reliable space for people to be productive and build amazing things without putting your ecosystem into any sort of detriment in any way.

The Power Platform contains several tools that allow us to govern the way people are using the tools. This includes functions such as Tenant Isolation, Data Policies, Monitoring, Data Auditing and MUCH more. As administrators, there are multiple options in the administration console that help ensure that your ecosystem is protected.

There are also add on options such as the Center of Excellence Starter Kit, which allows administrators to get a more granular view of what is being built within the Power Platform and what makers and users are doing. Ultimately, the visibility in the world of an administrator is extremely important and the Power Platform governance tools provide this.

The Power Platform enables operational excellence by focusing on people, platform, and processes. It aligns with the "Era of Enablement," where organizations can build their solutions without relying on external partners. This shift requires a cultural change, allowing individuals to optimize their work and drive efficiency. However, governance is crucial to protect the ecosystem from misuse. The Power Platform offers tools for monitoring, data policies, and auditing to ensure responsible and productive usage.

Summary

In this chapter, you have learned about the Power Platform, a suite of low-code/no-code tools that allow users to build custom applications, workflows, chatbots, and dashboards without writing complex code. You have seen how the Power Platform can help you achieve operational excellence by enabling you to solve business problems, improve efficiency, and enhance customer satisfaction. You have also learned about the importance of governance and the tools available to monitor, manage, and secure the Power Platform environment. You have learned how to use the Power Platform Admin Center, the Power Platform Center of Excellence, and the Microsoft Cloud App Security to ensure compliance, security, and quality standards for your Power Platform solutions. By reading this chapter, you have gained an overview of the capabilities and benefits of the Power Platform, as well as the best practices for ensuring its responsible and productive usage. This information may be useful to you if you are interested in exploring the Power Platform as a way to optimize your work, automate your processes, and leverage your data.

In the next chapter we will look at how to create a center for enablement which becomes a central hub, bringing together the people, processes and platforms in your organization and enables the creation of a useful portfolio of solutions that solve business problems.

Get This Book's PDF Version and Exclusive Extras

UNLOCK NOW

Scan the QR code (or go to packtpub.com/unlock). Search for this book by name, confirm the edition, and then follow the steps on the page.

Note: Keep your invoice handy. Purchases made directly from Packt don't require one.

4

Creating Your Center for Enablement

The **Center for Enablement (C4E)** plays a pivotal role in empowering individuals and teams to embark on their digital transformation journey within the Power Platform. It serves as a safe space where people can explore, experiment, and create innovative solutions without fear of failure. By providing training, resources, and support, the C4E enables users to unlock the full potential of the Power Platform and drive meaningful change in their organizations.

At the C4E, individuals have the opportunity to enhance their skills and proficiency in utilizing the Power Platform's suite of tools. Through comprehensive training programs and workshops, users can learn how to design, develop, and deploy applications, automate processes, and gain insights from data. The C4E fosters a learning environment that encourages continuous growth and knowledge sharing, ensuring that individuals are equipped with the necessary expertise to navigate the digital landscape with confidence.

Moreover, the C4E serves as a hub for collaboration and innovation, bringing together individuals from diverse backgrounds and skill sets. It provides a platform for cross-functional teams to collaborate, share ideas, and co-create solutions that address complex business challenges. By upholding a culture of inclusivity and collaboration, the C4E enables organizations to harness the collective intelligence and creativity of their workforce, driving digital transformation and facilitating a culture of continuous improvement.

We will cover the following topics in the chapter:

- Creating avenues for innovation and exploration within C4E
- Enabling individuals to unleash creativity with IT governance.
- Encouraging innovation and co-creation for digital transformation

Nurturing Creativity: Creating Avenues for Innovation and Exploration within C4E

In the past, we would often refer to the Power Platform central governance team as the "Center of Excellence". At the time, this was a fair point to make because that's exactly what it was. The Center of Excellence or CoE were the team of people who defined best practices and governed the power Platform Assets and technology stack. This was supported by a custom tool Microsoft released called the Power Platform **Center of Excellence (CoE)** Starter Kit, which provided many monitoring, governance and nurture tools, which assisted administrators with their management of the platform.

Although an extremely useful piece of technology, it was assumed that on installing the starter kit, all the organization's governance problems would be solved. Sadly, this is NOT the case. To drive *excellence*, software isn't the only ingredient in the recipe. One needs to consider people and processes as well. As this concept has become more relevant and more accepted the CoE has morphed into a center for Enablement or now known as the C4E. This focuses more on driving behavioral change within a maker community by implementing best practice processes and using technology as the facilitator for these changes. Ultimately, if people are enabled and shown the correct way to do things, there will be less need for hard governance. Ultimately, more well-thought-out guidance and enablement like community and training leads to less need for administrators to be hands-on and they can focus on enabling the wider user base.

How do you start creating your center for enablement?

Creating a safe space for makers

One of the core values of a C4E is to nurture creativity among the makers who use the Power Platform to solve business problems and innovate new solutions. To encourage this culture of creativity, a C4E needs to create a safe space for makers where they can experiment, learn, and collaborate without fear of failure or judgment.

Providing clear and consistent guidance on the governance and compliance policies that apply to the Power Platform, such as data security, privacy, accessibility, and quality standards is hugely important. The clearer these rules are, the easier it will be for people to follow them. A C4E should communicate these policies in a transparent and accessible way, using tools like the CoE Starter Kit, Power Platform Admin Center, and Microsoft Learn. A C4E should also provide training and support for makers to understand and follow these policies and monitor and audit their adherence using dashboards and reports. The best form of governance is applied when people do not know the platform is being governed and don't feel the need for governance.

We should be encouraging makers to explore the full potential of the Power Platform, leveraging its Pro code, low-code and no-code capabilities, integrations with other Microsoft products and third-party services, and extensibility with custom code and connectors. A C4E should provide makers with access to the latest features and updates of the Power Platform, as well as resources and best practices to help them learn and improve their skills. A C4E should also showcase successful examples and use cases of the Power Platform across the organization and celebrate the achievements and innovations of the makers.

Creating opportunities for makers to collaborate and share their ideas, feedback, and experiences with the Power Platform, both within and across teams and departments has proven hugely successful in the past. The more collaboration takes place the more people are likely to join in and share. A C4E should facilitate communication and knowledge sharing among makers, using platforms like Teams, Viva Engage, SharePoint, and GitHub. A C4E should also organize events and activities to drive community and engagement among makers, such as hackathons, workshops, webinars, and user groups.

By creating a safe space for makers, a C4E can encourage the creativity and potential of the Power Platform users and empower them to deliver value and impact for the organization. The more people use the tools in the platform, the more valuable the platform is.

A useful analogy is to compare Power Platform to Microsoft Office. People use the Office tools every day and these tools allow for people to be more productive, for the most part. Power Platform is essentially another business productivity tool that will allow people to do their jobs.

Creating Champions and Advocates

A C4E should not only create opportunities for makers, but also identify and nurture champions and advocates of the Power Platform within the organization. Champions are makers who have demonstrated advanced skills and knowledge of the Power Platform, and who are willing to share their expertise and best practices with other makers. Advocates are business leaders or influencers who can promote the value and benefits of the Power Platform to their peers and stakeholders, and who can sponsor and support Power Platform initiatives and projects.

Creating champions and advocates is crucial for scaling the adoption and impact of the Power Platform across the organization. A C4E should establish a clear and consistent process for identifying, recognizing, and rewarding champions and advocates, based on criteria such as:

- The number and quality of Power Platform solutions they have built or contributed to. This may be as a singular person or part of a fusion team. Most preferably the fusion team option.

- The level of engagement and activity they have shown in the maker community, such as answering questions, providing feedback, sharing tips and tricks, and mentoring new makers. These types of contributions can be tracked through feedback and monitoring. It's important to understand this impact as this will have a direct impact on adoption.

- The impact and outcomes they have achieved or enabled with the Power Platform, such as improving efficiency, productivity, customer satisfaction, revenue, or innovation. These types of metrics are both qualitative and quantitative.

- The feedback and testimonials they have received from other makers, users, customers, or stakeholders. Testimonials and feedback are great, and these makers / champions can build up a portfolio.

A C4E should also provide champions and advocates with various opportunities and incentives to grow and showcase their skills and influence. Again, a mechanism for them to build up a portfolio. There are several methods and strategies for rewarding these people and for keeping them engaged. It is key to ensure that their buy in remains constant. Losing the buy-in from a champion and having them leave the program is way worse than losing other people in the program as the champions are most visible.

- Giving champions access to advanced training and certification programs, such as Microsoft Learn, Power Platform Academy, or Microsoft Certified: Power Platform Developer Associate ensures that they are up to date with the most relevant content and technology updates.

- Including champions in Invitations to exclusive events and webinars, such as Microsoft Ignite, Power Platform Community Conference, or Power Platform User Groups has turned out to be a great way to keeping engagement. In fact, many champions have gotten on stage at these events and shared stories. This is a great way to highlight the innovative nature of your organization.

- Generating recognition and visibility on internal and external platforms, such as newsletters, blogs, podcasts, social media, or Microsoft Power Platform Community is a great way to share people's achievements. Obviously, ensure that there is consent from the person and the business/ Many of the Power Platform champions have been featured by Microsoft in articles, video content and some have even been on stage with Microsoft leadership teams. Support and sponsorship for speaking or presenting at internal or external events, such as town halls, showcases, demos, or conferences really is a great reward for hard work.

- Microsoft often release functionality and content early to certain smaller groups for testing. Getting this feedback from the community is crucial to the way products are built and released. Participation in feedback and beta testing programs, such as Microsoft Power Platform Adoption program, or Microsoft Product Feedback Loop is extremely valuable to champions as they get hands on with the products early and have much better knowledge of the roadmap. This is highly beneficial to them, the C4E and the organization.

By creating champions and advocates, a C4E can leverage the power of peer-to-peer learning and influence and create a culture of empowerment and innovation with the Power Platform. Champions and advocates can help drive the adoption and usage of the Power Platform, inspire and mentor other makers, and demonstrate the value and impact of the Power Platform to the organization.

Ultimately, your champions and advocates network become the core to the "People" part of your C4E.

Driving enthusiasm and encouraging creativity

One of the key challenges of a C4E is to drive and create enthusiasm for the Power Platform in an organization. This is extremely important as the more widely the platform is used, the more valuable it becomes. As people feel inspired to use the platform to solve problems, they will become a driving force in its wider adoption. Driving this enthusiasm takes place in many forms and there are several things that can be done to promote this creativity.

Ultimately, people need to be excited to do something that will help them. Power Platform needs to be seen as a tool that is AWESOME not something that is a chore.

Communicating the vision and benefits of the Power Platform to different stakeholders, such as business leaders, IT professionals, and end users is one of the most important first steps. A C4E can showcase how the Power Platform can help solve business problems, improve efficiency, and foster innovation across the organization. A great way of articulating this is by leveraging the standard monitoring in the CoE starter kit to show the actual live use of the various assets.

By providing learning opportunities and resources for potential and existing makers, such as training sessions, workshops, Hackathons, webinars, documentation, videos, blogs, and forums, you will show your community that this is something the organization has invested in. A C4E can also leverage the Microsoft Learn platform, which offers free online courses and certifications for the Power Platform. We have found that when internal C4E team members and the maker and champions community generate their own specialized content for the team, it is more widely adopted and leveraged.

Similarly to the champions, recognizing and rewarding the achievements and contributions of makers, such as creating badges, certificates, awards, or incentives is a great way to drive enthusiasm and it also gets other people into the spotlight. A C4E can also celebrate and promote the success stories and best practices of makers, such as featuring their apps and solutions on newsletters, intranets, or social media. Celebrating the success of the maker community will likely attract others to the community and to participate.

Creating a community of practice and collaboration among makers, such as forming user groups, clubs, or networks is one of the most useful and important aspects of a C4E. A C4E can also facilitate the exchange of ideas, feedback, and support among makers, such as hosting hackathons, events, or competitions. The more feedback and collaboration that can be gathered, the more likely it is that the community will grow. In fact, based on experience, it has proven that hackathons have been one of the MOST effective ways to drive enablement, engagement and enthusiasm. Getting people together in a creative setting and getting them to work together to build something useful has shown that fusion teams are one of the most effective ways to get something built at a rapid pace, that best solves the problem.

Empowering and trusting makers to experiment and explore the Power Platform, while providing guidance and governance will SHOW your community that this is a strategic area for your business. A C4E should enable makers to access the tools and data they need, while ensuring compliance and security standards. Ultimately, makers are going to find a way to be creative and to build things, therefore it is a better idea to give them the safe space to be creative.

By driving and creating enthusiasm for the Power Platform, a C4E can inspire creativity and innovation in the organization. Creativity involves coming up with new, useful and practical ideas that can POTENTIALLY be implemented. Innovation is about taking these ideas and making them real! Actually productionizing them for others to benefit. What we have seen in Power Platform maker communities is people of ALL backgrounds and skill sets, starting to use the tools available to create amazing solutions that solve often extremely difficult problems.

A key aspect of Power Platform is it lets makers work and innovate where they are most comfortable. Whether they chose to use the tools as they are without writing any code, to full on high code development. Now with the fusion of AI and copilot into the platform, makers can be even more creative. There has been an influx of solutions that are not JUST apps. Now makers are starting to use copilot studio to create conversational user experiences on their data. And not just data from the Microsoft stack, but data from other line of business solutions. This means that data from pretty much any solution that has an API can be connected too. This is how Microsoft has brought us the ability to microservice our data wherever it is, not just within the Microsoft ecosystem.

We are seeing makers think more outside the box now. In the past we have been wedded to this concept of "An App" which has an interface that we interact with but one of the most innovative approaches that many makers have adopted is leveraging automation to make those manual tasks a whole lot less manual. In most of the ecosystems that we work within, there is almost always more automations than applications. This is because sometimes the best user interface is NO user interface.

Organizations should promote a culture that will encourage makers to identify and prioritize the business problems or opportunities that they want to address with the Power Platform, and to define the goals and metrics of their apps and solutions. This type of ideation process is normally done best in a workshop type environment, where people closest to the problem can share struggles and requirements and even build out prototypes if needed.

It's important to challenge makers to think outside the box and explore different possibilities and alternatives with the Power Platform, and to seek feedback and validation from users and stakeholders. The platform is ever changing and with the introduction of AI tools, rethinking ways of working is even more important.

As a C4E team it's critical to support makers to iterate and improve their apps, automations and solutions based on data and feedback, and to share their learnings and findings with others. The introduction of clear feedback mechanisms and monitoring will help makers understand what to do next based on what works and doesn't work. Generating your C4E team should be top of Mind and a high priority. You can see the example of a C4E team represented in *Figure 4.1* as an example of what your team may look like.

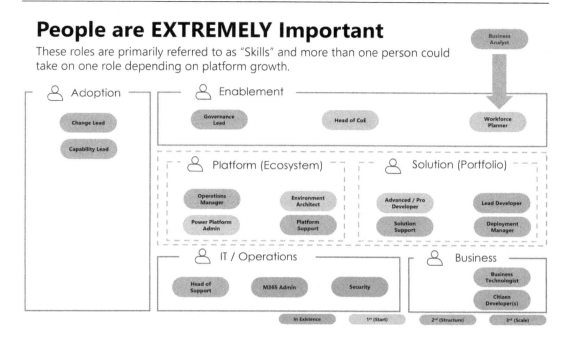

People are EXTREMELY Important

These roles are primarily referred to as "Skills" and more than one person could take on one role depending on platform growth.

Figure 4.1: Example of a center for Enablement team and skills

The evolution from the traditional CoE to the modern C4E focuses on nurturing creativity and innovation within the Power Platform community. The C4E's core values include creating a safe space for makers to experiment, learn, and collaborate without fear of judgment, providing resources for makers to explore the full potential of the Power Platform, and cultivating a community of practice and collaboration. Additionally, the C4E identifies and nurtures champions and advocates of the Power Platform, establishing a process for recognizing and rewarding their contributions. Furthermore, creating enthusiasm and promoting creativity is essential in driving the wider adoption and usage of the Power Platform, encouraging makers to think outside the box and seek feedback and validation from users and stakeholders. Ultimately, the C4E plays a vital role in empowering and supporting makers to deliver value and impact within the organization. In the next section we will explore how to enable guided empowerment and how to help your power platform community get involved.

Enabling individuals to unleash creativity with IT governance

How can you enable your Power Platform makers to let loose their creativity and innovation, while ensuring compliance and security with IT governance? This is the question that this section will address, by introducing the concept of guided empowerment and its benefits for both makers and the organization.

In this section, we will explore how to balance the need for IT governance and the desire for maker empowerment with the Power Platform. We will introduce the idea of guided empowerment, which is a way of providing makers with the freedom and support to create impactful solutions, while also aligning them with IT best practices and policies.

It can be a balancing act and it's important to ensure that the governance and risk rules of the business are respected, AND that makers are given the room and freedom to build things that are useful but SAFE.

Creating an environment of enablement

An environment of enablement is one that empowers individuals to express their creativity and potential with the Power Platform, while ensuring alignment with IT governance and best practices. It is important that ALL parties are comfortable with the governance and guidance framework and processes that have been set up. Typically, there can be rifts between what is technically possible in the platform and the expectations, therefore communication and setting expectations up front is important.

The first step is to Identify and engage the makers in your organization who are interested in using the Power Platform to solve business problems or improve processes. Provide them with resources, guidance, and support to help them get started and learn the basics of the platform. This can be done by leveraging the CoE Starter Kit, which lists top makers. By interacting with all these people, your C4E will quickly develop a community of engaged people and potential champions for your champions' network.

What are the rules people need to follow? Establish and communicate clear policies and guidelines for using the Power Platform, such as naming conventions, security roles, data sources, app sharing, and approval processes. Use the Power Platform admin center and the Center of Excellence (CoE) toolkit to manage and monitor the platform usage and performance across your organization. The earlier you establish these rules, the better. It's important to understand:

- What people are making?
- Where are people making things?
- Who is making things?

Understanding these three things will allow you to set up your ecosystem in a manner that best supports your makers. In *Figure 4.2* is an example of the monitoring of the CoE starter kit we can see the number of apps and flows built in certain environments.

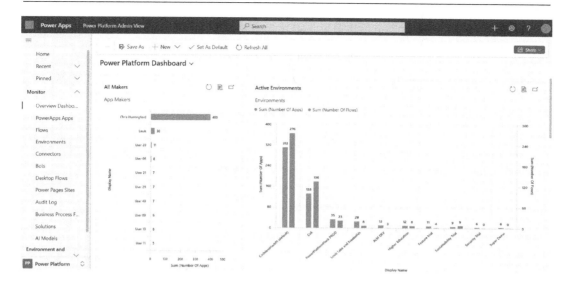

Figure 4.2: Center of Excellence Starter kit opening dashboard.

What are people making?

If you know what people are making then these as a C4E team, you can apply the right levels of support and governance to these solutions. Offering support to solutions that are more complex or critical and less support to solutions that may not be as critical is a great use of resources. Not every solution is made equal.

Where are people making?

Not all environments are made equal. Things created in the default environment should not be given all the support from IT. It's important to ensure that solutions are ring fenced within environments and this will be reflective of your environment strategy.

Who is making?

Understanding and defining your maker archetypes is essential to providing a safe space to makers. Less experienced makers require more stringent governance as they may not know that they are potentially doing something wrong. More experienced makers may have access to premium environments where they can build more freely. It's important to help people discover the right pathway for themselves and to guide them as much as possible.

If a culture of collaboration and knowledge sharing among the makers and other stakeholders, such as IT professionals, business analysts, and end users, is created, then makers are more likely to join the community. Leverage the existing Microsoft communities and forums, such as the Power Platform Community, the Tech Community, and the User Groups, to connect with other makers and experts around the world, then build on this. This will drive people to self-learn and become enabled to create useful things and troubleshoot problems without having to contact a support desk.

By shifting to a "learn it all" culture and by providing collaboration platforms and guidance, you can create an environment focused on Power Platform enablement, where people are motivated and capable of building useful and valuable solutions and learning along the way.

Ensuring data and people are safe

Data and people are ALWAYS top of mind when building solutions with the Power Platform. It's important to understand that data is a digital representation of YOU, your business and your customers so we MUST look after it and respect it. Data leaks do happen and sadly not everyone has the best intentions. We must always ensure that we have the correct people, processes and platforms in place that will ensure people and data are respected. One of the simplest ways to begin is to look at the CoE starter kit Power BI report and understand wat connectors are being used. This is visible in *Figure 4.3*.

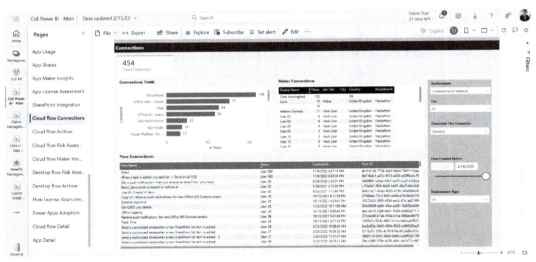

Figure 4.3: Power Automate Connector Review in the Power BI CoE Starter kit report

Once you understand the connectors, create an organization wide data policy and block the connectors NOT being used! This is managed through the Power Platform Admin center and is a fantastic way to stop connector sprawl within the ecosystem. In *Figure 4.4* you can see that MANY unused connectors are left in the blocked list and makers will not be allowed to build solutions with these.

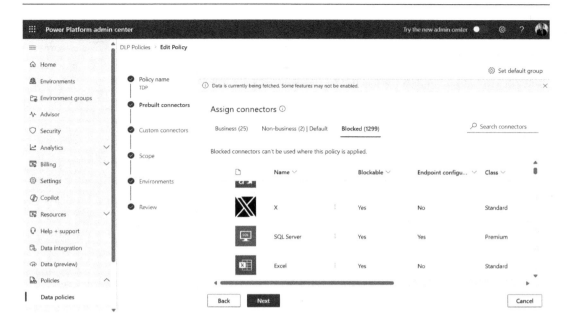

Figure 4.4: Blocking connectors with a tenant wide Data policy in the Power Platform Admin Center

Essentially, if people feel as if they can easily make a mistake and put the organization at risk, it will become more difficult for them to build on the platform as they will be nervous about making that mistake. Hard governance is important but doesn't always need to be overly visible.

There will always be a need for hard governance and soft governance in any ecosystem. The point is, it's important to know when to apply each one. Hard governance will be a physically enforced guardrail, like using Data Policies to block a connector and soft governance will be guidance and learning based. There should be a mix of the 2.

Establish clear policies and governance for the use of the Power Platform in your organization. Define the roles and responsibilities of the makers, admins, and end-users, and enforce the appropriate permissions and security settings. Educate the makers on the best practices and standards for developing and deploying solutions and monitor their compliance and performance. The right team in place will ensure that governance and guidance is adhered to.

Protect the data sources and connectors that the Power Platform accesses and integrates. Ensure that the data is securely stored, encrypted, and backed up, and that the access rights and data policies are consistent across the different platforms and applications. Use **data loss prevention** (**DLP**) policies to prevent the leakage or misuse of sensitive or confidential data and audit the data flows and usage regularly. An important point to make here is educating makes in the type of data they are building with. Often the maker community may not even understand that putting private data (**personally identifiable information** or **PII**) into tools such as excel, and SharePoint may be considered as risky.

Empower the makers to build solutions that are secure, reliable, and scalable. Provide them with the tools and resources to test, debug, and troubleshoot their solutions, and to address any issues or errors that may arise. Encourage them to use pre-built templates, components, and connectors that have been verified and approved by the admins or the Microsoft community. Support them to update and maintain their solutions as the requirements and technologies evolve.

Driving people to learn and grow

One of the key benefits of the Power Platform is that it enables people to learn and grow by building their own solutions without depending on specialized developers or IT professionals. Sure, fusion teams have grown out of this exact need, but there is nothing stopping people getting started on their own. However, this also means that the organization needs to create an environment where people are motivated and supported to focus on their own learning and development, and to leverage the full potential of the Power Platform.

Culture is always something that will be considered top of mind when encouraging learning and growth. Create a culture of curiosity and experimentation. Encourage people to explore the Power Platform and its features, and to try out different scenarios and possibilities. Celebrate the successes and learn from the failures. Reward the learners who share their knowledge and insights with others, and who seek feedback and improvement. The idea of failing fast can be tough to get used to but that's essentially what innovation is all about! Trying things out and finding what works best to solve a problem. Power Platform has just added more tools to our kitbag.

It's important to provide clear guidance and expectations. Define the roles and responsibilities of the makers, admins, and end-users, and communicate the best practices and standards for creating and using solutions. These best practices may not necessarily be physical rules that need to be adhered to, they may be concepts such as "Personal Development Days" where makers get time to learn and grow themselves. OR group training days where people can potentially attend hackathons or explore concepts outside of their specific remit. This has worked extremely well in the past and many organizations promote a culture of self-learning.

Create a space where people can connect, collaborate, and co-create solutions using the Power Platform. Provide opportunities for peer-to-peer learning, mentoring, and coaching. Leverage the existing Microsoft communities and resources, such as forums, blogs, webinars, and events, and encourage people to participate and contribute. Recognize and showcase the achievements and innovations of the makers and inspire others to follow their example.

By creating an environment where people focus on their own learning and growth, the organization can empower them to leverage the Power Platform and to transform the way they work and solve problems. This can lead to more innovation, efficiency, and customer satisfaction, and ultimately, to digital transformation.

This section aims to address the question of how to empower Power Platform makers to innovate while maintaining compliance and security with IT governance. The concept of guided empowerment is introduced, emphasizing the need to balance IT governance with maker empowerment. Key points include identifying and engaging makers, establishing clear policies and guidelines, and fostering a culture of collaboration and knowledge sharing. Additionally, the section highlights the importance of ensuring data and people's safety, driving learning and growth, and creating a supportive environment for individuals to leverage the Power Platform effectively. In the next section we will explore mechanisms to build the foundation for innovation and co-creation.

Encouraging innovation and co-creation for digital transformation

The introduction of Power Platform into the technical and transformation community has changed the way in which solutions are thought up and created. In the past, often solutions were built by a siloed group of developers who were working off a spec of sorts. As an example, an area of the business would share a requirement with a specification and the developers would create the solution, hoping that they understood the spec correctly. If the spec was not well defined or written the output or solution would not be fit for purpose.

As low-code development tools, specifically power Platforms, hit the market, organizations have been encouraged to allow people closest to the problem to be involved in creating these solutions. As mentioned in previous chapters, the person closest to the problem is often best able to define the solution and even participate in building it.

And thus, the concept of the Fusion team was born. A fusion team is a combination of people with varying skills, not all technical, who come together to create a solution to a problem.

Giving people a platform and a space to engage

One key aspect of establishing a culture of innovation and co-creation is giving people a platform and a space to engage with each other and with the Power Platform. This can be done by creating communities of practice, where people can share their ideas, challenges, solutions, and feedback on using the Power Platform. Communities of practice can also provide opportunities for learning, mentoring, recognition, and collaboration among peers and experts.

As ideas, problems and solutions are shared, people with specific skill sets or knowledge can engage one another and share information. This is often how these fusion teams are born. Someone with domain expertise will share a concept and others will identify with eh concept and share knowledge.

This leads to many other opportunities, such as the ability to build out **Minimum Viable Products** (**MVPs**) and **Proof of Concepts** (**PoCs**). These are not considered a full product but rather a part of a solution, containing specific aspects of what the full solution could do. Many of these MVPs and PoCs are built in innovation-type scenarios such as hackathons and now with Copilot, Promptathons (Using natural language prompting techniques and Microsoft Copilot, rather than physically writing code or building something).

By giving people, a platform and a space to engage, the organization can enable them to learn from each other, collaborate on solutions, and express their creativity and potential with the Power Platform. This can help to further a culture of innovation and co-creation that supports digital transformation.

Finding ways to inspire creativity and Innovation

To inspire creativity and innovation with the Power Platform, the organization can organize and participate in various events and activities that showcase the possibilities and benefits of the tools. There are so many opportunities to drive and inspire Innovation; we just must think out of the box and about the people we are engaging.

- **Hackathons**: A hackathon is a time-bound event where teams of developers, business analysts, domain experts, and end-users work together to create solutions using the Power Platform. Hackathons can be a great way to generate ideas, solve problems, learn new skills, and foster collaboration and innovation. The organization can host its own internal hackathons or join external ones, such as the Microsoft Power Platform Hack for Good, which aims to address social and environmental challenges with technology.

- **Workshops**: A workshop is a structured and interactive learning session where participants can gain hands-on experience with the Power Platform. Workshops can be tailored to different levels of expertise, from beginners to advanced users, and cover various topics, such as data modeling, app design, automation, AI, and security. The organization can offer workshops to its employees, customers, partners, or community members, either online or in person, to help them discover and explore the features and capabilities of the Power Platform.

- **In a Day labs**: There are several In a Day labs that Microsoft has created that enable users to build solutions by following a set of instructions. These are great mechanisms to get started with and for organizations wanting to understand the basics, these are highly recommended. The scenarios are generic, on purpose. Many partners and community members have built their own in a day lab that are far more custom.

- **Adoption of the tools**: To inspire creativity and innovation, the organization should also encourage and support the adoption of the Power Platform tools by its users. This can be done by providing training, documentation, guidance, and best practices, as well as creating a feedback loop and a recognition system. By empowering users to use the Power Platform tools effectively and confidently, the organization can enable them to create and share solutions that meet their needs and add value to the organization.

By engaging in these activities, the organization can inspire creativity and innovation with the Power Platform and build a vibrant and thriving community around it. The community and spirit of innovation will only be as good as the support that it gets from the wider team, so it is important to ensure that all stakeholders are aware and prepared for this movement to take place.

Ensuring progression

Another key aspect of inspiring creativity and innovation with the Power Platform is ensuring progression. This means that the organization should provide opportunities and resources for the makers to learn more about using the Power Platform tools to solve everyday problems and enhance their skills and knowledge. Some of the ways to ensure progression are:

- **Providing learning paths**: The organization can create or use existing learning paths that guide the makers through different levels of proficiency and complexity with the Power Platform tools. Learning paths can include online courses, videos, tutorials, quizzes, certifications, and hands-on projects that help the makers acquire and demonstrate their skills. For example, the organization can use the Microsoft Learn platform, which offers free and interactive learning content for various Power Platform tools and scenarios.

- **Creating challenges**: The organization can also create challenges that encourage the makers to apply their skills and creativity to solve real-world problems using the Power Platform tools. Challenges can be based on specific themes, domains, or business needs, and can have different levels of difficulty and reward. For example, the organization can use the Power Platform Community, which hosts monthly app challenges and hackathons for makers to showcase their solutions and win prizes.

- **Fostering collaboration**: The organization can foster collaboration among the makers by creating spaces and platforms where they can share their ideas, feedback, tips, and best practices with each other. Collaboration can help the makers learn from each other, discover new possibilities, and improve their solutions. For example, the organization can use the Power Platform User Groups, which are communities of users who meet regularly to network, learn, and exchange experiences with the Power Platform tools.

By ensuring progression, the organization can help the makers advance their learning journey with the Power Platform and unlock their full potential and creativity. The more people learn and the more curious they are, the more likely they are to engage in the platform and start problem solving.

The introduction of Power Platform into the technical and transformation community has revolutionized the approach to solution creation by driving collaborative and innovative practices. Previously, solutions were developed in silos based on specified requirements, often leading to misunderstandings and unfit solutions. With the advent of low code development tools like Power Platform, organizations are now embracing collaborative approaches, allowing individuals closest to the problem to participate in solution creation. The concept of Fusion teams, comprising individuals with diverse skills, has emerged to address this shift in approach. Creating communities of practice has been instrumental in providing a platform for sharing ideas, solutions, and feedback, resulting in the formation of fusion teams. Additionally, various events and activities such as hackathons, workshops, and "In a Day" labs have been organized to inspire creativity and drive innovation. Ensuring progression involves providing learning paths, creating challenges, and championing collaboration among makers, ultimately unlocking their full potential and creativity with the Power Platform.

Summary

The chapter discusses the evolution from the traditional Center of Excellence (CoE) to the modern Center for Enablement (C4E) and focuses on nurturing creativity and innovation within the Power Platform community. The C4E emphasizes creating a safe space for makers to experiment, learn, and collaborate without fear of judgment, providing resources for makers to explore the full potential of the Power Platform, and cultivating a community of practice and collaboration. Additionally, the C4E identifies and nurtures champions and advocates of the Power Platform and establishes a process for recognizing and rewarding their contributions. Moreover, creating enthusiasm and nurturing creativity is essential in driving the wider adoption and usage of the Power Platform, encouraging makers to think creatively and seek feedback and validation from users and stakeholders. The C4E plays a vital role in empowering and supporting makers to deliver value and impact within the organization.

The next section, "*Enabling individuals to unleash creativity with IT governance*," explores mechanisms for empowering Power Platform makers to innovate while maintaining compliance and security with IT governance. The concept of guided empowerment is introduced, emphasizing the need to balance IT governance with maker empowerment. It also highlights the importance of ensuring data and people's safety, driving learning and growth, and creating a supportive environment for individuals to leverage the Power Platform effectively.

Lastly, "*Encouraging innovation and co-creation for digital transformation*," discusses fostering a culture of innovation and co-creation by providing a platform for engagement, inspiring creativity, and innovation, and ensuring progression. It emphasizes the importance of creating communities of practice, organizing events such as hackathons and workshops, and providing opportunities for makers to learn and grow, unlocking their full potential and creativity with the Power Platform.

In the next chapter, we will be taking a look at how to build out multiple different types of solutions leveraging the tools in the power platform and how to connect these solutions to multiple data structures and services in order to scale across the wider organization.

5

Executing and Scaling Transformation Initiatives

Power Platform, with its low-code/no-code tools, helps organizations bring their ideas to life by executing and scaling transformation initiatives. Its user-friendly interface and intuitive design allow business users and citizen developers to quickly prototype, iterate, and deploy applications without relying heavily on traditional software development methods. This approach unlocks the potential for organizations to drive digital transformation at an accelerated pace.

One of the key advantages of Power Platform is its ability to scale solutions seamlessly. Organizations can start with small-scale initiatives and gradually expand to enterprise-wide deployments. Power Platform integrates with enterprise products from the Microsoft Azure suite, allowing organizations to leverage additional capabilities as their needs evolve. By leveraging Power Platform's advantages, organizations can confidently execute and scale their transformation initiatives, rapidly develop applications, automate processes, and integrate with enterprise products to drive meaningful change across the entire organization.

We will cover the following topics in this chapter:

- Getting started with your vision
- Rapid prototyping and deployment with Power Platform
- Unlocking solutions with Power Platform
- Driving tangible results and proving value

Getting started with your vision

Power Platform is an extremely powerful set of tools that can easily scale from smaller personal solutions to widely adopted organization initiatives that help manage and execute company-wide processes. This scale is only possible in a manageable state if the correct ecosystem is set up to support it. A number of approaches and processes can be undertaken to ensure that your organization's vision is turned into a reality. In this section, we will explore the process you might take to get started with turning your vision into a reality.

Setting your purpose

Many organizations do not have the opportunity to set their purpose for wanting to adopt Power Platform as it often just happens to them. Power Platform assets are often discovered within a digital ecosystem long after they are created. This is because Microsoft leaves the platform available as a standard and it is so deeply integrated with many other Office 365, Azure, and Dynamics 365 tools. Often, makers discover the platform by mistake and end up building amazing things with it.

There are scenarios in which IT admins have installed the **Center of Excellence (CoE) Starter Kit** and discovered thousands of cross-organizational solutions that have been adopted by many people. This means that people are already solving business problems with Power Platform in an ungoverned manner. In many scenarios, the platform has far surpassed the point of management and governance and if the platform is somehow turned off or blocked, people's assets break. This is called **the Scream Test**; if you shut it off, people will make a huge noise. So, *if* you try to do this and somehow succeed, please be prepared for a lot of support tickets. The point is that shutting it down is not an option in most cases, and this actually sends an unhealthy message to people who have been using these tools to solve problems. Regardless of where you may be in your Power Platform journey, it is important to at least decide what the next steps should be. Visibility and education are both important here. A clever idea is to get as many people into the room as possible and collectively define a purpose for Power Platform and your center for enablement. You may want to start by thinking about the following:

- *Who* is using the platform?
- *What* has been built on the platform?
- *Where* have things been built?

Progressing from there will be a great start as you can then decide what to do next. Often, organizations will take the approach of keeping the strategy simple to start with. Examples of this are as follows:

- Lock the platform down from a security perspective
- Let internal IT and pro developers build with it
- Roll out to a wider audience at a later point

These three simple strategy examples work well and are straightforward enough to stick to and map back to as you progress through the process of setting up and securing your ecosystem.

The idea here is to get everyone to agree on what the purpose is so that a plan can be put in place to ensure that the purpose is delivered on. The hardest part in all of this is to get the right people into one room or onto one call. This has historically been difficult.

The next tough part is getting people to agree on one thing! There are techniques to help facilitate this, such as changing management and designing thinking workshops facilitated over interactive tools, such as Mural, Miro, or Figma. This way, if people interact and share collaboratively, there is a stronger likelihood that they will reach a better-defined outcome faster.

As an example, your purpose statement could be as follows:

We would like to deploy Power Platform to an initial set of power users within the IT team and the business, which will enable rapid solution development. We would like to do this with a solid governance layer.

The purpose statement needs to be clear and defined! You should never do anything that does not support this statement. To drive this purpose, you need a plan!

What is your plan?

Your plan needs to map to your purpose as clearly as possible. This is where having a great program lead or project manager will help. Planning your project accurately will be important. Your plan should focus on specific areas that will help you reach your purpose. Typically, you can break your plan up into different pillars and each pillar would have specific workstreams (or categories) underneath it.

This plan, with an example illustrated in *Figure 5.1*, is referred to as an **ecosystem enablement program**, where you may want to consider the following pillars followed by specific allocated workstreams or categories as the core components of your plan. Each of these workstreams focuses on different aspects of your Power Platform ecosystem and each is important when ensuring that a safe space is being created for makers to build useful solutions.

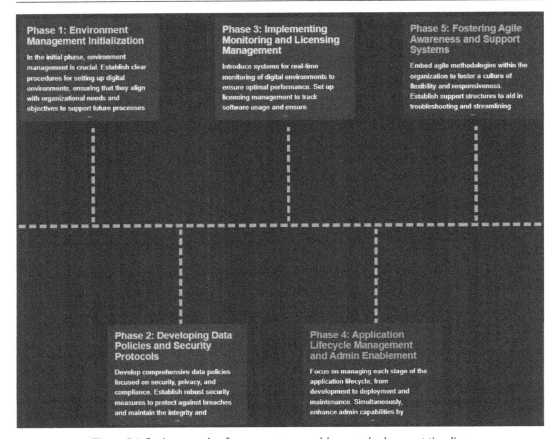

Figure 5.1: Basic example of an ecosystem enablement deployment timeline

Digital guardrails

Guardrails are the technical tools or platforms that are put in place to manage and maintain your ecosystem. Typically, in Power Platform, you may want to focus on the following digital guardrail workstreams as a starting point:

- **Environment strategy**: Environments form the core of your ecosystem and define *where* people will be building things. The environment strategy will form the basis of the digital guardrails and inform other workstreams within the strategy, such as data policies and security.

- **Data policies**: These policies form the core mechanism to manage the connectors that are available to each set of environments. These connectors are the core of Power Platform and require control across the environment estate.

- **Security**: The security within Power Platform and the wider Microsoft stack enables organizations to manage *who* has access to the relevant tools, environments, and connectors. A robust security strategy will enable the right people to access the correct tools and environments without worrying about data leakage. As an example, you may want to consider adding Dataverse to all environments as it has a much deeper set of security functionalities than what is available within environments without Dataverse.

- **Monitoring**: This is the ability to understand what is being leveraged in Power Platform. Typically, this process starts with the CoE Starter Kit installation to get visibility, and then wider monitoring functionality can be employed, such as Azure Application Insights and Compliance Center audit reporting.

Processes

The processes will define how people and technology within the ecosystem interact with one another. Processes within your ecosystem are extremely important as they will define and refine ways of working. Some of the key areas you would need to consider under the processes pillar are, but not limited to, the following:

- **Support and operations**: How are your support and operations structured and has a support wrapper been defined for the platform as well as the assets built on the platform? There are multiple processes that can be defined within the support wrapper, such as tracking of support tickets, feedback requests, event management, and more. It is important to ensure that these processes are well defined as they will directly impact your support desk and people's time.

- **Governance and compliance**: Governance is a very widely used word, but what is important in Power Platform is that governance and compliance standards are created and made available to everyone. Typically, governance and compliance align to ensure the platform and the tools created on the platform are done in a manner that correctly aligns with the rules set up by your organization. The rules of engagement that you create to ensure your ecosystem is protected are paramount to the success of the platform's adoption. As an example, you could create a governance rule in specific environments that dictates that apps can only be shared with less than 500 people.

- **Application life cycle management (ALM)**: This is not just about automatically moving solutions between environments but the initial idea of a solution to sunsetting it after it is no longer needed. It's important to understand how solutions will move through this process and how they will be managed. An important part of ALM is the tools used to move solutions between environments. Many organizations use Azure DevOps. However, Power Platform has its own capability with the pipelines functionality available within managed environments.

- **Ideation**: How are ideas managed and tracked into a proper backlog that can be fed to the relevant people for creation? This process defines your mechanism for workload management. Many organizations build a basic ideation solution based on SharePoint or may leverage the innovation backlog solution available in the CoE Starter Kit. Centralizing and managing ideas is important. The more assets that are built with the tools available in the platform, the more valuable the platform is.

- **Feedback**: It is important to ensure people can share their experiences when using the platform as it drives toward the constant growth and improvement of the platform and ecosystem. Feedback informs platform growth and adoption. When people's voices are heard, then the processes created to manage and govern the platform can be refined. A simple Microsoft form can be created and shared within your community collaboration platform for people to share feedback at any time.

Organization enablement

Organization enablement refers to methods of getting people in your organization to understand and use the platform to create useful things. Ways to start this process will typically be more change- and enablement-focused and will require knowledge of some frameworks, such as the **Professional and Science (PROSCI)** framework. The workstreams you may want to explore to start are, but not limited to, the following:

- **Community of practice**: How will makers and users interact with one another? A centralized hub where people can collaborate and communicate is especially important. Think about a Viva Engage site with your shared resources and the Power Platform guidance. This provides a central location for members of the Power Platform community to share knowledge and content that will help and support the growth of the wider community.

- **Champions**: The champions in your organization are typically the consistent makers who are actively building things and sharing them across the ecosystem. These people are enthusiastic and helpful. Champion programs are extremely beneficial to any organization as they become the core of the Power Platform community. Often, champions are viewed as heroes in the community and they help to motivate people around them.

- **Impacted group management**: How will groups of people be brought into the various maker and user communities? Which groups of people will be assigned Power Platform licenses? Think about the impacted groups of people and how this should be rolled out so the scale of platform adoption can be achieved.

- **Stakeholder management**: Stakeholders are particularly important in the realm of platform adoption. Your stakeholder management program should drive stakeholders to take responsibility and be bought in but also offer advice and leadership.

- **Training and enablement**: How will the best practice be disseminated across your organization? This is key because people want to learn. Where will training come from? A training and enablement plan is critical to the adoption of Power Platform across your business.

Portfolio

Your portfolio consists of the useful things you create and how you create an environment for makers to be creative and successful. There are several ways to start this program of work. Some of the key areas you would need to consider under the processes pillar are, but are not limited to, the following:

- **Maker archetypes**: As mentioned in previous chapters, makers are not all the same and not all makers have the same set of skills. It is important to set up your maker archetypes so that you can define where and what people can get access to. This will make the maker's life a lot easier.

- **Maker journey management**: Makers will participate in the platform differently and at various times. Some will really need to study and learn, while others will not. Defining what the maker archetype journeys could look like will help streamline the ways makers engage. A maker archetype journey is the journey a maker will take to create something useful. Typically, it is a set of steps that starts with the maker discovering the platform and results in a solution being created and productionized for consumption across the business.

- **Maker best practice**: There are always rules that need to be followed when making solutions. This type of practice should be shared across your entire maker base and makers need to understand that "this is how we do things here."

- **Data, connectors, and licensing**: This is a very important part of enablement and portfolio building. This is so different for many organizations as some see the platform as completely strategic and have invested in premium licensing and others see it as tactical and only use seeded licenses. It is important to understand the core fundamentals of data and connectors in order to make informed decisions on where data should be stored and managed so that compliance and risk policies in your organization are respected.

- **Architectural best practice**: This is a little different from maker best practice as it is far more technical. It involves an understanding of Power Platform at the platform level and not at the app or flow level. This is about setting the scene for all the makers.

The ecosystem enablement plan, as illustrated in *Figure 5.2*, should consolidate as many of these workstreams as possible as its core and can be executed as a *gather-and-implement* Agile approach where you focus on each workstream and ask as many questions as possible, and then define a mini-implementation plan for each workstream.

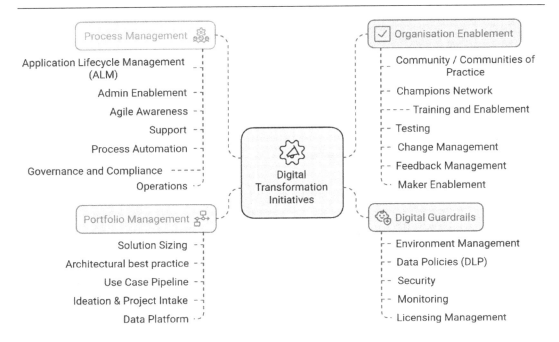

Figure 5.2: The breakdown of a classic ecosystem enablement program

As an example, for the communities of practice workstream, you would ensure that questions are asked about where people will collaborate, how they will get access, who will manage these areas, and how to onboard people.

The output would then be to do the following:

- Implement a viva engage or teams community site

- Appoint community leaders

- Define the community onboarding process

There are many other areas that can be focused on in each workstream and these will be discovered with your organization.

Setting up the foundations

Setting up the foundation is the most difficult phase. This is because there may already be things created on the platform that need to be reviewed. In more cases than not, these solutions need to not be impacted by any changes being made to the platform during an ecosystem enablement program. The foundational phase is important because it focuses on the technology (platform) as the initial mechanism to set up the governance needed. This is referred to in the market as *setting up the guardrails*.

Setting up the guardrails

Always start with guardrails! The workstreams in the guardrails pillar are vital and will provide the most value immediately. Whether your organization has thousands of assets or none, the guardrails pillar is the best place to begin. Figure out that environment strategy and get those data policies in place. Make sure you are protecting whatever is new. You can always go back and slowly clean up environments as you go. Getting in a core set of guardrails will bring peace of mind to Power Platform administrators.

The next steps are going to depend on what has already been set up in your ecosystem. If you already have high adoption, you should start with the processes as soon as you can. Getting the support and ops processes in place is the primary concern here.

If you have low adoption, move on to organization enablement workstreams, where you can start setting up communities of practice and champions networks. Ensure that the right people are in the right place and the infrastructure is in place to cater to a community of makers. This will be small to start and that is perfectly normal! Make sure you get your infrastructure ready for people.

Then, move on to process-focused workstreams, and ensure your support wrapper, ALM, operations, governance, ideation, and feedback processes are ready for implementation.

Finally, think about how to ensure makers understand the rules of engagement and "how we do things here." This will come through in the rules you set up under your portfolio creation workstreams.

Power Platform offers a flexible set of tools that can be scaled from individual solutions to enterprise initiatives. To ensure successful implementation, it is crucial to establish a clear purpose for using the platform and involve relevant stakeholders in the planning process. This involves defining the platform's purpose, creating a comprehensive plan, and focusing on key pillars, such as digital guardrails, processes, organization enablement, and portfolio. By following a structured approach and setting strong foundations, organizations can effectively execute and scale their transformation initiatives using Power Platform. In the next section, we will explore how to get started with your ability to prototype and deploy rapidly with Power Platform.

Rapid prototyping and deployment with Power Platform

One of the greatest and most widely adopted concepts with the Power Platform ecosystem is the ability to fail fast! Yes, this is not a bad thing at all. The ability to rapidly prototype and create meaningful solutions quickly is an enormously powerful tool. It does, however, involve a shift in mindset and culture. We cannot look at this the same way we did before when we used custom code for everything and applied these intensely complex release cycles and testing patterns. Sure, there is a time and a place for all of this but not all problems are at the same level of complexity and therefore not all solutions are made equally.

In real life, we do not apply the same level of attention and detail to every problem or requirement because the fact of the matter is that not all of them are as important or critical as the next. If a problem is weighted with higher risk or danger, that problem will get far more attention than one that carries less risk. This concept is applied to the creation and management of solutions as well.

Let us take two use cases:

- A kudos solution that allows people to send their colleagues free coffee vouchers
- The health and safety logging solution, where issues from all around the building are reported to prevent accidents

If the kudos solution breaks, the worst thing that will happen is people will not be able to send each other free coffee vouchers. However, if the health and safety solution goes down, a critical issue is ignored, and someone is hurt, there are legal ramifications, and someone is at risk.

These two solutions may be built in a comparable manner and the kudos solution may even have more technical complexity but the health and safety solution is more important. Therefore, the kudos solution will not require as much support and architectural rigor as the health and safety solution.

Solution sizing

A fantastic method of managing or cataloging what people create is the concept of solution sizing. This concept can be used at any phase of the application conception and creation of your solution. Because you can create millions of assets with Power Platform, there must be some commonalities in structure and therefore, there could be a way solutions are placed into buckets to be categorized. As an example, we could break down our solutions into small, medium, or large, or you may have bronze, silver, or gold. You may even have more than three categories, such as extra small, small, medium, large, or extra-large. There are so many methods to achieve this, and it will depend on what people want to build.

There are also characteristics for each size, which will then dictate what bracket a solution may fall into. This will also depend on how your organization works and the current IT governance. Let us look at a method of sizing your solutions. There are many criteria, some of which are as follows:

Category	Small	Medium	Large
Data	Public	Internal	Private
Support	By Maker	By Team	By IT
No of Users	<50	51 – 500	501 +
Criticality	Low	Medium	High
ROI	Low	Medium	High
Tech Complexity	Low	Medium	high

Table 5.1: Solution sizing criteria used when determining the impact of a solution

You may find that when reviewing your solution, it may be a mixture of small and medium, in which case it is best to select the larger of the two options as this will drive best practice once again and is more likely to respect the scale framework you put in place in the future.

A great way to build out all solutions is to rapidly prototype the smaller solutions based on the architectural best practice and then grow them into larger solutions should they require it.

Applying architectural best practices

It is especially important to define what architectural best practice looks like to you and your team of makers. This is not just about how to build a Canvas app; it is much larger and focuses on how to best prepare the platform for solutions that will be built using the tools provided. One of the most important questions to ask is this: "Where will we be storing data?"

As you will discover later in this chapter, data is always the most important part of the architectural process. It is key to start thinking about where your data is and how best to provide it to the makers. We often refer to this as data micro-servicing, and when this is done well, it creates a robust mechanism for many solutions to be built on top of it. Starting any solution design and development process with a well-thought-out data architecture is a great way to mitigate problems later on.

One of the most well defined enterprise architecture approaches is a focus on the concept of "Ecosystem Architecture", which focuses on splitting the various solution and tool types into groups known as digital neighborhoods.

You can see in *Figure 5.3* that there is a clear distinction between core business systems and the Application Portfolio neighborhood. The solutions built then leverage data from the core business systems or generate data and store this in Dataverse. This is an extremely scalable reference ecosystem architecture and creates a platform for rapid prototyping and scalable solutions.

Reference Ecosystem

Notional Ecosystem Map in the Microsoft Cloud

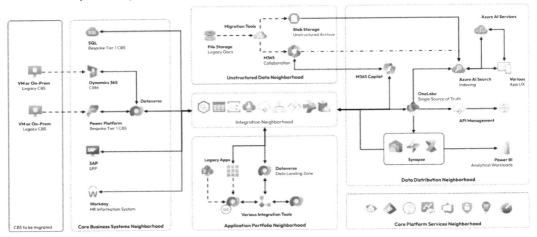

Figure 5.3: A reference ecosystem developed by the Cloud Lighthouse team

The definition and management of a strong ecosystem architecture are essential to the wider utilization and adoption of Power Platform. Many areas of the ecosystem can draw from both data and functionality within the platform, making it more useful and overall, a critical part of any digital ecosystem.

Prototyping in an Agile manner

Often, the culture and approach of prototyping can be a little daunting because we are so used to being bound into this extremely long and complicated development process. The idea with this approach is not everything needs to be kept, and sometimes the solution is less complex than it seems. Prototyping allows us to create more freely and again, fail fast. If something does not work well on the platform, that is fine, move on.

We have seen a huge shift since the inception of low-code tools such as Power Platform, where developers/makers are far more inclined to just try something out and then either build on it or move on, depending on the outcome. Before we even think about technology, we need to understand that this is a cultural shift and are you and your organization ready to think like this?

There are several delivery methodologies that can be leveraged to deliver projects in an organization. The two main delivery methodologies, as indicated in *Figure 5.4*, are Waterfall and Agile.

The Waterfall delivery methodology is a linear project management approach consisting of sequential phases: requirements analysis, system design, implementation, testing, deployment, and maintenance. Each phase must be completed before moving to the next, making it ideal for projects with clear, stable requirements. However, this method is less adaptable to changes during development.

The Agile delivery methodology is an iterative approach to project management that emphasizes flexibility, collaboration, and customer feedback. It allows for continuous improvement and adaptation throughout the development process. Agile is well suited for projects where requirements are likely to change or where a quick time to market is essential.

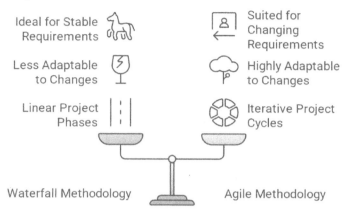

Waterfall and Agile methodologies in project management.

Figure 5.4: The difference between Waterfall and Agile project delivery methodologies

It is best to engage in a change management function or advisory function before this is released to the world because the approach is incredibly Agile. Organizations locked into a waterfall methodology often struggle with the speed and change of the solution build process. It is important to ensure people are ready to think differently.

The hyper-agility strategy advocates for rapid prototyping and deployment using low-code/no-code tools within the Power Platform ecosystem. It emphasizes the importance of embracing failure as a natural part of the development process and encourages a shift in mindset and culture. The strategy emphasizes that not all solutions require the same level of complexity and attention and introduces the concept of solution sizing to categorize solutions based on factors such as data, support, number of users, criticality, **return on investment** (**ROI**), and tech complexity. Additionally, it highlights the significance of applying architectural best practices, particularly focusing on data micro-servicing, and defining a scalable architecture for rapid prototyping. The strategy also promotes a cultural shift toward a more Agile approach to solution building and suggests engaging change management or advisory functions before implementing these practices to ensure the organization is ready for the transition. In the next section, we will explore methods of unlocking the potential to grow solutions with Power Platform.

In this section, we emphasize the importance of embracing failure as a natural part of the development process within the Power Platform ecosystem. It introduces the concept of solution sizing to categorize solutions based on factors such as data, support, number of users, criticality, ROI, and tech complexity. Additionally, it highlights the significance of applying architectural best practices, particularly focusing on data micro-servicing and defining a scalable architecture for rapid prototyping. We also promote a cultural shift toward a more agile approach to solution building and suggest engaging change management or advisory functions before implementing these practices to ensure the organization is ready for the transition. In the next section, we will explore mechanisms for unlocking the potential to grow solutions in the Power Platform ecosystem.

Unlocking solutions with Power Platform

Power Platform is designed to hyperscale! What this means is that it is designed and built in such a way that allows for multiple solutions of multiple types to be created with and on the tools provided by the platform. In fact, this is the primary and core design of many Microsoft (Microsoft Office or Microsoft Azure) tools. They are fantastic platforms that have grown hugely and have stood the test of time. Office alone has 1.2 billion users and is growing. Power Platform is built on top of the Microsoft productivity stack and therefore actually leverages tools within this stack.

There are organizations out there with quite literally hundreds and thousands of assets built with Power Platform. They have rich ecosystems of these assets that help their business run and help people and teams be more productive. It is incredible to look at some of these organizations' centers for enablement and to witness the growth of the platform.

In comparison, when you look at tools such as Purview and see the number of Excel documents that exist in your Office ecosystem, it is not surprising that Power Platform has had such wide adoption. People are interested in solving problems.

Starting with an idea

Ideation is one of the most underestimated and most powerful tools an organization can promote when leveraging platforms such as Power Platform. The concept of ideation involves thinking outside of the box and giving people the ability to do so. The more ideas that are generated, the more opportunity there will be to fulfill these ideas using Power Platform.

There are many methods that drive ideation, and we will explore two simple methods that really can get any organization going rapidly. These two methods are lightly summarized in *Figure 5.5*, indicating the differences between active and passive ideation.

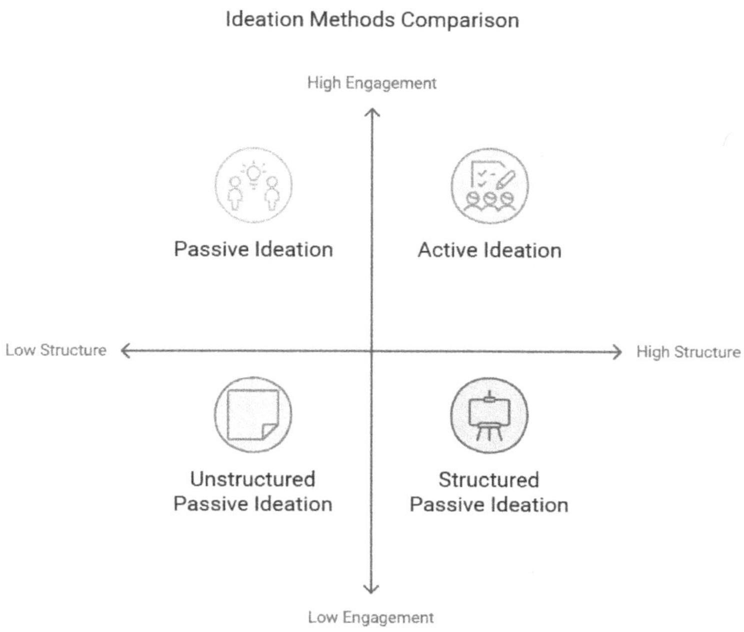

Ideation Methods Comparison

Figure 5.5: Highlighting the difference between passive and active ideation

Passive ideation

This is the simplest yet rewarding mechanism to drive ideation. It fosters a culture of idea generation without being held to account. Passive ideation gives people the opportunity to capture and store any ideas they may have in a central location. These ideas are explored once every X time and then either retired or approved. You can download solutions made from Power Platform tools, or you could even simply use a Microsoft form that is made available to the organization. There are tools that even allow other people to upvote your idea instead of capturing a new one themselves.

Active ideation

This is a less generic form of ideation and is far more intentional and targeted. It is usually conducted with a number of people over a set period of around four to eight hours. There are tools that help facilitate these types of engagement, such as the Microsoft Catalyst program. The process works in an interactive collaborative style where people come together to share their ideas, which are then formalized in an interactive manner and tracked into a central location as a predefined backlog. These are great ways to drive a group-wide adoption of Power Platform.

How to scale your idea

Once your ideas have been captured, it is important to make them real! Often, it is expected that all ideas will be taken through a review process, and after this has been completed, the idea selected for build is then placed into an effectively managed backlog and created. This is a perfectly reasonable process to run, though, and if it works well, it creates a mechanism for other people across the organization to put their ideas forward for review and creation.

A less formal method is the **minimum viable product** (**MVP**) and the **proof of concept** (**PoC**) approach. Both focus on the requirement of minimum effort for maximum output and are, in fact, great ways to scale ideas into working solutions.

The MVP

This process focuses on examining the requirement and identifying key parts that are deemed more important than other areas. These key parts of the solution are then built as an MVP, which means the solution can run and fulfill some core requirements but is not complete. These MVPs are then used as a baseline or foundation to scale out at whatever pace works for your organization or team. It is important to architect these MVPs for scale and growth, and this is where solid and well-thought-out architectural best practices are important.

The PoC

The PoC approach is an amazing fail-fast approach that allows the freedom of creativity in solution development. As an idea is selected, elements of the idea can be built based on best practices and pattern recognition. Certain known requirements fit well into several tools within Power Platform. A maker can easily try something out quickly in a number of ways, find the best result, and move on fast. This proves the concept and can then be moved into an MVP-type scenario if necessary.

The data up approach – preparing your solution for scale

One of the most important design principles that we recommend looking at is the **data up approach**. This is a great way to drive a best practice to solution design and the way you develop the assets on top of data.

This approach comes from a number of scenarios where solutions have not been approved to be productionized, and this is mostly down to data and security. Most makers have no idea that Excel is not a suitable place to store personally identifiable information, and in most cases, this is true for SharePoint lists. Both tools are incredibly powerful; however, both serve a specific purpose.

In *Figure 5.6*, you can see the data-driven design approach where we always start with data. Starting with data allows you to lay a solid foundation for your solution and then build upward into your technical asset. If your data is reviewed and approved, then whatever you build on top of that will respect the data. This avoids many productionization scenarios and keeps the information security team happy.

This approach also allows you to treat data as a microservice and build many assets on top of that data. It is a scalable approach to designing and building solutions with Power Platform.

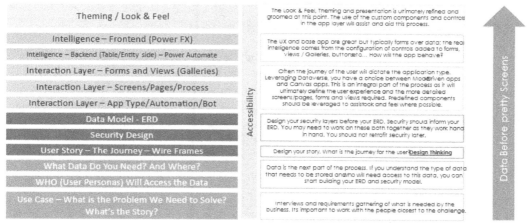

Figure 5.6: The data up approach to building solutions

Power Platform is designed for seamless scalability, allowing for the creation of multiple solutions of several types. By leveraging tools within the Microsoft productivity stack, it enables organizations to build rich ecosystems of assets that help streamline business processes and enhance productivity. Ideation plays a crucial role in driving solution development, with passive and active ideation methods fostering a culture of idea generation. Once ideas are captured, they can be scaled into working solutions through processes such as MVP and PoC approaches. Furthermore, the data up approach is emphasized to ensure that solutions are designed and developed on a solid foundation of data, promoting security and scalability. In the next section, we will be exploring the gradual expansion and integration with Power Platform.

Gradual expansion and integration with Power Platform

Sometimes, solutions get adopted more widely than planned. This is both a wonderful thing and a tough endeavor. Sometimes, your solution size is not at all what was anticipated, and sometimes, the thing you make is so impressive that more and more people want to use it. Congratulations, but now, we need to learn to grow our solutions so they can scale.

Luckily, Power Platform does cater to solutions that may need to be scaled out. Sadly, this is not always as easy as it seems, and it will come down to your architectural best practices implemented in your business. It is better to plan upfront than try to retrofit scalability later.

Often, people build things with Power Platform and complain about speed or scalability, but this is not always the platform's fault; this is down to the way the solution is designed. As an example, using SharePoint lists as a highly relational data structure and storing thousands of records will not scale, as this is not what it is built for. Or, adding thousands of controls to a canvas app and then wondering why it is not running at an optimum pace, is simple: the more controls, the more memory is used and the slower the app will run. It is logical. So, how do we ensure that what we create is scalable?

Understanding your solution and its impact

Impact is always a difficult metric to define, and what does "impact" even mean? Impact can be different in many organizations, and it is important for you to define what this means. What defines an impactful solution? It is not always about ROI from a monetary perspective; it could have to do with how the solution impacts the lives of the people using it. If a solution goes down, how are people and your organization affected? The more negative the impact of a solution, the more critical and impactful the solution is. This may sound slightly tough to absorb, but think about it for a second. If a solution that is on Power Platform is mistakenly taken offline and people and your business are negatively impacted, that means the solution is of high importance.

You may have other metrics and rules that define this, and this may differ per organization. In *Figure 5.7*, you can observe a basic summary of three methods to define the impact of a solution. It will be important to compare this metric to your solution sizing rules and ensure that there is alignment. Understanding the criticality of the solution will require consistent user feedback.

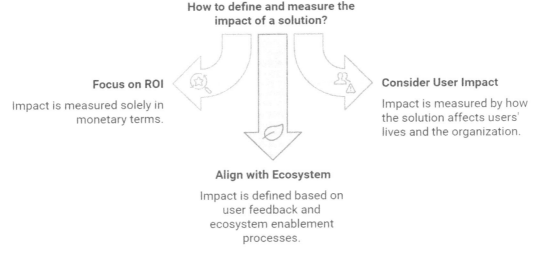

Figure 5.7: Methods to define and measure the impact of a solution

By listening and responding to the voices of the users and customers, you can understand the solution's impact from their perspective and discover their needs, expectations, and preferences. You can also build trust and loyalty with the users and customers and increase their adoption and advocacy of the solution. This all links up to your ecosystem's user feedback processes that you define in your ecosystem enablement program.

Architectural best practices

If the architectural best practice framework is adhered to, it is much easier to scale a solution more widely, especially if the data is in a reliable, robust data storage facility. It can be difficult to scale a solution built on Excel and SharePoint to tools such as Dataverse and SQL Server. This is because, typically, the data is stored and managed in a unique way. The data model may need to be completely redesigned to get the data into a tool that can scale more widely, and this will require work.

The data up approach pushes makers to think about the scalability of their solution and the potential adoption from the wider business. Building on free data structures may be fine as a PoC but later this will not scale, hence the need to understand the potential impact of the solution being created. It is highly recommended that guidance is created around this concept and is shared widely with the making community as it will prove invaluable in future Power Platform solution endeavors.

If your architectural best practices are respected and followed, it becomes much easier to "upgrade" solutions as they are more widely adopted.

Your scale framework – putting in the controls

Your scale framework will be defined by the controls and processes you implement when running your ecosystem enablement program. A scale framework is a set of rules that are defined "on purpose" and promote solutions through the framework into a well-defined micro-ecosystem.

As an example, if a solution is built in the default environment and is on SharePoint, should *everyone* be accessing that solution? Well, the answer is, do you, as IT, support *everything* built in the default environment? (You should not; that is like supporting every Excel workbook that gets created.)

The framework should focus on progressing well-adopted solutions to a well-defined, well-managed production environment with the correct ALM, governance, and compliance.

The way to think about a scaling framework is the more you can do upfront to mitigate massive changes in the solution as it scales, the better. Doing it the most appropriate way the first time is often easier said than done as not all makers will understand how to scale.

A suggestion in this scenario is to start thinking about how to help makers understand how to build for scale. As *Figure 5.8* suggests, many organizations implement controls around these scenarios, such as the following:

- **Solution registration**: When a maker has created something, they then need to register their solution in a central catalog. This helps admins understand what has been created and its intent.

- **Ideation process**: The ideation process allows people within the organization to leave an idea. This allows admins and backlog managers/workforce planners to pick off ideas, get them correctly architected, and build for scale.

- **Design review process**: Makers of all types can register a design for review and advice. This can be easily managed within the CoE Starter Kit using the innovation backlog solution, or a custom Power App can be built to facilitate this.

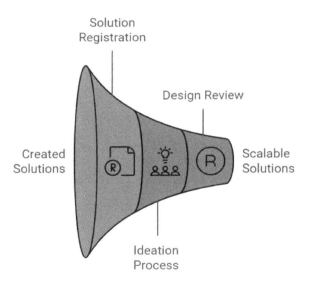

Figure 5.8: Three key aspects of managing scalable solutions

There are many ways to manage your scale framework, but it is important to align this to your architectural best practices.

The excerpt discusses the challenges and considerations involved in scaling solutions on Power Platform. It emphasizes the importance of understanding the impact of the solution, following architectural best practices, and implementing a scale framework with controls and processes. The key points include the need to plan for scalability upfront, understand the impact of the solution on users and the organization, adhere to architectural best practices, and implement a scale framework to promote well-managed production environments. The excerpt also highlights the importance of user feedback and suggests implementing controls for solution registration, ideation, and design review to manage the scale framework effectively. In the next section, we will explore the ability to execute and scale your transformative initiatives.

Driving tangible results and proving value

In every organization, when deploying Power Platform, there are questions about results and value. There is always discussion of ROI, tangible benefits, and value when delivering a Power Platform solution. Why have we done this? How does this benefit us? These are good questions! There is no point in implementing a strategic platform if we do not play to the strengths of the platform and get some seriously strong benefits.

There is a discussion to be had in parallel to this and that is the fact that Power Platform should not be seen or perceived as a tactical platform. Once viewed as a strategic platform, it is way easier to have benefit discussions, and vice versa. It is a bit of a chicken and egg scenario… which one came first?

Tactical versus strategic

When you talk about a tactical platform, we refer to it as something temporary that will solve a specific set of problems or point scenarios in one go. It is not the whole show; it is only a part of it and will be replaced. A lot of the time, this is something prebuilt that you buy off the shelf or something that is specifically created for a targeted outcome. These tactical solutions often create technical debt in organizations but are great for the immediate need.

As *Figure 5.9* indicates, strategic platforms are typically platforms that are put in place with the wider business strategy in mind. They are normally implemented to solve more than one problem and often need to go through a much longer approval cycle as they are much larger and pricier.

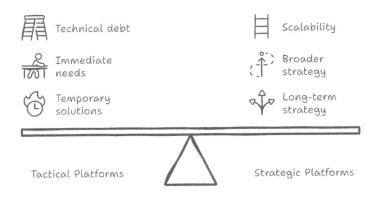

Tactical vs. Strategic Platforms

Figure 5.9: Tactical versus strategic platforms

Each of the preceding has its own value, however, when looking at the way Power Platform is leveraged and adopted, for it to work well and to be scalable, it needs to be seen and established as a strategic platform. Most of the time, it starts as a tactical solution and then grows into something much more in demand and strategic.

The value

When reviewing the value, often, it is done on a per use case basis (e.g., if we make this app and save X hours, we save X money). This is fine, but that is still a very tactical approach; it may not work for the wider platform.

Let us backtrack a bit! Let us compare Microsoft Office! Do you ask every person in your business to log the ROI of the spreadsheet they made in Excel? Or the email they send? Probably not, because the entire platform may have already gone through a value-based overview and it was quickly determined that it is a useful tool, and it is needed for business productivity. So, the platform is strategic. Its value is widely understood and it is core to the function of most organizations. There may be other parts of the office that require a discussion so organizations may dial up or dial down the license depending on what is needed.

Because Power Platform at its non-premium level is included within a lot of the Office / Microsoft 365 **Stock Keeping Units (SKU)**, it's seen as a business productivity tool. This tool is then connected to many of the tools in the Office stack, such as OneDrive and SharePoint. So, the value is absorbed by the Office license.

This has spoiled us as a user base. No other low-code tool does this! They all charge for this. So, the moment we must have the value discussion and talk about connecting to more robust data sources and APIs, we get upset because what we have had is "free."

So, this is about proving the value of using the premium tools in Power Platform and driving it into a more scalable, premium-focused strategic and supported platform within an organization. Often, simply moving data to a preferred data source and derisking that data is enough.

We often place ROI and value based on quantitative metrics, such as time and money, because that is what hits the bottom line. How many hours did this flow save me? How much money did I save? However, we often forget that there are hundreds of these invisible metrics that we do not count and are important and can also be quantified, such as risk!

Your data is valuable! Respect it!

Your data is a digital representation of you, your business, and your customers! It is extremely valuable and should be cared for and looked after. If this is the case, why do so many organizations disrespect their data? There is always legacy data in places that shall not be mentioned. Data exfiltration is rife in so many businesses. Often, we focus on doing what is cheap and not what is right. As an example, storing our personal and confidential data in public SharePoint lists because it is easy! Or, leaving critical data in an Excel document on someone's desktop. This just does not cut it, and, in fact, many organizations have been in trouble because of the lack of respect for data.

There are many aspects that need to be considered when respecting data. Not respecting your customer's data is not respecting your customer. There have been instances in the past, and names cannot be mentioned for legal reasons, where organizations have been caught out when not managing and storing their customers' data correctly. In particular, fines have been issued under the **General Data Protection Regulation** (**GDPR**). When building solutions with Power Platform, it is important to place value on the data. Placing data in proper scalable premium data storage facilities, such as SQL Server or Dataverse, removes risk from that data. This is a fact!

Your ROI value framework

It's good to take your solutions through a value framework to see if they are worth building and if they require the same level of rigor as the other solutions in your ecosystem., In fact, it's an even better idea to have these solutions registered somewhere where you can actually track and manage value. However, it's important not to confuse the value of a solution and the outright value of the platform.

In many organizations, part of the platform being considered strategic is to implement an ROI and value framework. This will allow you to benchmark solutions based on their value and ROI. It is not all about money and time saving; there can be many metrics, such as staff retention, effort, well-being, risk management, and business impact. Your framework should consider both qualitative and quantitative metrics that drive your organization forward. Put weightings on them; in your business, derisking something is worth way more than time spent. This is up to you to decide! There is no fixed rule and depending on who you speak to in your organization, you will get different answers.

The excerpt discusses the importance of viewing Power Platform as a strategic tool rather than just a tactical one. It emphasizes the need to recognize the value of the platform beyond just immediate ROI, highlighting the significance of strategic implementation and long-term benefits. Additionally, it underscores the importance of respecting and effectively managing data within the platform to mitigate risks and maximize its value. The need for implementing a value framework and considering both quantitative and qualitative metrics to measure the overall impact of solutions within the organization is also highlighted.

Summary

In conclusion, to fully leverage the potential of Power Platform, you need to implement it with an unobstructed vision, respect and manage your data, and measure the value and impact of your solutions using a comprehensive framework. By doing so, you will be able to create innovative, scalable, and secure solutions that empower your organization and drive it forward. We hope this chapter has given you some insights and guidance on how to view and use Power Platform as a strategic tool. Power Platform is an extremely powerful set of tools that can be used to solve business problems of varying types and sizes; it's not only used to build simple, small apps. If organizations are to drive Power Platform adoption across their business, it is important to understand the state of the digital ecosystem and undertake a proper ecosystem enablement program, consisting of several workstreams that focus on the platform, people, process, and portfolio of solutions. Following the guidance in this chapter will help you get started in creating a thriving Power Platform ecosystem filled with enabled makers and useful solutions. In the next chapter, we will focus on orchestrating success and some of the key considerations that organizations will need to understand to drive wider adoption of Power Platform.

Further reading

You can find more information on the Cloud Lighthouse site here: `https://cloudlight.house/blog/strategic-pyramid`.

Get This Book's PDF Version and Exclusive Extras

UNLOCK NOW

Scan the QR code (or go to `packtpub.com/unlock`). Search for this book by name, confirm the edition, and then follow the steps on the page.

Note: Keep your invoice handy. Purchases made directly from Packt don't require one.

Orchestrating Success: Key Considerations for a Digital Transformation Strategy Using Power Platform

Embarking on a digital transformation using Power Platform requires a structured approach, divided into three stages: envision, onboard, and scale. During the envision phase, several key considerations are essential.

Organizations should clearly outline their goals and objectives, define a vision, and establish a dedicated project team. Executive sponsorship is crucial for securing resources and fostering a culture of adoption.

An adoption strategy is necessary to guide efforts, including outlining the roadmap, setting milestones, and aligning with business objectives. Establishing success criteria enables measurable outcomes.

Managing resistance involves identifying and addressing challenges proactively, ensuring a smoother transition. Assessing technical capabilities, infrastructure, and data governance is vital for readiness. A comprehensive training strategy will empower employees to leverage the platform effectively.

By considering these aspects during the envision phase, organizations can lay a solid foundation for a successful digital transformation with Power Platform.

In this chapter, we will discuss the following topics:

- Charting the path for Power Platform adoption
- Empowering success through executive sponsorship and buy-in
- Navigating IT and leadership challenges during adoption
- Empowering teams with Power Platform skills

- Change management
- Accelerating the adoption journey

Charting the path for Power Platform adoption

In *Chapter 5*, we spoke about "setting your purpose" and how a clear vision is needed and understood across the organization. This is important as it is a collective view of what the overall strategic vision is. What is also key is building out a plan that you will then need to execute. This plan will map to your vision and will allow you to build an amazing Power Platform center of enablement that provides a safe space for people to create amazing things.

In setting up your enablement program, you will have gone through a number of the workstreams mentioned in *Chapter 5*, *What is your plan?* section. This creates a fantastic central ecosystem where you will be able to drive wider adoption of the platform across your organization.

Setting your program's scope of work can be tough. We will now explore how to define the scope of your program of work and, most importantly, how to get started.

Setting your adoption scope

In reviewing your purpose statement, it is important that this drives your adoption plan and acts as a "North Star," so to speak. There are varying scopes that can be applied to any adoption program and what is important is to make sure that you are set up for success rather than failure.

A fantastic quality of a well-thought-out adoption program is a well-defined scope. If the scope is set early and clearly and aligns with your purpose and vision, then the Power Platform rollout will be much more seamless and easier to manage.

There are a number of aspects that need to be reviewed that will allow you to clearly define and refine the scope before your adoption program is started. We will discuss these aspects in the following sections.

Clear objectives

A clear set of objectives needs to be defined and set immediately. These need agreement from *everyone* participating in the program as they will be one of the metrics used to define overall success. The clearer the objectives, the easier it will be to manage the program outcomes. It is an innovative idea to keep the goals and objectives as simple as possible and to have as many quantitative or binary (yes/no) outcomes as possible. This is not going to be the case every time, so please bear that in mind. An example of a strong objective could be to ensure that all people in the organization have access to the tools on Power Platform. This is true or false. Another example is that everyone in the IT department has access to the tools in Power Platform and is actively building solutions with these tools. The steps required for program success are visible in *Figure 6.1*. Typically, these objectives are defined by the wider Power Platform stakeholder team with the program manager being the lead.

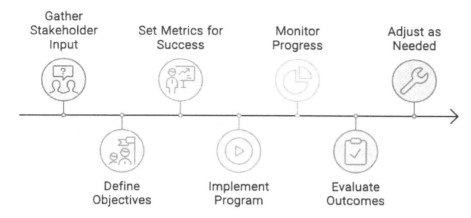

Figure 6.1: A process defining the clear objectives for program success

Microsoft provides several fantastic resources on the Microsoft Learn site when talking about strategy goals and metrics. These can be found at this location:

```
https://learn.microsoft.com/en-us/power-platform/guidance/adoption/
strategy-best-practices
```

In *all* projects, timing and milestones are extremely important. The clearer these are and the more focused they can be, the easier it will be to manage project outcomes. Typically, this adoption timeline will map to the goals that have been set out by the project team. As an example, you may want to roll out Power Platform to the HR department by the end of month X. You then work to establish *how* to do this and how to get the HR department engaged. The plan you set out for adoption will have many of these milestones attached to dates, and each milestone will have actions that need to be completed to achieve the milestone and the overall goal.

Stakeholder management

In *any* program of work, there needs to be a sponsor. Someone who pays the bills. Someone who agrees that the project is running smoothly, and things are on track. The sponsor is one of the most important stakeholders; however, this extends more widely across the organization to other leaders in each area. It is important to maintain clear communications with all these people and to manage all your stakeholders' expectations. It is a particularly good idea to conduct a stakeholder mapping exercise to ensure you understand how your project will impact people in the organization. *Figure 6.2* shows some basic steps that can be taken to manage stakeholders effectively.

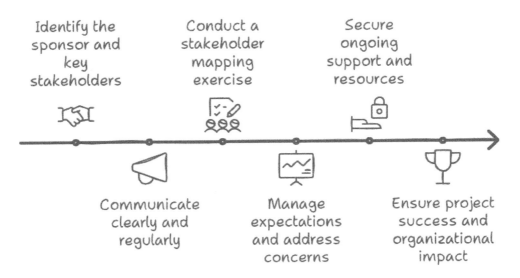

Figure 6.2: A process defining key points in managing stakeholders successfully

It is important to note that stakeholder management should be undertaken by a smaller but well-defined Power Platform ecosystem team. This is mentioned in the *Chapter 2* section, *Driving digital maturity with the CoE*.

Baselining

This is an extremely important exercise to go through. It involves establishing a clear and measurable starting point, which serves as a reference for tracking progress and evaluating the impact of the adoption efforts. Here are some key reasons why baselining is important. You would want to baseline the organization to understand Power Platform usage and adoption and then look department by department, depending on how you define your impacted groups. Then, you work from there, ensuring each part of the organization adopts the tools and then you will need to do a comparative baseline review after the adoption program to check whether numbers have increased. This will involve an element of monitoring/auditing as one of the mechanisms to understand utilization and adoption.

As mentioned in the *Navigating maturity levels in Power Platform adoption* section in *Chapter 2*, the Power Platform maturity model is a great place to start. You may want to extend this into a more detailed maturity and baseline assessment. This can be found at the following link:

```
https://learn.microsoft.com/en-gb/power-platform/guidance/adoption/
maturity-model
```

A great mechanism for baselining an organization's portfolio landscape is to leverage the Power Platform CoE Starter Kit. This tool allows the administration team the ability to gain the visibility they need into the portfolio and maker landscape and to truly understand what has been created and by whom. More information can be found on the Microsoft Learn site at this location:

```
https://learn.microsoft.com/en-gb/power-platform/guidance/coe/
starter-kit
```

Governance framework

Establishing a robust governance framework is crucial before driving Power Platform adoption in a business. This framework acts as the backbone, ensuring that the adoption process is structured, compliant, and aligned with the organization's strategic goals. The governance framework should do the following:

- Provide guidelines and policies for consistent and standardized Power Platform usage
- Facilitate resource allocation by defining roles, responsibilities, and access levels
- Identify potential risks and set up mitigation strategies in advance
- Establish clear structures for reporting, feedback, and decision-making
- Set benchmarks and monitor performance for continuous improvement

Having a governance framework in place before driving Power Platform adoption is fundamental to achieving a seamless, secure, and successful integration that aligns with the organization's broader strategic objectives. The framework is part of the adoption program and provides a set of rules that people follow. Implementing a governance framework can be quite a process; however, there are great tools out there such as the CoE Starter Kit, which will provide the visibility you require. The Power Platform governance team is responsible for ensuring this is in place and is required to work with the organization-wide governance team to drive the framework and processes forward. The team structure can be found in *Chapter 2*, in the *Driving digital maturity with the CoE* section.

The Microsoft team has provided some fantastic governance resources, which can be found on the Microsoft Learn site:

```
https://learn.microsoft.com/en-gb/power-platform/guidance/adoption/
admin-best-practices
```

Resource allocation

Resource allocation is paramount during any Power Platform adoption project for several critical reasons. It ensures that the right resources, whether they be human, financial, or technical, are available at the right time. This strategic alignment of resources prevents bottlenecks and ensures that the project stays on track and within budget.

Effective resource allocation also enhances productivity by ensuring that team members have the tools and support they need to accomplish their tasks efficiently, and by clearly defining roles and responsibilities. This will later be explored in the *Expanding the team* section.

Resource allocation is integral to risk management. By identifying the resources required for each phase of the project, potential gaps can be identified and addressed proactively. This foresight helps in mitigating risks associated with resource shortages or misallocations that could derail the project.

A well-structured resource allocation plan fosters accountability and transparency. When team members are aware of their specific responsibilities and the resources at their disposal, it promotes a sense of ownership and commitment toward achieving the project goals. This clarity is essential for maintaining motivation and ensuring that all stakeholders are aligned with the project's objectives.

Effective resource allocation supports continuous improvement. By regularly reviewing and reallocating resources based on project needs and performance metrics, the governance framework can adapt to changing circumstances and ensure the sustained success of the Power Platform adoption.

Impacted group management

Impacted group management is often one of the tougher areas to focus on when thinking about adoption. This area helps define how people in the organization will be given access to the tools and over what period within your adoption program.

You may not want to go with a big-bang approach and release all the tools to everyone immediately; a better approach is to portion it out across groups or departments and have a more targeted adoption focus. Many refer to this approach as *rings of release*. The analogy is when you throw a pebble into a pond, there are ripples; this is how a more targeted adoption program works. You start small with a targeted group and grow your presence more widely as you go. This is highlighted in *Figure 6.3*, showing how to start with a small core group and release more widely over time.

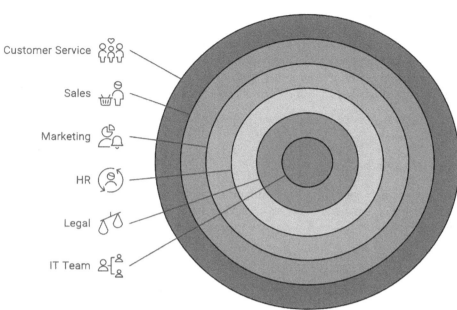

Figure 6.3: The release rings of a specific organization's impacted group management program

This approach also helps you localize and mitigate any risk that may arise with specific groups in the adoption program. Some groups of people are more difficult to drive adoption with, and that is just a fact, so keeping your program focused is important.

Your impacted groups will be a large factor in defining the overall scope of your Power Platform adoption program.

Risk management

Effective risk management in a Power Platform adoption program involves identifying, assessing, and mitigating risks throughout the project. Start by identifying potential risks such as technological challenges, resource constraints, stakeholder resistance, and security vulnerabilities. Engaging key stakeholders during this phase is crucial. Assess risks based on their impact and likelihood. Prioritize them to focus on the most critical ones. Use your risk register to document and track identified risks.

Develop strategies to manage risks, which may include the following:

- **Risk avoidance**: Altering project plans to eliminate risks
- **Risk transfer**: Outsourcing certain project components

- **Risk mitigation**: Reducing the likelihood or impact of risks, such as through additional training
- **Risk acceptance**: Proceeding with the project while closely monitoring the risk

Continuously monitor risks and report on their status to keep stakeholders informed. This fosters trust and collaborative problem-solving. Prepare contingency plans to address risks that materialize despite mitigation efforts. Allocate reserve resources for unforeseen issues. Regularly review and adapt the risk management process based on lessons learned, ensuring continuous improvement and resilience.

By incorporating these practices, you can safeguard your Power Platform adoption program and drive its overall success.

Communications plan

Building and managing a communications program is crucial when defining the scope of a Power Platform adoption program. Clear communication guarantees that all stakeholders remain aligned, well-informed, and actively involved during the entire project.

Begin by clearly defining the objectives of your communication efforts. Identify the key stakeholders, including executive sponsors, project managers, IT teams, end users, and external partners. Understanding their needs and expectations will help tailor your communication strategies.

Develop a comprehensive communication plan that outlines the methods, frequency, and channels of communication. Determine the types of information to be shared, such as project updates, milestones, risk status, and success stories. Utilize various channels such as emails, meetings, newsletters, and intranet portals to ensure the information reaches all stakeholders effectively.

Assign specific roles and responsibilities for communication tasks. Designate a communications manager or team to oversee the execution of the plan. Ensure that all team members understand their roles in disseminating information and gathering feedback.

Implement feedback loops to capture stakeholder input and concerns. Frequently gather feedback using surveys, focus groups, and individual meetings. Apply this input to refine communication strategies and swiftly resolve any concerns.

Track the effectiveness of your communication efforts by setting **key performance indicators** (**KPIs**) such as stakeholder engagement levels, feedback response times, and information retention rates. Regularly review these metrics and adapt the communication plan as needed to ensure continuous improvement.

All the components mentioned have been summarized in *Figure 6.4*, showing that a communications program is not just about sending emails but needs to be clearly thought out.

Components of an Effective Communications Program

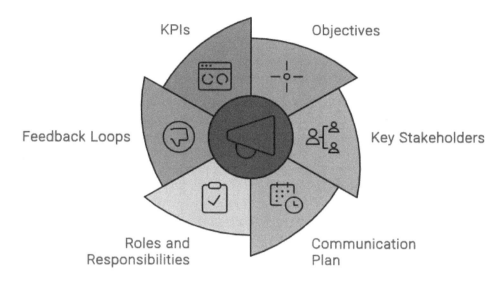

Figure 6.4: The components of an effective communications program

Platforms

Before embarking on the Power Platform adoption program, several foundational platforms must be established to ensure a seamless and successful implementation. These platforms serve as the bedrock upon which the entire program's infrastructure and strategy are built. These platforms are typically selected when building out the center of enablement workstreams.

An advanced collaboration platform must be implemented to enable efficient communication and teamwork across different departments and stakeholders. This platform should support various modes of interaction, such as instant messaging, video conferencing, and document sharing, enhancing productivity and supporting a culture of collaboration. People will need to be directed to a central place to interact with the various resources available to them and to leverage the governance and guidance materials. A notable example of this is to leverage Microsoft Teams or Viva Engage.

A comprehensive project management platform is crucial for tracking progress, managing tasks, and ensuring that timelines and milestones are met. This platform should include features such as Gantt charts, resource allocation tools, and real-time reporting to provide clear visibility into the project's status and performance. A popular tool used for this type of program is Microsoft Project.

A training and development platform is vital to equip all users with the necessary skills and knowledge to leverage Power Platform effectively. This platform should offer a range of learning resources, including tutorials, webinars, and hands-on workshops, tailored to different user roles and proficiency levels. It is a clever idea to surface the training and adoption platform through your collaboration portal (Microsoft Teams or Viva Engage).

By focusing on all the aspects mentioned in this section and clearly defining your scope, you are ready to drive much wider Power Platform adoption in your organization.

In this section, we emphasized the need for a more governed scope of work when building your Power Platform adoption program. It is important to ensure that you are as clear as possible on *what* it is you are going to be delivering and over which specific timeline. Getting your ecosystem ready for Power Platform adoption will set you up for success and ensure your people, platforms, and processes are ready for much wider, scaled use of the platform. In the next section, we will focus on managing stakeholder expectations and building a team around your adoption program.

Empowering success through executive sponsorship and buy-in

In *Chapter 2*, in the *Assemble the team* section, basic team structures for a center of enablement are shared. This team structure is essential when preparing your digital ecosystem for Power Platform. In this same section, there is also a brief excerpt on stakeholder mapping and the importance of aligning the correct stakeholders as you prepare for your center of enablement.

A critical element in the successful adoption of the Power Platform is securing executive sponsorship and assembling the right team. Executive sponsorship is vital as it provides the necessary authority and resources to drive the initiative forward, ensuring that organizational goals remain aligned with the project's objectives. An influential sponsor can champion the cause, influence key stakeholders, and facilitate the removal of obstacles that may hinder progress.

Equally important is the composition of the team tasked with spearheading this transformation. The team should be a cohesive blend of skilled professionals, including project managers, IT specialists, and business analysts, each bringing a unique perspective and expertise to the table. This diversity ensures that all facets of the implementation are covered, from technical intricacies to strategic alignment and user adoption.

Working with stakeholders to drive buy-in

Engaging stakeholders and ensuring their buy-in is critical to the success of your Power Platform adoption program. This process begins with identifying and mapping out all relevant stakeholders, which may include executive leaders, department heads, IT staff, end users, and external partners. Each of these groups has unique interests, concerns, and objectives that must be addressed to secure their support.

One of the first steps in collaborating with stakeholders is to clearly communicate the vision and benefits of the Power Platform adoption. This involves articulating how the platform will solve existing problems, enhance efficiency, and drive innovation within the organization. Tailoring this message to address the specific needs and pain points of different stakeholder groups can significantly enhance their engagement and willingness to support the initiative. This message should map to your purpose and vision statement that was defined in *Chapter 5*'s *Getting started with your vision* section.

It is essential to involve stakeholders in the planning and decision-making process. This can be achieved by conducting workshops, meetings, and focus groups where stakeholders can provide input and feedback on the implementation plan. By actively involving them, you demonstrate that their opinions are valued, which can foster a sense of ownership and commitment to the project's success. Stakeholders need to feel part of the process.

Creating a detailed stakeholder engagement plan is another key component. This plan should outline the communication strategies, frequency, and channels for keeping stakeholders informed and engaged throughout the project life cycle. Regular updates, progress reports, and success stories can help maintain momentum and reinforce the value of the initiative. Being as open and clear as often as possible is important.

It is important to address and manage any resistance that may arise. This can be done by identifying potential sources of resistance early on and developing strategies to mitigate them. Typical sources of resistance you may encounter are often based on a lack of understanding and support. Often, people simply fear something new that they need to do or learn and this can lead to high resistance to change. Equipping stakeholders with the needed training and resources can ease concerns and boost confidence in the new platform.

Building strong relationships with key influencers within the organization can further aid in gaining buy-in. These individuals can function as advocates for the project, helping to spread positive messages and encourage support from their peers and subordinates.

Recognizing and celebrating milestones and achievements is crucial in maintaining stakeholder engagement. Acknowledging their contributions and the progress made can boost morale and reinforce their commitment to the project's success.

The steps to a successful stakeholder management program are summarized in *Figure 6.5*; it's important to understand that this is a process. Each step will require planning and action in order to ensure stakeholders are kept in the loop and engaged.

Figure 6.5: The process for stakeholder management consists of various steps

Expanding the team

To build, grow, and expand a Power Platform team during a Power Platform adoption program, it is essential to follow a structured and strategic approach. This begins with understanding the goals and requirements of the initiative and aligning them with the skills and expertise needed within the team. As an example, if one of your goals is to ensure that all members of the HR team are trained in creating solutions with Power Platform, then you will need people who are able to help with this, or a training team.

Bearing in mind that the team focusing on adoption will be a part of the wider Center for Enablement team mentioned in *Chapter 2, Assemble the team* section. At this point, the center of enablement should be in the process of being created and these roles should already be mapped.

Define the key roles and responsibilities necessary for the successful adoption of the Power Platform. These roles may include the following:

- **Project managers**: Oversee the entire adoption process, ensuring that timelines, budgets, and deliverables are met.

- **Program managers**: Manage the relationships with stakeholders and ensure that the project moves forward in a successful direction.

- **Power Platform admin team**: Manage the digital ecosystem of Power Platform and ensure that the technical elements of the platform are working correctly.

- **Trainers and support staff**: Provide ongoing education and assistance to end users, ensuring smooth adoption and utilization of the platform. This should not be underestimated. The more people engage in the community and use the platform, the more support staff you will need.

- **Change managers**: Understand the wider change culture in the organization and manage the aspects of change across the teams.

Encourage a culture of collaboration and continuous learning within the team. This can be achieved by organizing regular team meetings, workshops, and training sessions where team members can share knowledge, discuss challenges, and brainstorm solutions. Promote open communication and provide platforms for team members to voice their ideas and concerns.

Invest in ongoing training and development programs to keep the team updated with the latest features, best practices, and industry trends related to Power Platform. This can include attending conferences, enrolling in online courses, and participating in webinars and community events. Encourage team members to pursue relevant certifications to enhance their skills and knowledge. Many organizations invest in creating bite-sized videos internally of people undertaking tasks or using Power Platform to solve problems. This is known as "nano training."

As the adoption program progresses, continuously assess the team's capacity and capabilities. This may be done in the same way the baselining assessment was undertaken. Be prepared to scale the team by hiring additional staff or engaging external consultants to address any gaps or increased workload. Ensure that the team structure remains flexible and adaptable to meet the evolving needs of the project.

Maintain open lines of communication with key stakeholders, including executive leaders, department heads, and end users. Regularly update them on the progress of the adoption program and seek their feedback and input. Involving stakeholders in the decision-making process can help build trust and ensure that the team's efforts align with the organization's overall objectives.

Define specific metrics and KPIs to assess the team's advancement and achievements. Regularly review these metrics to identify areas for improvement and celebrate achievements. Recognizing and rewarding the team's hard work and accomplishments can boost morale and motivate them to continue delivering high-quality results.

By following the steps highlighted in *Figure 6.6*, you can build, grow, and expand a highly effective Power Platform team that is well-equipped to drive the successful adoption and long-term utilization of the platform within your organization.

Power Platform Team Expansion Cycle

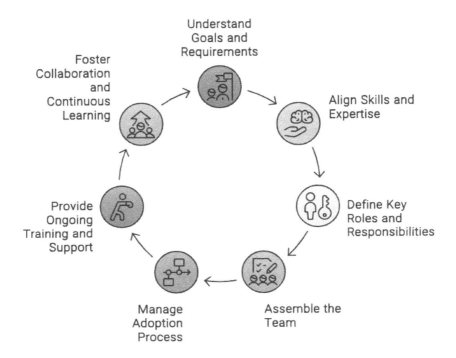

Figure 6.6: Process to drive the expansion of the team in your organization

Assembling the right team and securing executive sponsorship for the successful adoption of the Power Platform is so important. The right team should include a mix of professionals with diverse skills and expertise to cover all aspects of the implementation.

Engaging stakeholders and ensuring their buy-in is also crucial, involving clearly communicating the vision and benefits of the Power Platform adoption, involving them in the planning process, creating a stakeholder engagement plan, and addressing any resistance that may arise.

Additionally, it is essential to expand the team strategically by defining key roles and responsibilities, attracting top talent, promoting collaboration and continuous learning, investing in ongoing training and development, assessing the team's capacity, and maintaining open communication with key stakeholders. These steps are key for building a highly effective Power Platform team and driving successful adoption within the organization. In the next section, we will focus on how to navigate IT and leadership challenges during your adoption program.

Navigating IT and leadership challenges during adoption

The road to successful technology adoption often exposes various challenges, particularly when it comes to navigating IT leadership and managing resistance within the organization. Adoption is not easy because it involves people and people are complicated at the best of times.

Effective communication plays an important role in the success of an adoption program. Transparent and consistent communication with all stakeholders, from executive leaders to end users, ensures that everyone is aligned with the program's objectives and progress. This alignment not only builds trust but also engenders a sense of ownership and collaboration across the organization.

It is crucial to define clear metrics and KPIs to monitor progress and celebrate achievements. Regularly reviewing these metrics allows leaders to pinpoint areas for improvement and recognize the hard work and accomplishments of their teams, thereby boosting morale and motivation.

Metrics and KPIs can be tracked in multiple ways. Many organizations will simply use spreadsheets to do this; however, tools such as Power BI are far more effective and expose data in a more meaningful way. It is suggested that monitoring outputs are fed into a central location such as Dataverse and then Power BI can be used to visualize the data.

Another important aspect is the need for a clear understanding of the current team's capacity and capabilities. Additional people/talent may be required, and this may mean bringing more people into the fold. Often, these team members come from other departments. Many organizations grow their Power Platform teams by including champions/heroes from other departments who have shown a deep interest in the platform and want to be part of the wider program. Investing in ongoing training and development programs is also highlighted as a cornerstone of successful adoption. Keeping the team updated with the latest features, best practices, and industry trends related to technology ensures that they remain proficient and innovative in their roles. Encouraging a culture of collaboration and continuous learning further enhances the team's ability to navigate challenges and devise creative solutions. This can be managed by the champions who have an active interest in growing the Power Platform ecosystem.

Defining and managing resistance

Resistance to change is a natural human response, particularly in the context of adopting technologies such as Power Platform. Understanding and managing this resistance effectively is crucial to the success of any adoption program.

The first step in managing resistance is to identify its sources. There can be many sources, stemming from entrenched work habits, fear of the unknown, or concerns about job security. Employees might worry about their ability to learn new skills or the potential for increased workload. By recognizing these concerns, IT leaders can develop targeted strategies to address them.

To mitigate resistance, it is essential to implement targeted approaches tailored to address specific concerns. For instance, if employees are worried about their ability to learn new skills, offering comprehensive training programs and resources can alleviate these fears. Regular workshops, online courses, and hands-on sessions can help build confidence and competence.

Building a supportive environment is another key strategy. This involves transparent communication about the benefits of Power Platform and how it will positively impact the organization and its employees. Highlighting success stories and case studies can help illustrate the platform's value. Providing a clear roadmap and timeline for the adoption process can also reduce uncertainty and build trust. This is typically undertaken by the champions and with the communities of practice that have been set up.

Strong leadership involvement is critical in managing resistance. Leaders should actively advocate for the adoption program, demonstrating their commitment and support. They should also be visible and accessible, addressing any concerns and providing reassurance. Engaging leaders from different departments can help create a unified front and reinforce the message that adoption is a strategic priority for the entire organization.

Promoting a culture of collaboration and continuous learning can further ease resistance. Encouraging knowledge sharing and teamwork can help employees feel more engaged and invested in the adoption process. Creating forums for feedback and suggestions can also give employees a sense of ownership and involvement, making them more likely to embrace the change. The more people are seen to be learning in public, the more likely others will be to join the movement and participate.

By following the steps highlighted in *Figure 6.7* and promoting people to feel included and part of something, the less likely they are to be resistant. Creating a fan out of a person who is resistant is one of the most amazing things that can happen because that person will become a fan for life.

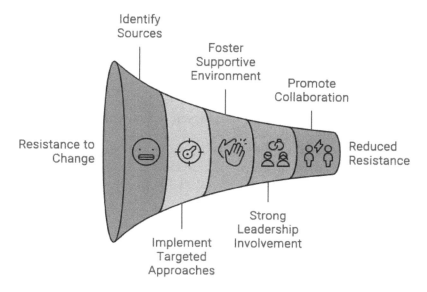

Figure 6.7: Reducing resistance

Understanding and navigating the challenges

Understanding the challenges inherent in adopting Power Platform is pivotal for ensuring a smooth transition and maximizing the potential benefits of the technology. Challenges can arise from various sources, each requiring a nuanced approach to address effectively.

One of the primary challenges is resistance to change, as mentioned in the *Defining and managing resistance* section. Leaders should take the time to understand the specific anxieties and reservations employees may have. This understanding will allow for a level of empathy and a more targeted approach to helping. "*What specifically are you worried about?*" is a useful conversation to have with a person or a team when engaging in an adoption program.

Another significant challenge is the technical preparedness of the organization. This involves ensuring that the existing IT infrastructure can support Power Platform and that there is sufficient technical expertise within the team to manage and maintain the new system. Conducting a thorough baseline assessment of the current technological landscape is crucial. This assessment should identify any gaps in infrastructure or skills and outline a plan to address these gaps through investment in technology upgrades and staff training. The baseline assessment is focused on in the *Chapter 2* section, *The importance of baselining*.

Cultural readiness is also a vital aspect of understanding the challenges during adoption. Organizational culture plays a crucial role in how innovative technologies are received and integrated. A culture that promotes innovation, continuous learning, and collaboration is more likely to embrace Power Platform. Conversely, a culture resistant to change may pose significant barriers. Leaders should work to cultivate a supportive environment that values and encourages adaptability, learning, and open communication. This can be achieved by encouraging a culture of collaboration, promoting knowledge sharing, and creating forums for feedback and suggestions.

Strong leadership involvement is critical in navigating the challenges of adopting Power Platform. Leaders should actively advocate for the adoption program, demonstrating their commitment and support. They should also be visible and accessible, addressing any concerns and providing reassurance. Engaging leaders from different departments can help create a unified front and reinforce the message that adoption is a strategic priority for the entire organization. By understanding and addressing these challenges, organizations can better navigate the complexities of adopting Power Platform and ensure a successful transition.

The more unified the approach and the clearer vision, the more targeted the adoption program and the clearer the scope will be.

In summary, we focused on some of the resistance that may crop up from certain parts of the business and some of the challenges that may be faced. It's important to be empathetic to these and to understand that, sometimes, people just need to be given more information. Risks can be mitigated and challenges can be solved if there is strong leadership and an actual plan and team that support these leaders. In the next section, we will look at how to set up a training strategy so that the people using the platform are given the skills they need to be successful.

Empowering teams with Power Platform skills

Crafting a robust training strategy is a foundational step in ensuring that employees are not only equipped with the necessary skills but also motivated to embrace this transformation.

Many assume that the focus on training is about how to technically use a set of tools, but it is *so* much more than that and can be complex when delving into various areas and aspects of a training and education program. Thinking about technology is especially important, but what is also crucial is to help people understand culturally that there is a change in the way "we do things here." What used to be an acceptable way of working is now changing and people should be excited to get on board with that.

As mentioned in the *Defining and managing risks* section, people are often just so used to doing things a certain way and not thinking about how to refine *how* they do things. This is no fault of theirs. It is human nature to learn and adapt, so in this training, it will be important to ensure that anyone adopting the platform understands *why* they are doing this, not just *what* it is they are doing. As an example, in regular day-to-day working practices, people are used to using tools such as spreadsheets to manage data.

Instead, by leveraging Power Platform, you may create a canvas app on top of a SharePoint list to interact with this data in a more refined way. Making a canvas app is easy, but *why* are we doing this instead of using an Excel sheet? A lot of the time, the training misses this extremely valuable point. If people understand why, adoption will be much easier for them.

Change management

Change management is extremely important in the successful implementation of a Power Platform adoption program. It involves a structured approach to transitioning individuals, teams, and organizations from their current state to a desired future state. Embracing change management ensures that the adoption of new technologies is as smooth and effective as possible, minimizing resistance and maximizing the potential for success.

One key aspect of change management is communication. Open, transparent, and frequent communication helps to alleviate fears and uncertainties, providing a clear vision of the benefits and the roadmap ahead. This communication should address the *why* behind the change, helping everyone understand the strategic importance and the positive impact it will have on their work and the organization as a whole.

Involving stakeholders at all levels in the planning and implementation process promotes a sense of ownership and commitment. When people feel they are part of the movement, they are more likely to support and engage with the new systems and practices. This inclusive approach also helps identify potential issues early on and develop solutions collaboratively.

Providing adequate training and resources is another critical element. Ensuring that employees have the skills and knowledge they need to use Power Platform effectively reduces frustration and enhances productivity. Continuous learning opportunities and support systems help maintain momentum and encourage ongoing development.

Recognizing and celebrating successes along the way reinforces positive behavior and motivates the team. Acknowledging the efforts and achievements of individuals and teams strengthens their commitment and encourages a culture of continuous improvement.

By integrating change management principles into the Power Platform adoption program, organizations can navigate the complexities of digital transformation with greater confidence and achieve long-lasting, impactful results.

Forming a training strategy

Designing and creating a comprehensive training program that empowers teams, fosters a culture of continuous learning, and drives the successful adoption of Power Platform often becomes one of the central aspects of a business's adoption program.

The process begins with a thorough baseline assessment to understand the current skill levels and knowledge gaps within the organization. This assessment should involve surveys, interviews, and performance reviews to gather detailed insights into what specific areas require attention.

Once the needs are identified and a baseline has been created, the next step is to develop a structured curriculum or program that covers both the basics and advanced functionalities of Power Platform as well as any cultural areas that have been identified. The curriculum should be tailored to distinct roles within the organization, providing role-specific training that ensures each team member can leverage the platform effectively in their context. Incorporating hands-on workshops, real-world scenarios, and interactive modules can make the learning experience more engaging and practical.

Another fantastic mechanism to drive adoption and training is through hackathons or makeathons. These events allow offer makers of all types to get together to build out solutions that the organization may need. Typically, they will focus on proof-of-concept type solutions that can be further enriched. The important part is that people are building together to achieve a common goal.

Establishing a support system is crucial for maintaining momentum and addressing any challenges that may arise during the training process. This can include creating a repository of learning resources, setting up a mentorship program, and providing access to expert guidance. Regular feedback sessions should be conducted to assess progress and make necessary adjustments to the training approach.

Establishing a culture of continuous learning is another key aspect of the training strategy. Encouraging employees to participate in ongoing professional development and keeping them informed about the latest updates and features of Power Platform can help sustain their engagement and proficiency. Recognizing and rewarding those who demonstrate exceptional commitment and improvement can further motivate the team.

Leadership involvement is also paramount. Leaders should actively participate in the training initiatives, demonstrating their commitment and setting an example for the rest of the organization. Their endorsement and involvement can significantly enhance the credibility and importance of the training program.

A well-crafted training strategy not only equips teams with the necessary skills but also fosters an environment where continuous improvement and innovation are ingrained in the organizational culture. By investing in comprehensive and effective training, organizations can maximize the benefits of Power Platform and drive successful digital transformation. The steps in *Figure 6.8* summarize the steps that need to be taken to start driving a well-crafted training strategy.

Figure 6.8: A comprehensive training program for Power Platform adoption

Driving a culture of learning

Building and nurturing a culture of learning when adopting the Power Platform involves several crucial steps. Firstly, organizations must create an engaging and comprehensive training strategy that aligns with their digital transformation goals. This strategy should be designed to equip teams with the necessary skills and encourage a mindset of continuous learning and innovation.

A well-developed curriculum and strong leadership support play integral roles in this process. Leaders are not only advocates but also active participants in the learning journey, demonstrating their commitment to the program. They facilitate an environment where learning is valued and encouraged, making resources readily available and accessible.

To implement the training program effectively, it should be piloted with a select group to gather feedback and refine the approach. Once tested and improved, the program can be scaled across different departments, ensuring widespread adoption and proficiency.

A fantastic way to support a culture of learning in public is to ensure that a mentorship program is set up. Mentorship in an organization is a fantastic way of helping people across the business learn and grow into positions or roles that they aspire to be in. A key part of getting this right is through guidance and teaching. This is great for both mentors and mentees.

Encouraging ongoing professional development and keeping employees informed about the latest updates and features of Power Platform further sustains their engagement and proficiency. Recognizing and rewarding those who show exceptional commitment and improvement incentivizes continued participation and effort.

In conclusion, by creating a culture of continuous learning and implementing strategic training programs, organizations can drive the successful adoption of Power Platform, ensuring long-term sustainability and growth.

We understand the importance of developing a robust training strategy to empower employees. The primary goal here is to provide people with the skills needed to embrace the transformation brought about by Power Platform. We discuss how training should not only focus on technical aspects but also on cultural change within the organization.

The process of forming a training strategy involves assessing current skill levels, designing a tailored curriculum, and establishing a support system to address challenges and maintain momentum. It also highlights the significance of fostering a culture of continuous learning and leadership involvement in driving the successful adoption of Power Platform. Overall, the article underlines the value of investing in comprehensive and effective training to maximize the benefits of Power Platform and facilitate successful digital transformation. In the next section, we will be exploring how to accelerate your Power Platform adoption journey by starting small and growing to scale.

Accelerating the adoption journey

The journey toward full adoption and capability building is rarely straightforward. It necessitates a strategic approach that balances immediate needs with long-term objectives, and that fosters an environment conducive to continuous learning and innovation. It is important to understand that building capability does not just happen, it relies on strong, robust frameworks to be put in place and a cultural shift toward learning and growth.

Following the ecosystem enablement approach and ensuring and setting up the Center for Enablement with the right team is a great start and a step in the right direction toward ensuring that adoption grows across your organization.

Start small

Starting small when building capacity to accelerate Power Platform adoption is not merely a tactical approach; it is a strategic necessity. This method embraces the principle of incremental progress, allowing organizations to implement changes at a manageable pace, thereby reducing resistance and enhancing the likelihood of success.

The initial phase involves identifying pilot projects that are well-suited to demonstrate the tangible benefits of Power Platform. These projects should be carefully selected based on their potential impact and the readiness of the teams involved. By starting with smaller, manageable projects, you can create a proof of concept that highlights the platform's capabilities and value, providing a motivating example for the rest of the organization.

Getting hands-on with the platform and building smaller solutions is a fantastic way for people to learn as well as drive tangible outputs.

As these pilot projects progress, it is critical to document lessons learned and best practices. This process of continuous evaluation and improvement ensures that subsequent initiatives can build on the successes and avoid the pitfalls of earlier efforts. This iterative method boosts the success of the adoption program and promotes ongoing improvement and learning.

Starting small allows for the development of internal champions who can advocate for the Power Platform and support their peers through the adoption journey. These champions, equipped with hands-on experience and a deep understanding of the platform, become invaluable resources for training and mentoring others in the organization. Their enthusiasm and expertise help to build momentum and drive wider adoption across departments.

As confidence in Power Platform grows and initial projects demonstrate success, organizations can gradually expand the scope of their adoption efforts. This may involve scaling the program to incorporate more complex projects and additional departments. Throughout this process, maintaining a focus on continuous learning and improvement is key, ensuring that the organization remains agile and responsive to new challenges and opportunities.

Starting small and building capacity incrementally provides a solid foundation for the successful adoption of Power Platform. By leveraging pilot projects, developing internal champions, establishing a **Center for Enablement** (C4E), and maintaining clear communication, organizations can create a sustainable path to digital transformation and long-term success. *Figure 6.9* shows a summary of key aspects you can focus on to drive that capacity growth in your Power Platform team.

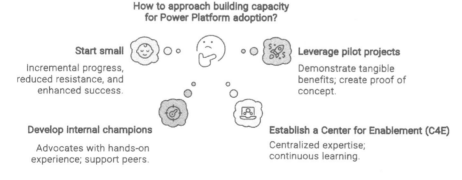

Figure 6.9: Key points to building capacity in your business

Understanding true adoption

Understanding true Power Platform adoption within an organization involves recognizing the importance of incremental capability growth. By starting with smaller projects and gradually increasing the complexity and scope of Power Platform initiatives, organizations can build a solid foundation for broader adoption. This also means that there is a focused approach to these smaller projects, and this makes it much easier to support people.

True adoption is not just about making one app or automation, it's about using the tools in Power Platform at scale to solve business problems.

Capability growth plays a crucial role in this journey. It entails developing the necessary skills, knowledge, and resources to effectively utilize Power Platform. This includes investing in training programs, encouraging a culture of continuous learning, and providing ongoing support to employees. As individuals and teams become more proficient with the platform, they can tackle more sophisticated projects and drive innovation across the organization.

Most of the time, the training is relatively driven by self-sufficient makers and users, then governed by the central Power Platform adoption and enablement team (or administration team). However, sometimes, the need for training is much higher and more formal, and in these cases, it's important to potentially bring in vendors to conduct more defined training programs.

Capability growth allows organizations to adapt to evolving business needs and stay ahead of the competition. By continuously enhancing their Power Platform capabilities, organizations can leverage new features and functionalities, streamline processes, and deliver greater value to customers. This iterative approach ensures that the organization remains agile and responsive to changing market dynamics.

Ultimately, understanding true Power Platform adoption is about recognizing the strategic importance of capability growth. By starting small, building capacity incrementally, and favoring a culture of continuous improvement, organizations can unlock the full potential of the Power Platform and achieve long-term success in their digital transformation journey.

Scaling your strategy

Scaling a Power Platform adoption program as capability is built requires a strategic and phased approach. As organizations develop the necessary skills, knowledge, and resources, they can begin to undertake more ambitious projects and expand their Power Platform initiatives. Start by identifying and training internal champions who can advocate for the platform and provide support to their colleagues. This scale approach is all facilitated from within the **C4E** where the governance and the adoption program are successfully managed in a defined manner.

As confidence in Power Platform grows through successful pilot projects, gradually scale the program to encompass more complex initiatives and additional departments. Maintain clear and regular communication with all stakeholders to keep them informed and engaged, establishing an environment of continuous learning and improvement.

This iterative approach not only builds capability but also ensures that the organization remains agile, responsive, and well-equipped to leverage the full potential of Power Platform.

Potential pitfalls

Despite the vast opportunities presented by Power Platform, several common pitfalls can hinder the successful implementation of an adoption program. A significant challenge is underestimating the cultural shift required within the organization. Resistance to change is a natural human response, and without a concerted effort to uphold a culture of learning and growth, employees may be hesitant to embrace new tools and processes. Do not underestimate the need for well-thought-out change management.

Inadequate training and support can lead to a lack of proficiency and confidence in using the platform, resulting in suboptimal utilization of its features. It is crucial to invest in comprehensive training programs and provide continuous support to ensure that employees are well-equipped to leverage the platform effectively.

Another common pitfall is the absence of a clear and strategic plan. Without a phased approach that starts with smaller projects and gradually scales up, organizations may find themselves overwhelmed by the complexity and scope of the initiatives. This can lead to project delays, budget overruns, and, ultimately, failure to achieve the desired outcomes.

Insufficient governance and oversight can result in inconsistent practices and fragmented efforts across different departments. Establishing a C4E to provide governance and manage the adoption program in a structured manner is essential for maintaining coherence and alignment with organizational goals.

Failing to maintain regular communication with all stakeholders can lead to disengagement and a lack of buy-in. It is vital to keep everyone informed and involved throughout the process, cultivating an environment of continuous learning and improvement. In this section, we learn that building capability relies on strong frameworks and a cultural shift toward learning and growth. Starting small and building capacity incrementally is necessary, allowing for incremental progress and reducing resistance. This approach helps in developing internal champions and promoting a culture of continuous improvement and learning. Scaling a Power Platform adoption program involves a strategic and phased approach, identifying and training internal champions, and gradually expanding the program. Regular communication is essential for nurturing a culture of continuous learning and improvement.

Summary

In summary, building capability within an organization heavily relies on establishing robust frameworks and nurturing a culture of learning and growth. The process should begin on a small scale, incrementally building capacity to allow for steady progress and reduced resistance. This method aids in developing internal champions and establishing a culture of continuous improvement. A strategic and phased approach is essential for scaling a Power Platform adoption program, where identifying and training internal champions plays a crucial role. Regular and clear communication is vital to ensure all stakeholders are informed and engaged, fostering an environment of continuous learning and improvement.

As organizations gain confidence in Power Platform through successful pilot projects, they should gradually scale the program to include more complex initiatives and additional departments. This incremental approach not only builds capability but also ensures that the organization remains agile, responsive, and well-equipped to leverage the full potential of the Power Platform. The C4E provides governance and manages the adoption program in a structured manner, facilitating this scaling approach from within.

Capability growth is critical for staying ahead of the competition and adapting to evolving business needs. Through continuous enhancement of Power Platform capabilities, organizations can leverage new features, streamline processes, and deliver greater value to customers. This iterative approach ensures agility and responsiveness to market changes. Investing in training programs, encouraging a culture of learning, and providing ongoing support are key to developing the necessary skills and resources for effective platform utilization.

True Power Platform adoption is not merely about creating a single app or automation but involves using the tools at scale to solve business problems. By starting with smaller projects and gradually increasing their complexity and scope, organizations can build a solid foundation for broader adoption. This focused approach to incremental capability growth makes it easier to support and guide individuals and teams, leading to successful and widespread implementation of Power Platform within the organization.

In the next chapter, we will be exploring in more detail how Power Platform can be positioned to various stakeholders and how aspects of change management are applied in a Power Platform adoption program.

Join our community on Discord

Join our community's Discord space for discussions with the authors and other readers:

`https://packt.link/powerusers`

7

Collaboration and Change in Digital Transformation

In this chapter, we'll be focusing on the crucial importance of stakeholder analysis, alignment, and effective change management in the digital transformation era. We'll delve into the roles of different stakeholders, including the Executive Sponsor, Success Owner, Champions, Training Lead, Department Leads, Communication Leads, Power Platform Admin Team, and Power Platform Nurture Team in successfully adopting Power Platform within organizations. We'll also explore how citizen developers can contribute innovative ideas from various departments, going beyond traditional IT roles.

It's vital to get buy-in from managers and executives for these individuals to effectively use Power Platform. We'll discuss strategies for gaining buy-in from different stakeholders by showing the positive impacts Power Platform can have on their roles. Executives are concerned about cost reductions, managers about time savings, and individuals about learning opportunities. We'll also emphasize the importance of addressing concerns and clarifying how the transformation will impact various parts of the organization in both the short and long term. To facilitate this transformation, organizations rely on their Microsoft Power Platform admin team. We'll explore the admin team's responsibilities, which include establishing an environment strategy, implementing data loss prevention policies, managing users, capacity, and licensing, and enabling data access through connectors and integrations.

In this chapter, we will explore the following topics:

- Stakeholder analysis and alignment
- Strategies for stakeholder buy-in
- The role of the Power Platform admin team
- Fusion team collaboration and beyond
- Building a digital culture

Stakeholder analysis and alignment

The success of any Power Platform adoption program relies on the effective engagement of stakeholders. Stakeholder mapping is a critical initial step in this process, enabling organizations to identify, analyze, and categorize all individuals and groups who have an interest in or are affected by the program. By understanding their needs, concerns, motivations, and influence, organizations can tailor their engagement strategies to ensure widespread support and minimize resistance. This introduction provides an insight into the importance of stakeholder mapping and how it sets the stage for successful Power Platform adoption. Let us explore how to effectively map and manage stakeholders successfully.

Stakeholder mapping

Stakeholder mapping is a crucial initial step in any Power Platform adoption program, acting as the cornerstone for successful implementation and long-term sustainability. It involves identifying, analyzing, and categorizing all individuals and groups who have an interest in or are affected by the program. By understanding their needs, concerns, motivations, and influence, you can tailor your engagement strategies to ensure wide-ranging support and minimize resistance.

The first phase of stakeholder mapping is identifying all potential stakeholders. This includes not only the primary users of the Power Platform but also the secondary stakeholders who might be indirectly impacted. It's important to understand that stakeholders are NOT just senior people in the organization. A stakeholder can be *anyone* who is engaging the platform. Typical stakeholders might include the following:

- **Executive leadership**: Their buy-in and continuous support are vital for resource allocation and driving organizational change
- **IT department**: They play a critical role in the technical enablement and maintenance of the platform
- **End users**: The employees who will be using the platform daily – their feedback and user experience are crucial for iterative improvements
- **Business unit managers**: They need to see the strategic advantages and efficiencies the platform will bring to their operations
- **Pro-code and low-code developers**: Both groups need to collaborate effectively to leverage the full potential of the platform
- **External partners**: Third-party vendors and consultants who might be involved in the implementation and support phases

Once stakeholders are identified, the next step is to analyze their influence and interest in the Power Platform adoption. This can be visualized using a stakeholder matrix, which helps categorize stakeholders into diverse groups based on their level of influence and interest. The table in *Table 7.1* is an example of how stakeholder influence can be tracked.

Influence/Interest	High Influence, High Interest	High Influence, Low Interest	Low Influence, High Interest	Low Influence, Low Interest
Examples	Executive Leadership, Business Unit Managers	IT Department	End Users, Citizen Developers	External Partners

Table 7.1: Stakeholder influence mapping table

Different stakeholder groups require tailored engagement strategies to address their unique needs and concerns. As an example, you wouldn't share the same information with a senior executive as you would with an end user. They both require different pieces of data at different intervals. Here are some strategies for each category:

- **High Influence, High Interest**: Engage them through regular updates, strategic discussions, and involvement in key decision-making processes. Their support and advocacy can drive the platform's adoption across the organization.

- **High Influence, Low Interest**: Focus on demonstrating the platform's strategic value and how it aligns with their goals. Use concise, impact-driven communication to capture their attention.

- **Low Influence, High Interest**: Provide comprehensive training and resources to equip them with the knowledge and skills to use the platform effectively. Their positive experiences can create grassroots support.

- **Low Influence, Low Interest**: Keep them informed through general communications and updates. Their support might not be critical, but their awareness is beneficial.

Stakeholder mapping is not something you do once; it is a constant action you perform throughout the delivery program. As the Power Platform adoption progresses, stakeholder roles, interests, and influence might change. Regularly revisit and update the stakeholder analysis to ensure continued alignment and support.

By constantly mapping and engaging stakeholders, organizations can navigate the complexities of Power Platform adoption, promoting a collaborative environment that drives innovation and transformation.

As an example, in organization X, stakeholder mapping may be completed for many of the various levels of stakeholders, but it is very typical for stakeholders to move around and move roles. It's important to ensure that these stakeholders' movements are tracked and managed as well.

Defining success

Defining success in a stakeholder mapping exercise requires a clear understanding of the goals and objectives of the Power Platform adoption program. Success can be gauged by the extent to which the stakeholder engagement strategies promote collaboration, drive innovation, and facilitate transformation across the organization.

The more engaged the stakeholders are and the more feedback you receive, the likelihood of the program being more successful is higher. Engaged stakeholders drive more defined outputs.

A successful stakeholder mapping exercise should identify all relevant stakeholders and categorize them based on their influence and interest, as mentioned in the previous section. This categorization helps tailor engagement strategies to ensure each stakeholder group is effectively addressed. Here are some key metrics to consider:

- **Stakeholder Awareness and Understanding**: Measure the increase in stakeholder awareness and understanding of the Power Platform's capabilities and benefits. This can be done through surveys, feedback sessions, and participation rates in training programs.

- **Stakeholder Engagement Levels**: Track the level of engagement from different stakeholder groups. Elevated levels of participation in strategic discussions, feedback sessions, and decision-making processes indicate successful engagement.

- **Support and Advocacy**: Assess the degree of support and advocacy from key stakeholders, especially those with high influence and high interest. Their endorsements and active promotion of the platform within the organization are crucial for widespread adoption.

- **Alignment with Organizational Goals**: Ensure that the stakeholder mapping and engagement strategies align with the broader organizational goals and objectives. Regularly review and adjust the strategies to maintain alignment and address any emerging concerns or opportunities.

- **Feedback and Iteration**: Collect ongoing feedback from stakeholders to refine and improve the engagement strategies. Success is an iterative process that involves continuous learning and adaptation.

By systematically defining and measuring the success metrics shown in *Figure 7.1*, organizations can effectively navigate the complexities of Power Platform adoption. A well-executed stakeholder mapping exercise not only drives the platform's adoption but also promotes innovation and continuous improvement.

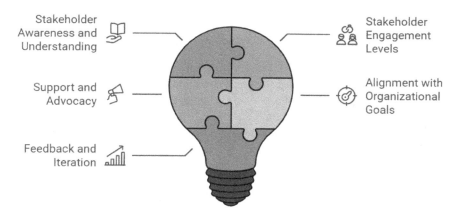

Success Metrics for Stakeholder Mapping

Stakeholder Awareness and Understanding

Stakeholder Engagement Levels

Support and Advocacy

Alignment with Organizational Goals

Feedback and Iteration

Figure 7.1: Success metrics for stakeholder mapping

Stakeholder mapping and management are crucial for successful implementation and long-term sustainability. They involve identifying and analyzing all potential stakeholders, including executive leadership, the IT department, end users, business unit managers, pro-code and low-code developers, and external partners. Once stakeholders are identified, their influence and interest can be analyzed and visualized using a stakeholder matrix, allowing for more refined engagement strategies to address their unique needs.

Stakeholder mapping is an ongoing process, requiring regular revisiting and updating as stakeholder roles and influence may change. Success metrics to consider include stakeholder awareness and understanding, engagement levels, support and advocacy, alignment with organizational goals, and feedback and iteration. By systematically defining and measuring these success metrics, organizations can effectively navigate the complexities of Power Platform adoption. In the next section, we will explore strategies to manage and drive stakeholder buy-in.

Strategies for stakeholder buy-in

When undertaking any program of work, ensuring that your stakeholders buy into it is extremely important. The more buy-in you have from the various stakeholders you have, the more successful the program of work will be. What is key here is to understand *what* your stakeholders are looking for and what success and impact mean to them. If you can show impact and actual quantifiable outcomes, your stakeholders' requirements will be satisfied and they will be more bought in. Let us look at how you can highlight impact. As an example, a maker really wants to get to a working solution as fast as possible, whereas a CIO will want to see time savings and a productivity impact across a *much* wider group.

Showcasing impact

Displaying the impact of Power Platform to stakeholders is pivotal for its successful adoption and integration within an organization. Demonstrating the platform's value requires a strategic approach that encompasses clear communication, tangible outcomes, and continuous engagement.

Once you have mapped out your stakeholders and their interests, you can define and refine your strategies to the needs and concerns of each group to ensure comprehensive engagement. Stakeholders of varying levels may perceive impact and value differently, so it is important to ensure this is understood and relevant metrics are set. As an example, a stakeholder in senior management may be looking for the number of hours saved by a person when solving a problem, whereas a developer may be looking for wider technical breadth from a platform.

After identifying each group's value statements, clearly articulate the unique value propositions of Power Platform. This includes its capabilities in enhancing productivity, automating processes, and driving innovation. Use real-world examples and case studies to illustrate these points convincingly.

Present data-driven evidence of the platform's impact. Metrics such as time saved, cost reductions, and efficiency improvements should be highlighted. Visual aids such as graphs, charts, and dashboards can make these outcomes more compelling. A great method of doing this is tracking any monitoring and feedback data in a Power BI data model, which then allows the data to be visually understood.

A great method to achieving this is through the proactive monitoring of the assets created and then tracking against user feedback such as time saved per asset. The monitoring and active feedback from makers and users will allow for much more detailed reporting to take place. An actual active example is the maker of an automation could share the number of minutes saved per flow and the number of flow runs could be counted to understand the number of minutes saved. If 1 flow saves a user 10 minutes and that flow runs 10 times a day, then 100 minutes are saved daily.

Share success stories from within the organization or from similar industries. Testimonials from early adopters or key users can provide authentic insights into the benefits of Power Platform, promoting trust and credibility. The Power Platform customer stories site that Microsoft has set up is a suitable place to share your success story. A great example on the Microsoft site is the story of Chevron and how they have been successful with the Power Platform. You can access the customer stories at this URL: https://www.microsoft.com/en-us/power-platform/blog/power-apps/power-platform-stories.

Organize interactive workshops and live demonstrations to display the platform's capabilities. Allow stakeholders to experience firsthand how Power Platform can solve specific business challenges and streamline operations – the more visual and interactive, the better.

Establish a continuous feedback process to gather stakeholder input and make iterative improvements. Regular surveys, feedback sessions, and engagement activities ensure that stakeholder concerns are addressed promptly and effectively. An engaged stakeholder, sharing actively will always mean that the program is going well. One of the methods that has worked well is one-to-one stakeholder calls and discussions. Typically, a stakeholder may be more inclined to share in a private forum; however, this can take a lot of time, so it's important to be targeted in *who* you interview.

Ensure that the showcased impacts align with broader organizational goals and objectives. This helps in reinforcing the relevance of Power Platform in achieving strategic priorities and enhances stakeholder buy-in.

Engage and empower influential stakeholders to function as advocates for the platform. Their endorsements and initiative-taking promotion can significantly boost adoption rates and drive organizational change. Creating hero stories and putting people in the spotlight often drives others to be part of the wider movement.

Acknowledge that showcasing impact is an ongoing process. Continuously refine your strategies based on feedback and evolving organizational needs. Demonstrating a commitment to continuous improvement can strengthen stakeholder confidence in Power Platform.

By adopting the strategies summarized in *Figure 7.2*, organizations can effectively display the transformative impact of Power Platform to their stakeholders, driving engagement and encouraging a culture of innovation and collaboration.

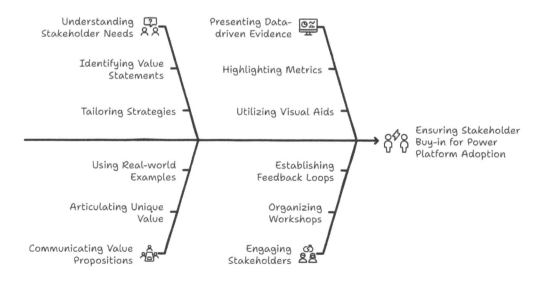

Figure 7.2: Strategies for showcasing Power Platform impact

When implementing a work program, gaining buy-in from stakeholders is crucial for success. Refining your approach to each stakeholder group ensures comprehensive engagement. Providing data-driven evidence, sharing success stories, and aligning impacts with organizational goals enhances stakeholder buy-in. Empowering influential stakeholders as advocates significantly boosts adoption rates. Continuous refinement of strategies based on feedback is essential for strengthening stakeholder confidence in the Power Platform. In the next section, we will explore the role of the Power Platform admin team in the Power Platform program of work.

The role of the Power Platform admin team

In this section, we will be focusing on the essential roles and responsibilities of the admin team in a Power Platform adoption program. Understand how their strategic planning, technical proficiency, and ongoing support form the cornerstone for successful execution and ready the ecosystem for expansion and growth. Explore how the admin team's proactive methodology is pivotal in enhancing efficiency through automation and securing lasting value for the Power Platform adoption initiative.

The roles and responsibilities of the admin team

The roles and responsibilities of the admin team in a Power Platform adoption program are multifaceted, encompassing strategic planning, technical expertise, and continuous support. The admin team is tasked with laying the foundation for a successful implementation and ensuring the platform's sustainability and scalability over time.

Often, the primary user or maker in the Power Platform ecosystem ends up becoming the Power Platform admin, which can prove to be difficult since the platform can rapidly grow organically. It's key to formalize the roles of the people in the admin team to drive some sort of structure. One person cannot be responsible for everything. There are organizations out there where the platform is essentially tactical, and the owner of the platform is overrun with tasks as the platform expands. This is not a scalable solution.

One of the primary responsibilities of the admin team is to establish a governance framework that aligns with the organization's overall strategic objectives. This involves setting policies, standards, and best practices to ensure the effective and secure use of Power Platform. The team must also define roles and responsibilities, ensuring that there is clear accountability and oversight.

The admin team is responsible for creating and managing the various environments within the Power Platform. This includes setting up development, testing, and production environments (relevant to the determined environment strategy), managing data policies, and ensuring that environments are correctly configured to support business needs while maintaining security and compliance requirements.

Ensuring the security and compliance of the Power Platform is a critical responsibility. The admin team must implement robust security measures to protect sensitive data and prevent unauthorized access. This involves configuring security roles, managing user permissions, and regularly monitoring for any potential security threats. Compliance with industry standards and regulations must be continuously assessed and maintained. As an example, a key consideration in managing security in an environment is determining whether it requires Dataverse or not. Dataverse gives a *much* more granular approach to environment security management. This will become part of the wider environment strategy.

To drive the adoption and effective use of Power Platform, the admin team (and the wider center for enablement team) must provide comprehensive training and support to end users and citizen developers. This includes developing training materials, conducting workshops, and offering ongoing support to address any issues or questions that arise. By empowering users with the knowledge and skills they need, the admin team helps to build a culture of innovation and self-sufficiency. This is hugely important when promoting adoption across an organization.

Effective collaboration and communication with other departments and stakeholders are vital for the success of the Power Platform adoption program. The admin team must work closely with IT, business units, and executive leadership to ensure alignment and address any cross-functional challenges. Clear and consistent communication helps to build trust and ensures that the platform's benefits are fully realized across the organization.

The admin team must stay abreast of the latest developments, innovations, and best practices in Power Platform and related technologies. This involves continuous learning, experimentation, and adaptation to drive ongoing improvements and innovation within the organization. By promoting a culture of continuous improvement, the admin team can ensure that Power Platform remains a valuable and dynamic tool for driving business transformation. *Figure 7.3* shows a summary of the roles and responsibilities of the Power Platform admin team. A point to note is that the team often may get allocated more things to do, so it is important to set up some guardrails at the start to ensure that the team does not take on too much.

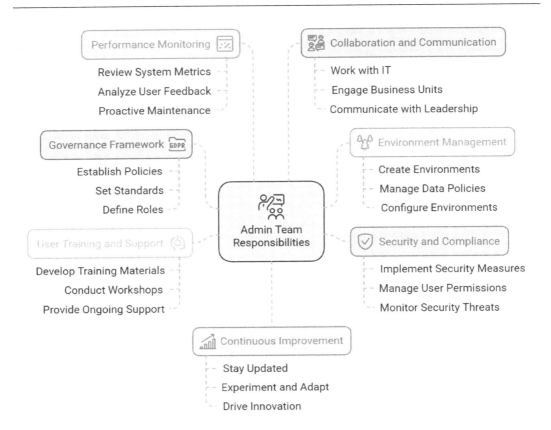

Figure 7.3: Summary of the roles and responsibilities of the Power Platform admin team

The Admin team is the center of the Power Platform solar system, with many tasks and activities orbiting them. These will increase as the ecosystem grows from tens to hundreds to thousands of assets. It is also important to ensure that the team grows in parallel so that these responsibilities can be picked up by others and not have a single point of failure in one person.

Considering the concepts of continuous improvement within an organization adopting Power Platform is key. Ultimately, the admin team should want makers to be self-sufficient and to support their own creations. The admin team can't always be responsible for every problem's solution and every person's learning; therefore, building a culture of continuous improvement is key. Helping makers to understand that learning in public and with others is a great start and driving this sort of messaging through the community sites and portals will help. It's okay to not know everything, but let's share what we learn and *how* we come to solutions. This creates an environment for others to learn openly and *want* to become better makers.

Preparing your ecosystem for scale and growth

To prepare your ecosystem for scale and growth, your power platform admin team will need to ensure that open and effective collaboration and communication with other departments and stakeholders is at the heart of the program of work. The admin team must work closely with IT, business units, and executive leadership to ensure alignment and address any cross-functional challenges. Clear and consistent communication helps to build trust and ensures that the platform's benefits are fully realized across the organization.

Continuous monitoring of the platform's performance and usage is essential to identify areas for improvement and optimization. The admin team must regularly review system metrics, user feedback, and other data sources to ensure the platform is operating efficiently and effectively. Initiative-taking maintenance and updates are necessary to address any issues and to leverage new features and capabilities as they become available. This is no different from a Microsoft 365 program, where understanding *how* the users are leveraging the tools and for what purposes will help in applying governance and compliance strategies. The monitoring is typically available within the admin center and Microsoft 365 compliance center; however, it is imperative to ensure the Microsoft CoE starter kit has been installed for more granular monitoring.

As the Power Platform ecosystem expands within the organization, it is essential to empower the varying levels of makers. By providing them with the right tools, training, and support, they can create solutions that meet their specific needs, reducing their dependency on IT. Promoting a culture of fusion team collaboration—where IT and business units work together—can drive innovation and ensure that solutions are aligned with business objectives.

Building a fusion team culture within the organization can enhance collaboration and communication, leading to more effective problem-solving and innovation. The role of fusion teams is to bridge the gap between IT and business units, ensuring that both technical and business perspectives are considered.

While scaling and growing the Power Platform ecosystem, the admin team may face several challenges, including resistance to change, skill gaps, and integration issues. When speaking of integration in this scenario, we refer to the integration of teams and people rather than technology. Addressing these challenges requires an initiative-taking approach, including continuous learning, stakeholder engagement, and leveraging best practices. By overcoming these hurdles, the organization can fully realize the benefits of the Power Platform and drive a much wider level of adoption across a business.

By preparing the Power Platform admin team and ecosystem for scale and growth, organizations can ensure that they are well-positioned to drive business transformation and innovation. The admin team's strategic planning, technical expertise, and continuous support are critical to the platform's long-term success and sustainability.

In addition to the roles mentioned, automation plays a significant role in scaling and growth. Automating routine tasks and workflows can save time, reduce errors, and ensure consistency across the platform. The admin team should leverage Power Automate and other tools to streamline processes, allowing team members to focus on more strategic initiatives. Essentially, the more tasks that are automated, the less manual work the team will need to undertake.

Automation and efficiency

Driving efficiency through automation within your Power Platform ecosystem requires a well-orchestrated strategy that combines technological tools, structured processes, and an empowered team. During a Power Platform adoption program, the admin team plays a pivotal role in identifying and implementing automation opportunities, which can significantly enhance organizational performance. As you can see in *Figure 7.4*, there are many other benefits to driving efficiency through automation. There may be a resource commitment up front to realize the true benefits of automation.

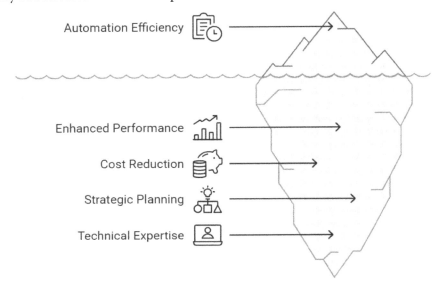

Figure 7.4: Driving automation efficiency drives many other benefits that can be realized as a result

The first step toward driving efficiency is to conduct a thorough analysis of existing workflows and processes. The admin team should collaborate with various business units to map out routine tasks, identify bottlenecks, and pinpoint areas where automation could deliver the maximum impact. This requires a keen understanding of both the technical capabilities of the Power Platform and the operational needs of the organization.

The admin team should focus on developing automated solutions that streamline repetitive tasks, such as data entry, approval processes, and notifications. By using templates and connectors available in Power Automate, the team can quickly deploy automation solutions that integrate seamlessly with existing systems. Automating as much as possible means that the admin team can focus on driving wider adoption of the platform. Tools such as Power Automate are fantastic for these types of scenarios and can help a business realize extremely rapid value.

To ensure the success and sustainability of automation initiatives, it is crucial to establish best practices. This includes setting guidelines for designing, evaluating, and deploying automated workflows. The admin team should create a repository of reusable components and templates, which can accelerate the development of new automation solutions and promote consistency across the organization.

Automation is the continuous improvement of processes you have already created or are creating. The admin team must implement monitoring mechanisms to track the performance of automated workflows and identify areas for improvement. Regular reviews and feedback sessions with stakeholders can provide valuable insights into the effectiveness of automation solutions and help refine them further. This is not "One Off!" automation – the automation of processes is a continuous process.

As automation touches various aspects of the business, ensuring security and compliance becomes paramount. The Admin Team should enforce strict access controls and regularly audit automated workflows to prevent unauthorized actions and ensure that they adhere to regulatory requirements. Additionally, maintaining a secure environment for automation tools and data is crucial for protecting sensitive information.

By strategically leveraging automation within the Power Platform ecosystem, organizations can achieve significant efficiency gains, reduce operational costs, and enhance overall productivity. The admin team, with its expertise and initiative-taking approach, is central to driving these outcomes and ensuring that the Power Platform adoption program delivers long-term value.

The admin team in a Power Platform adoption program is responsible for strategic planning, technical expertise, and continuous support to ensure the successful implementation and sustainability of the platform. Roles include establishing governance, managing environments, ensuring security and compliance, providing training and support, monitoring performance, and staying updated with the latest best practices. They also play a crucial role in preparing the ecosystem for scale and growth by promoting collaboration, empowering citizen developers, and driving efficiency through automation. The admin team's initiative-taking approach is essential for maintaining long-term value and driving business transformation. In the next section, we will explore how organizations can build and maintain a fusion team culture as Power Platform scales across the business.

Fusion team collaboration and beyond

Creating a fusion team culture is crucial for the successful adoption of the Power Platform within an organization. A fusion team, consisting of both IT professionals and business users, encourages collaboration, innovation, and shared ownership of digital transformation initiatives and assets.

By embracing these strategies, organizations can lay the groundwork for cohesive and effective fusion teams, driving the successful implementation of solutions and contributing to the organization's overall digital transformation journey.

Building a fusion team culture

Building a fusion team culture within your organization may be a bit of a change from what people are used to. Typically, a fusion team consists of a mixture of people from across the business. Some may be more technical than others; however, the main goal is for them to all work together to build useful solutions with the tools available in the Power Platform.

Encouraging open communication channels between IT and business units is vital. Regular meetings, workshops, and collaborative platforms can help break down silos and facilitate the exchange of ideas and expertise. By promoting a culture of transparency and mutual respect, teams can work together more effectively to develop and implement automation solutions. This can be a struggle sometimes as IT has not historically co-developed solutions with the business. They may have received lists of requirements from the business, but this can be considered disconnected from the actual problem that needs solving.

It is important to establish clear roles and responsibilities for each member of the fusion team. This ensures that everyone understands their contribution to the project and can leverage their unique skills and knowledge. By defining these roles early on, the team can operate more smoothly and avoid potential conflicts or overlaps in responsibilities. As an example, a person who is non-technical but clearly understands an area of the business would be considered a subject matter expert, but a person who is more technical and is proficient at writing code may be called a "developer."

A shared vision and common goals are crucial for uniting the fusion team. By aligning the team's objectives with the organization's overall strategy, members can work toward a common purpose and stay motivated. Revisiting and refining these goals can help maintain focus and drive progress throughout the adoption program.

Empowering team members with the necessary skills and resources is key to building a capable fusion team. Offering training sessions, access to knowledge repositories, and hands-on workshops can help both IT and business users become proficient in using the Power Platform. This investment in education not only enhances individual capabilities but also strengthens the team's overall performance.

Innovation should be at the heart of a fusion team culture. By creating an environment where experimentation and creative problem-solving are encouraged, teams can develop novel solutions to business challenges. Celebrating successes, learning from failures, and continuously iterating on ideas can help sustain a culture of innovation.

By involving a diverse group of stakeholders in the adoption program, the fusion team can gain a holistic understanding of the organization's needs and priorities. This cross-functional approach ensures that automation initiatives are aligned with business objectives and deliver maximum value.

Acknowledging the efforts and achievements of fusion team members is important for maintaining morale and motivation. Implementing a recognition and rewards program can help reinforce positive behaviors and encourage continued engagement. Whether through formal awards, public acknowledgments, or informal gestures of appreciation, recognizing contributions can strengthen the team's sense of ownership and commitment. *Figure 7.5* summarizes the six key aspects of building a strong fusion team culture in your organization.

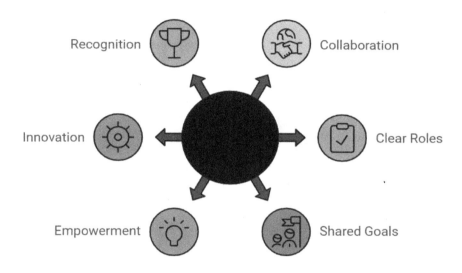

Figure 7.5: Six key aspects of a fusion team culture

Many organizations have embraced a fusion team culture without even knowing it. This can be given a bit more process and formality by focusing on the types of areas mentioned in *Figure 7.5*.

Creating a supportive environment where team members feel valued and empowered is crucial for the success of a fusion team. Providing access to mentors, promoting a culture of continuous learning, and promoting work-life balance can help ensure that team members remain engaged and productive. A supportive environment also encourages team members to take risks and innovate without fear of failure.

This collaborative and empowered approach not only enhances the effectiveness of automation initiatives but also contributes to the organization's overall digital transformation journey.

The role of fusion teams

Fusion teams play a pivotal role in driving the successful adoption of the Power Platform within organizations. By integrating IT professionals and business users into a cohesive unit, fusion teams leverage diverse skills and perspectives to address the complicated challenges of digital transformation. Their role is varied, encompassing strategic planning, execution, and continuous improvement across various stages of the adoption program.

At the outset, fusion teams are instrumental in aligning the Power Platform adoption program with the organization's strategic objectives. They facilitate the identification of key business processes that can benefit from automation and low-code/no-code solutions. This strategic focus ensures that the adoption efforts are not only aligned with business goals but also deliver tangible value. By engaging stakeholders from different departments, fusion teams develop a comprehensive roadmap that highlights priorities, timelines, and resource requirements.

During the implementation phase, fusion teams serve as the driving force behind the development and deployment of automation solutions. Their collaborative nature allows for the seamless integration of technical expertise and business acumen, resulting in solutions that are both technically robust and aligned with business needs. Fusion teams are responsible for configuring and customizing the Power Platform and associated tools to suit specific organizational requirements, overseeing the development of applications, workflows, and dashboards that enhance operational efficiency.

The importance of creating a supportive environment cannot be overstated. Fusion teams thrive in settings where members feel valued and empowered. This is achieved by providing access to mentors, promoting a culture of continuous learning, and promoting work-life balance. Such an environment encourages innovation and risk-taking, enabling team members to explore creative solutions without fear of failure. A supportive culture also ensures sustained engagement and productivity, which are critical for the long-term success of the adoption program.

Innovation lies at the heart of fusion teams. By cultivating an environment that encourages experimentation and creative problem-solving, fusion teams drive the development of novel solutions to business challenges. Celebrating successes, learning from failures, and iterating on ideas are key practices that sustain a culture of innovation. This focus on continuous improvement ensures that the organization remains agile and responsive to evolving business needs.

Empowering team members with the necessary skills and resources is paramount. Fusion teams invest in training and development to enhance individual capabilities and overall team performance. Offering training sessions, access to knowledge repositories, and hands-on workshops enables both IT and business users to become proficient in using the Power Platform. This investment in education not only boosts technical competency but also generates a culture of self-reliance and continuous learning.

A shared vision and common goals unite fusion teams around a common purpose. By aligning team objectives with the organization's strategic goals, fusion teams ensure that all members are working toward the same end. This alignment generates a sense of ownership and commitment, driving progress and maintaining focus throughout the adoption program. Regularly revisiting and refining these goals helps keep the team aligned and motivated.

Clear roles and responsibilities are essential for the smooth operation of fusion teams. By establishing well-defined roles early on, fusion teams can leverage the unique skills and knowledge of each member, avoiding potential conflicts or overlaps. This clarity ensures that everyone understands their contribution to the project, facilitating efficient collaboration and execution. *Figure 7.6* summarizes the roles of a fusion team.

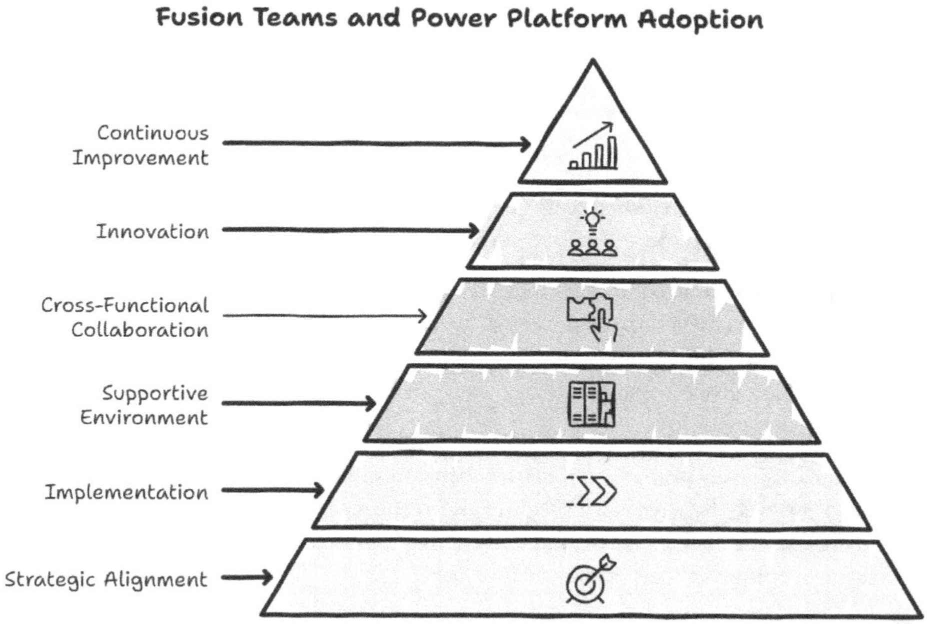

Fusion Teams and Power Platform Adoption

Figure 7.6: Key aspects of the role of a fusion team

Organizations can build a robust fusion team culture that drives the successful adoption of the Power Platform. This collaborative and empowered approach not only enhances the effectiveness of automation initiatives but also contributes to the organization's overall digital transformation journey.

Collaboration and communication

Open communication channels are vital for the success of fusion teams and building a collaborative culture. Regular meetings, workshops, hackathons, and collaborative platforms facilitate the exchange of ideas and expertise, breaking down silos and promoting transparency. A culture of open communication and mutual respect enables teams to work together more effectively, ensuring that automation solutions are developed and implemented cohesively.

One effective method for driving collaboration and communication among fusion teams is to establish designated collaboration platforms. These platforms can include tools such as Microsoft Teams, Slack, or other digital workspaces that allow team members to share updates, discuss challenges, and brainstorm solutions in real time. Additionally, setting up regular touchpoints, such as daily stand-ups, weekly syncs, or bi-weekly retrospectives, ensures that communication remains consistent, and any issues are promptly addressed.

Fusion teams can benefit from creating cross-functional working groups, pods, or task forces. These groups can be composed of members from various departments such as IT, business units, and other stakeholders, who bring diverse perspectives and expertise to the table. By working together on specific tasks or projects, these cross-functional teams can generate a deeper understanding of distinct roles and responsibilities, leading to more cohesive and integrated solutions.

Fusion teams should be encouraged to share their experiences, lessons learned, and best practices with one another. This can be achieved through regular feedback sessions, peer reviews, and knowledge-sharing workshops. By creating an environment where feedback is valued and acted upon, teams can continuously refine their processes and enhance their performance.

Lastly, leadership plays a pivotal role in facilitating collaboration and communication within fusion teams. Leaders should actively promote and model open communication, transparency, and inclusivity. They should also provide the necessary support and resources to ensure that team members can collaborate effectively. This includes investing in training programs, providing access to collaboration tools, and creating a culture of trust and mutual respect.

Clear roles and responsibilities are essential for the smooth operation of fusion teams. By establishing well-defined roles early on, fusion teams can leverage the unique skills and knowledge of each member, avoiding potential conflicts or overlaps. This clarity ensures that everyone understands their contribution to the project, facilitating efficient collaboration and execution.

Challenges and solutions

During the development of fusion teams during a Power Platform adoption program, organizations often face several challenges. Addressing these challenges effectively is crucial to ensure the success and sustainability of the initiative.

One of the major challenges is identifying "who does what." If this isn't defined, there *will* be a communication barrier that is created and there may even be no clear leadership and support. By establishing well-defined roles early on, fusion teams can leverage the unique skills and knowledge of each member, avoiding potential conflicts or overlaps. This clarity ensures that everyone understands their contribution to the project, facilitating efficient collaboration and execution.

To continue the thread of roles and responsibilities, leadership plays a pivotal role in facilitating collaboration and communication within fusion teams. Leaders should actively promote and model open communication, transparency, and inclusivity. The concept of fusion teams is relatively new so it's important to establish a clear direction for each person in the team. Without well-defined leadership, the fusion team will be a ship without a rudder – directionless.

Communication is *key*! A fusion team with well-defined communication and active members will perform well. This means that there needs to be processes and channels put in place for people to communicate. Getting these frameworks in place early will avoid many challenges later. A key challenge is when the technical members and non-technical members split apart into smaller teams. If this happens, the fusion team has failed. *Figure 7.7* highlights some of the pros and cons of leveraging fusion teams.

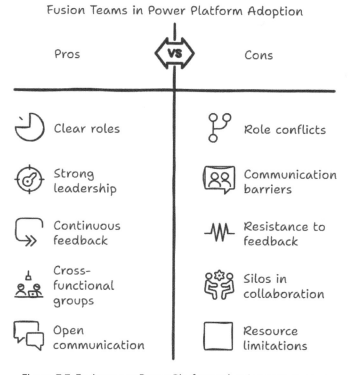

Figure 7.7: Fusion team Power Platform adoption pros vs cons

In conclusion, creating a robust fusion team culture is essential for the successful adoption of the Power Platform within an organization. Fusion teams, which integrate IT professionals with business users, are instrumental in driving collaboration, innovation, and shared responsibility in digital transformation initiatives. To build such a team, organizations must prioritize several strategies. Aligning team objectives with the organization's strategic goals helps maintain motivation and focus. Investing in the necessary skills and resources, such as training and access to knowledge repositories, enhances both individual and team performance. Promoting a culture of innovation by encouraging experimentation and learning from both successes and failures drives the development of creative solutions. Recognizing and supporting team members through recognition programs and a supportive work environment boosts morale and productivity. By addressing these aspects, organizations can establish a fusion team that not only enhances the effectiveness of automation initiatives but also significantly contributes to the overall digital transformation journey. In the next section, we will explore methods for building a digital culture in your organization.

Building a digital culture

Examining your organization's culture is a pivotal step during the adoption of the Power Platform. It begins with an honest assessment of the current state, identifying existing cultural norms, values, and behaviors that could impact the program's success. Surveys, interviews, and focus groups can be effective tools to gather insights from employees at all levels. These methods help uncover perceptions, attitudes, and potential resistance toward the innovative technology.

Understanding the underlying dynamics of your organization's culture allows leaders to tailor their strategies to address specific cultural barriers and leverage strengths. For instance, if a culture of innovation and collaboration already exists, the focus can be on enhancing these traits to support the Power Platform adoption. If silos and resistance to change are prevalent, efforts should be geared toward openness and cross-functional collaboration.

Examining organizational culture involves recognizing and celebrating early adopters, champions, and success stories. Highlighting these examples can serve as powerful motivators for the rest of the organization, highlighting tangible benefits and promoting a positive narrative around the adoption process.

A thorough examination of your organization's culture not only aids in smoothing the transition but also lays the foundation for sustainable digital transformation. By understanding and nurturing the cultural elements that align with the goals of the Power Platform program, organizations can drive more effective and lasting change.

Cultural change management

Successful adoption of the Power Platform hinges on careful cultural change management within the organization. This involves an approach that begins with an assessment of the current cultural landscape.

Once these cultural elements are understood, the next step is to actively cultivate a culture that supports and enhances the adoption of the Power Platform. Addressing specific cultural barriers is crucial. If the organization already has a culture of innovation and collaboration, these traits can be further amplified to support the Power Platform implementation. Conversely, if the organization suffers from silos or resistance to change, efforts should be focused on building bridges between silos.

It is essential that leaders tailor their strategies to leverage the organization's existing strengths while addressing its weaknesses. This might involve targeted training programs, workshops, and other initiatives designed to build the necessary skills and confidence among employees. By strategically focusing on these areas, organizations can build a robust fusion team culture that drives the successful adoption of the Power Platform. This collaborative and empowered approach not only enhances the effectiveness of automation initiatives but also contributes to the organization's overall digital transformation journey.

Getting people on board

Getting people on board a digital change management program during a Power Platform adoption initiative requires a strategic approach. It begins with leaders understanding the unique cultural dynamics of their organization. By leveraging existing strengths and addressing weaknesses, a refined strategy can be created that resonates with the team's needs and aspirations.

Addressing specific cultural barriers is also crucial. If the organization already has a culture of innovation and collaboration, these traits can be amplified to support the Power Platform implementation. If there are silos or resistance to change, these areas should be further explored, and work done to resolve this resistance and to educate people through various programs.

Recognizing and celebrating milestones and adoption is important. Highlighting these positive examples serves as a powerful motivator, demonstrating the tangible benefits of the platform and creating a positive narrative around its adoption.

Successful adoption of the Power Platform hinges on careful cultural change management. This involves a comprehensive assessment of the current cultural landscape. Existing norms, values, and behaviors must be identified that could either propel or hinder the implementation process. Tools such as surveys, interviews, and focus groups can provide valuable insights into employee perceptions and attitudes toward the innovative technology, helping to pinpoint areas of resistance and opportunities for engagement.

A thorough examination of the organization's culture not only aids in smoothing the transition but also lays the foundation for sustainable digital transformation. By understanding and nurturing the cultural elements that align with the goals of the Power Platform program, organizations can drive more effective and lasting change. *Figure 7.8* shows six of the core pillars that should be explored when examining an organization's digital culture.

Navigating Cultural Dynamics for Power Platform Adoption

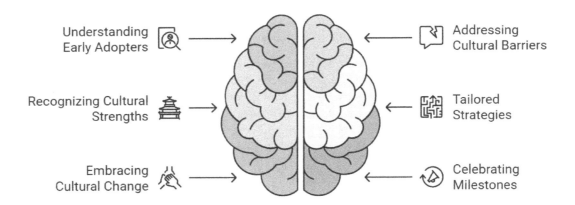

Figure 7.8: Understanding the various dynamics when navigating a digital culture

The focus is on the critical role of organizational culture in the successful adoption of the Power Platform. It emphasizes the need for an honest assessment of the current cultural state, using tools such as surveys, interviews, and focus groups to uncover existing norms, values, and potential resistance. Understanding these cultural dynamics allows leaders to tailor their strategies, either by reinforcing existing strengths such as innovation and collaboration or by addressing barriers such as silos and resistance to change. Celebrating early adopters and success stories can motivate others and build a positive narrative around modern technology. Effective cultural change management involves open communication, targeted training, and strategic adjustments to support the adoption process. By aligning cultural elements with the goals of the Power Platform, organizations can facilitate a smoother transition and foster a sustainable digital transformation.

Summary

The successful adoption of the Power Platform hinges on a strategic approach to change management that leverages an organization's strengths and addresses its weaknesses. Leaders must understand their organization's unique cultural dynamics and tailor their strategies accordingly, which may involve targeted training programs and initiatives to build necessary skills and confidence among employees.

Addressing specific cultural barriers is crucial. If the organization has a culture of innovation and collaboration, these traits should be amplified to support the Power Platform implementation. Conversely, if there are silos or resistance to change, these areas must be explored and resolved through educational programs. Recognizing and celebrating milestones and adoption is important as it serves as a motivator and creates a positive narrative around the platform's adoption.

A comprehensive assessment of the current cultural landscape using tools such as surveys, interviews, and focus groups is necessary to understand existing norms, values, and potential resistance. Effective cultural change management involves open communication, targeted training, and strategic adjustments. Aligning cultural elements with the goals of the Power Platform facilitates a smoother transition and fosters sustainable digital transformation.

Ultimately, understanding and nurturing the cultural elements that align with the goals of the Power Platform program can drive more effective and lasting change, enhancing the effectiveness of automation initiatives, and contributing to the organization's overall digital transformation journey.

In the next chapter, we will explore how organizations can embrace Power Platform and build useful solutions as they progress through the maturity model levels.

Get This Book's PDF Version and Exclusive Extras

UNLOCK NOW

Scan the QR code (or go to packtpub.com/unlock). Search for this book by name, confirm the edition, and then follow the steps on the page.

Note: Keep your invoice handy. Purchases made directly from Packt don't require one.

8

Power Platform Solutions for Digital Transformation

In the dynamic landscape of digital transformation, organizations increasingly acknowledge the pivotal role of the Power Platform in fostering innovation and facilitating growth. Comprising Microsoft technologies such as Power BI, Power Apps, and Power Automate, the Power Platform presents unparalleled potential for crafting solutions that tackle intricate business challenges. However, the effective integration and utilization of the Power Platform demands a strategic approach, considering the organization's maturity level and the alignment of diverse stakeholders. In this chapter, we will explore the following:

- Key elements of stakeholder analysis and alignment
- Using the Capability Maturity Model Integration (CMMI) to guide successful digital transformation
- Strategies for stakeholder buy-in
- Establishing fusion team collaboration

Stakeholder analysis and alignment – driving successful Power Platform adoption

Exploring the Capability Maturity Model Integration (CMMI)

The **Capability Maturity Model Integration (CMMI)** serves as a framework for evaluating an organization's maturity in managing processes and practices. This model provides a roadmap to understand an organization's readiness and capacity to effectively utilize the Power Platform. The CMMI outlines five levels of maturity, each indicating the organization's progress in adopting best practices and achieving success. The following figure shows the levels of maturity according to the CMMI and the respective abilities associated with each level. Leaders should be aware of where their organizations sit within this spectrum.

Figure 8.1 – CMMI maturity levels

- **Initial Level**: At this stage, organizations have encountered sporadic successes with the Power Platform, albeit without a cohesive strategy or governance. The focus is on exploring capabilities rather than systematically utilizing them. Stakeholders might be unaware of the platform's potential, hindering its broader adoption.

- **Repeatable Level**: Progressing to this stage involves implementing initial controls and recognizing widely used applications. However, a sense of unregulated usage may persist. Stakeholders are beginning to realize the platform's value, but there's a need for more structured approaches.

- **Defined Level**: Organizations at this level standardize repeatable practices and achieve measurable success in digital transformation. Establishing a Power Platform **Center of Excellence (CoE)** team becomes crucial, indicating a growing understanding of the platform's impact. However, organic growth might still overshadow formal strategies.

- **Capable Level**: Moving further along the maturity curve, organizations standardize practices and leverage Power Platform capabilities for broader business transformation. Enterprise-critical applications and integrations depend on the platform, and Platform Champions emerge, creating vital communication channels.

- **Efficient Level**: At the pinnacle of the maturity model, organizations have harnessed the Power Platform's potential to transform mission-critical functions. An expert community thrives, and fusion teams emerge to integrate legacy capabilities with modern cloud architecture, ensuring optimal efficiency.

Strategic stakeholder analysis

Stakeholder analysis is a crucial element in the Power Platform adoption journey, as it helps organizations identify and engage key individuals and groups affected by the initiative. Effective stakeholder engagement ensures buy-in, support, and alignment throughout the process. Identifying the stakeholders begins with understanding their roles, responsibilities, and expectations.

- **Executive Leadership**: These decision-makers hold the power to allocate resources and approve strategic initiatives. Demonstrating the Power Platform's potential to drive transformation aligns their interests with the adoption goals.

- **Business Units and Departments**: Different departments have unique needs and challenges. Engaging with leaders and teams across these units helps tailor solutions that directly address their pain points, fostering enthusiasm for the platform.

- **IT Department**: The IT team plays a critical role in implementation, integration, and support. Collaborating with IT early on ensures a smooth adoption process and addresses any concerns related to security, compliance, and governance.

- **End Users**: These are the individuals who will directly interact with the solutions built on the Power Platform. Involving end users in the design and testing phases enhances usability and drives engagement.

- **Power Platform CoE Team**: This team, at the Defined and Capable levels, becomes the driving force behind best practices and knowledge sharing. Their input is invaluable in guiding stakeholders and ensuring alignment with platform objectives.

Alignment strategies for each maturity level

The journey to achieving Power Platform maturity involves a series of strategic alignment stages, each building progressively upon the last. In the Initial Level alignment, the aim is to generate early enthusiasm and support by highlighting quick wins and internal success stories, underscoring the platform's potential. Moving to the Repeatable Level alignment, the emphasis shifts to developing governance and engaging IT to ensure sustainable, secure use of the platform.

As organizations reach the Defined Level alignment, collaborating with the CoE and gaining executive backing becomes essential, focusing on standardization and strategic resource allocation. In the Capable Level alignment, the Power Platform's significance in critical operations and integration is highlighted, with Platform Champions playing a more central role in decision-making. Finally, at the Efficient Level alignment, the focus is on fully leveraging the platform to revolutionize core functions, utilizing an expert community to showcase advanced applications and achieving seamless integration with legacy systems. Each level represents a stepping stone toward fully aligning stakeholders with the Power Platform's transformative potential.

- **Initial Level Alignment**: At this stage, the focus is on raising awareness among stakeholders. Demonstrating quick wins and illustrating the potential of the Power Platform can help secure initial support. Highlighting success stories within the organization showcases the platform's capabilities.

- **Repeatable Level Alignment**: As organizations progress, aligning stakeholders involves showcasing the platform's impact on efficiency and productivity. Developing a governance framework and involving IT in discussions addresses concerns related to unregulated usage.

- **Defined Level Alignment**: Here, the focus shifts to collaboration with the CoE team. Engaging executive leadership becomes crucial to secure resources for CoE initiatives. Demonstrating the CoE's role in standardizing practices can further align stakeholders.

- **Capable Level Alignment**: At this stage, emphasizing the platform's strategic impact is key. Engaging with Platform Champions and involving them in decision-making reinforces alignment. Demonstrating how critical applications and integrations rely on the platform reinforces its significance.

- **Efficient Level Alignment**: The emphasis is on showcasing the Power Platform's ability to transform core functions. Leveraging the expert community to showcase innovative use cases and integrating legacy systems reinforces the alignment of stakeholders at this stage.

In the journey toward digital transformation through Power Platform adoption, stakeholder analysis and alignment are fundamental pillars for success. By assessing an organization's maturity level using the CMMI and strategically engaging stakeholders at each stage, organizations can ensure that their Power Platform initiatives are well-structured, supported, and positioned for optimal impact. Recognizing the significance of stakeholders' roles and perspectives while aligning them with the platform's potential is a key driver of successful Power Platform adoption and, ultimately, digital transformation.

The Power Platform dream team

In the CMMI context, roles are defined within the framework of process improvement and organizational maturity. These roles are not specific to a particular technology adoption but rather focus on improving an organization's processes and practices across various domains. Successful Power Platform adoption requires specific roles and responsibilities.

Executive sponsor – visionary leadership

At the core of the dream team stands the Executive Sponsor—a beacon of high-level vision and values. This influential leader communicates the strategic significance of the Microsoft Power Platform to the entire organization. By painting a compelling picture of the transformation journey, they inspire buy-in and secure necessary resources. The Executive Sponsor serves as the driving force behind organizational alignment and continuous support for the adoption process.

Success owner – nurturing business goals

The Success Owner shoulders the responsibility of ensuring that the organization's business goals are not only acknowledged but also realized through the adoption process. This individual translates strategic objectives into actionable steps, guiding the team toward measurable outcomes. By maintaining a laser focus on business results, the Success Owner guarantees that the Power Platform adoption is more than just a technological initiative—it is a vehicle for tangible success.

Champions – catalysts of evangelism

Champions emerge as vital catalysts of Power Platform evangelism. These passionate advocates help create a circle of influence within the organization, actively promoting the platform's potential. Their role extends beyond enthusiastic endorsement; they serve as a bridge between end users and the adoption team. Champions provide critical feedback, sharing insights on what works and what doesn't, ultimately shaping the adoption strategy.

Training lead – knowledge dissemination maestro

The Training Lead takes center stage in managing and communicating training content about the Power Platform. Whether through internal resources or external vendors, this role ensures that knowledge dissemination is organized, effective, and accessible. By equipping users with the necessary skills, the Training Lead empowers them to harness the Power Platform's capabilities confidently, thereby enhancing engagement and adoption.

Department leads (stakeholders) – advocates of engagement

Department Leads are pivotal stakeholders who bridge the gap between the Power Platform and specific operational needs. Their role involves identifying how their respective departments can effectively leverage the platform's features. These advocates of engagement align business processes with the platform's capabilities, ensuring that the adoption journey addresses department-specific challenges, and fostering enthusiasm from the ground up.

Communication lead – amplifier of awareness

Communication is the lifeblood of successful adoption, and the communication lead takes on the crucial responsibility of overseeing company-wide communications about the Power Platform. This role ensures that messages are clear, consistent, and aligned with the transformation narrative. By disseminating information effectively, the communication lead fosters a culture of open communication, dispelling myths and promoting understanding.

Power Platform admin team – guardians of technical enablement

The Power Platform admin team stands as the guardians of technical enablement. Their realm encompasses establishing an environment strategy, implementing **data loss prevention** (**DLP**) policies, managing users and licensing, and facilitating data availability through connectors, integrations, or migration. Their expertise provides makers with the tools they need to turn ideas into impactful solutions.

Power Platform nurture team – sowers of innovation

The Power Platform nurture team embodies innovation evangelists who sow the seeds of creativity within the organization. They organize app-in-a-day events and hackathons, and provide mentorship to makers. By nurturing newcomers and guiding them through the initial stages, the nurture team cultivates a culture where experimentation and learning thrive, ultimately driving the adoption of the Power Platform.

The Power Platform dream team represents a harmonious ensemble of roles, each contributing distinct expertise to create a symphony of successful adoption. Assembling this team is not just a matter of organizational structure; it's about fostering collaboration, alignment, and a shared commitment to driving digital transformation. By recognizing the value that each stakeholder brings to the table and embracing their unique contributions, organizations can navigate the complexities of Power Platform adoption with clarity, purpose, and confidence.

In this chapter, we explored two key aspects crucial to the successful adoption of the Power Platform: understanding the CMMI and assembling the Power Platform dream team. Through our examination of the CMMI, we gained valuable insights into the various maturity levels that organizations may progress through on their path to effectively utilizing the Power Platform. From the Initial Level, marked by sporadic successes without a cohesive strategy, to the Efficient Level, characterized by the platform's full utilization to transform core functions, each stage presents distinct challenges and opportunities.

Additionally, we delved into the essential roles within the Power Platform dream team, each contributing unique expertise to facilitate successful adoption. From the visionary leadership of the executive sponsor to the innovation-fostering efforts of the Power Platform nurture team, every role plays a crucial role in advancing digital transformation.

It's important to recognize that understanding the CMMI and assembling the Power Platform dream team are interconnected components of a comprehensive adoption approach. By grasping an organization's maturity level and aligning stakeholders effectively, we lay the groundwork for a structured, supported, and impactful journey toward digital transformation.

Moving ahead, the subsequent section will explore *Strategies for stakeholder buy-in – showcasing Power Platform's impact*. This section is pivotal for the success of the Power Platform adoption journey. By effectively demonstrating the platform's potential to key individuals and groups, organizations can ensure that their initiatives are not only well-structured but also positioned to drive substantial change. We'll delve into strategies for engaging stakeholders and aligning their perspectives at each maturity level, thereby enhancing our understanding of navigating the complexities of Power Platform adoption successfully.

Strategies for stakeholder buy-in – showcasing Power Platform's impact

In the journey towards digital transformation, organizations often encounter the need for stakeholder buy-in to effectively implement Power Platform solutions. These solutions, driven by citizen developers, have the potential to revolutionize business processes, enhance productivity, and streamline operations. However, for these benefits to be realized, it is crucial to secure buy-in from various stakeholders, ranging from executive leadership to individual contributors. This section delves into the strategies and approaches for gaining stakeholder buy-in by showcasing the impact of Power Platform across different levels of the organization.

The Dynamics of stakeholder buy-in

Citizen developers, individuals who possess domain expertise but may not be traditionally associated with IT roles, form the cornerstone of Power Platform's transformative potential. However, since these individuals report to managers who are vested in their primary responsibilities, the process of securing buy-in becomes multifaceted. The challenge lies in convincing executives, managers, and individual contributors to recognize the value of Power Platform and allocate time and resources to its implementation:

- **Executive buy-in**: To engage executive leadership, it is essential to translate the potential of Power Platform into tangible business value. Executives are often motivated by factors such as cost reduction, increased efficiency, and competitive advantage. By presenting data-driven projections that demonstrate how Power Platform can lead to substantial cost savings, streamlined processes, and enhanced customer experiences, you can create a compelling case for executive buy-in. Additionally, highlighting success stories and real-world examples can illustrate the platform's transformative impact on a strategic level. Executive buy-in is instrumental in driving transformative initiatives. To secure this crucial support for Power Platform adoption, one of the most compelling arguments centers around the substantial financial gains it can yield.

The evolution of low-code development, exemplified by Power Platform, has dramatically reshaped the application development market. This section delves into how showcasing Power Platform's impact on financial gains, backed by statistics on the remarkable growth of low-code development, can resonate with executive leaders.

- **Manager buy-in**: Managers are responsible for the productivity and performance of their teams. They are concerned with optimizing processes and ensuring that resources are utilized efficiently. When seeking manager buy-in, emphasize how Power Platform solutions can save valuable time and empower teams to focus on strategic tasks. Showcasing how automation, data integration, and self-service capabilities can alleviate repetitive tasks and enable managers to make data-driven decisions can resonate strongly. Additionally, stressing the potential for managers to become champions of innovation within their departments can encourage their support.

- **Individual buy-in**: For individual contributors, the prospect of contributing to the creation of apps, flows, and chatbots presents exciting opportunities for learning and personal growth. By highlighting the platform's user-friendly interface and the potential for acquiring valuable technical skills, you can pique the interest of those who are eager to expand their horizons. Showcasing success stories of individuals who have transitioned from being end users to citizen developers can inspire others to embrace the platform with enthusiasm. While showcasing the positive impact of Power Platform is essential, it's equally important to address potential concerns and uncertainties. People often fear change, and the introduction of new technologies can trigger apprehensions about job security, changes in responsibilities, and disruptions to established routines. By proactively addressing these concerns and illustrating how Power Platform's implementation aligns with the organization's goals, you can foster a sense of security and encourage a smoother transition.

Short-term and long-term impacts

When gaining stakeholder buy-in, it's crucial to discuss both short-term and long-term impacts. Highlight how Power Platform can quickly address immediate pain points and provide rapid returns on investment. Simultaneously, discuss the platform's long-term potential to catalyze ongoing innovation, adaptability, and agility within the organization. Demonstrating how the platform can grow with the organization and serve as a foundation for future advancements can resonate with stakeholders who are concerned about sustainability.

Securing stakeholder buy-in for Power Platform initiatives is a pivotal aspect of the digital transformation journey. By tailoring your approach to the unique motivations and concerns of executives, managers, and individual contributors, you can build a coalition of support that propels the platform's adoption and success. By showcasing Power Platform's transformative impact, addressing concerns, and emphasizing the learning and growth opportunities it offers, you can navigate the intricacies of stakeholder engagement and set the stage for a successful digital transformation journey.

The paradigm shift – the rise of low-code development and its financial impact

Traditional application development has been synonymous with complex coding, extensive development cycles, and high costs. The emergence of low-code development platforms, epitomized by Power Platform, has revolutionized this landscape. Low-code platforms empower citizen developers to create functional applications with minimal coding knowledge, significantly reducing the time and resources required for development. This paradigm shift aligns perfectly with executive goals of efficiency and cost reduction.

To underscore the potential financial gains from Power Platform, consider the explosive growth of the low-code development market. By 2030, over 85% of new enterprise apps will be built with low-code or no-code, up from under 25% in 2020. AI-driven tools will further speed up development, automating nearly 50% of repetitive coding tasks. This growth is indicative of the increasing recognition and adoption of low-code platforms as organizations seek streamlined and cost-effective ways to develop applications.

Furthermore, studies have shown that low-code development can lead to substantial savings. Organizations adopting low-code platforms are reported to achieve up to a 90% reduction in application development time compared to traditional methods. This accelerated development process directly translates into cost savings by minimizing labor and resource expenditures. Moreover, the agility provided by low-code platforms allows organizations to respond rapidly to market changes and emerging opportunities, further enhancing their financial resilience.

Power Platform's contribution – translating potential to reality

Power Platform, as a prominent player in the low-code arena, offers a compelling case for executive buy-in by presenting demonstrable results. Share case studies and success stories from organizations that have harnessed Power Platform to develop applications in record time, significantly cutting down development costs. Highlight instances where citizen developers, with minimal technical backgrounds, have created impactful solutions that directly contributed to revenue growth or operational efficiency.

When engaging with executives, frame the discussion around how Power Platform's low-code capabilities directly align with their financial objectives. Emphasize the reduction in development time, associated cost savings, and the ability to rapidly respond to market demands. Present the statistics on low-code growth as evidence of a widespread shift towards platforms such as Power Platform, underscoring its relevance in the current business landscape.

Securing executive buy-in for Power Platform can be significantly bolstered by showcasing its impact on financial gains. The rise of low-code development platforms has reshaped the application development market, offering organizations the potential for remarkable cost savings and agility. By presenting statistics on the growth of low-code development, backed by real-world success stories of Power Platform implementations, you can paint a compelling picture of its financial impact. Aligning the platform's capabilities with executive goals and highlighting its potential to drive substantial returns on investment positions, Power Platform is an invaluable tool for the organization's financial success.

Securing citizen developers' buy-in – showcasing Power Platform's impact on career projection and growth

In today's fast-paced business landscape, career projection and growth are paramount for professionals seeking to advance their skills and opportunities. For citizen developers – individuals who possess domain expertise but may not have traditional IT backgrounds – embracing the Power Platform offers a unique avenue to not only contribute meaningfully to their organizations but also elevate their own careers. This section delves into how showcasing Power Platform's impact on career projection and growth, bolstered by salary statistics reflecting the robust growth of low-code development, can be a compelling catalyst for citizen developer buy-in.

Empowering career aspirations – the Power Platform advantage

Power Platform opens doors for citizen developers by democratizing application development. This empowerment resonates strongly with professionals who aspire to expand their skill sets, embrace innovative roles, and explore new horizons within their organizations. By enabling them to create apps, flows, and chatbots with minimal coding expertise, Power Platform nurtures a culture of continuous learning and skill development, which is crucial for career growth in the rapidly evolving tech-driven landscape.

Career projection – seizing the opportunity

For citizen developers, embracing Power Platform is not only about addressing immediate business needs but also about capitalizing on the opportunity for career projection. By showcasing the platform's potential to create valuable, user-centric solutions, organizations can encourage citizen developers to step into roles that involve innovation and leadership. Highlighting examples of individuals who started as end users and transitioned into impactful roles as citizen developers can inspire others to envision their own career progression.

Growth in application development – statistics tell the story

The application development landscape has been significantly impacted by the rise of low-code platforms such as Power Platform. According to industry data, the low-code development market is expected to experience substantial growth, with a projected compound annual growth rate (CAGR) exceeding 20% over the next few years. This growth reflects the increasing recognition of low-code's potential to accelerate development and drive digital transformation.

Salary statistics further underscore the impact of this growth on career projection. Salaries for professionals with low-code development skills are on the rise, reflecting the demand for individuals who can leverage these platforms to create efficient and innovative solutions. As organizations increasingly prioritize digital transformation, citizen developers armed with Power Platform proficiency are well-positioned to become invaluable assets, driving both technical and business success.

Cultivating a growth mindset – framing the discussion

When engaging with citizen developers, frame the discussion around how Power Platform can serve as a launchpad for career advancement. Illustrate how the platform's user-friendly interface, coupled with its ability to rapidly create functional solutions, aligns perfectly with their aspirations for growth. Present the salary statistics on low-code professionals as tangible evidence of the industry's recognition of these skills, emphasizing the potential for elevated earnings and career trajectories.

Elevating skill sets – empowering career growth

Power Platform not only empowers citizen developers to create functional solutions but also equips them with a valuable skill set that can enhance their overall career trajectory. As organizations recognize the role citizen developers play in fostering innovation, these individuals can become sought-after contributors in cross-functional teams. The ability to conceptualize, design, and implement solutions using Power Platform sets them apart and positions them as key players in driving digital transformation initiatives.

Framing the discussion – navigating career growth

When engaging citizen developers, it's crucial to frame the discussion around how Power Platform can contribute to their career growth. Emphasize the potential for these individuals to transition from being end users to becoming catalysts for change. Present the salary statistics and growth trends in the low-code development market as indicators of the value attached to their skill set.

Securing buy-in from citizen developers for Power Platform is a strategic move that can have profound implications for an organization's digital transformation journey. By showcasing the platform's impact on career projection and growth, backed by compelling salary statistics and growth trends in the low-code development market, organizations can tap into the aspirations of these individuals. Empowering citizen developers not only benefits the organization but also propels these individuals towards fulfilling and rewarding career paths, where they play a pivotal role in shaping the future of the business.

Securing IT professionals' buy-in – Power Platform's impact on career projection and growth for system administrators

In the rapidly evolving landscape of technology, IT professionals, especially system administrators, play a crucial role in maintaining and optimizing an organization's digital infrastructure. Securing their buy-in for Power Platform, despite their traditional roles, can be achieved by showcasing how this low-code platform can propel their career projection and growth. By presenting the platform's potential to expand skill sets and responsibilities and supporting it with salary statistics reflecting the robust growth in the low-code application development market, organizations can effectively engage and enlist the support of their IT experts.

Expanding horizons – from system administration to innovation

System administrators are the backbone of an organization's IT infrastructure, ensuring smooth operations and troubleshooting technical issues. However, in today's technology-driven environment, their role can extend beyond conventional system maintenance. Power Platform offers an opportunity for system administrators to embrace innovation and broaden their skill sets. By enabling them to design and implement solutions using a low-code approach, the platform empowers them to contribute to digital transformation initiatives and become catalysts for positive change.

Career growth through versatility – unleashing Power Platform's potential

Power Platform's low-code environment equips system administrators with a unique advantage – the ability to develop applications and automate processes without extensive coding expertise. This versatility not only streamlines operational efficiency but also expands career possibilities. As organizations increasingly adopt Power Platform, system administrators who master its functionalities become invaluable assets capable of bridging the gap between traditional IT roles and emerging technological demands.

A statistical reality – low-code's remarkable growth and impact on compensation

To reinforce the potential for career projection and growth, consider the remarkable growth trajectory of the low-code development market. As mentioned before, industry reports project a CAGR of over 20% from 2021 to 2027 for the low-code market. This exponential growth reflects the increasing recognition of low-code platforms as a pivotal driver of digital transformation. Moreover, salary statistics substantiate this trend, with professionals skilled in low-code development witnessing an uptick in demand and compensation.

The burgeoning low-code application development market directly impacts salary trends, favoring IT professionals who embrace this transformative approach. As organizations rely more on low-code platforms such as Power Platform, the demand for skilled professionals to leverage these tools intensifies. Consequently, system administrators who master Power Platform's capabilities can position themselves for salary growth and new career opportunities. These salary statistics serve as a tangible representation of how Power Platform proficiency can positively influence career advancement.

Embracing the evolution – fostering career resilience and promoting career growth

By encouraging system administrators to embrace Power Platform, organizations empower them to evolve with the ever-changing technological landscape. The platform not only offers new skill acquisition opportunities but also demonstrates an organization's commitment to nurturing talent. This creates an environment where system administrators feel valued, supported, and equipped to contribute to the organization's growth.

When engaging IT professionals, especially system administrators, emphasize how Power Platform aligns with their aspirations for career projection and growth. Highlight the expanding role that these professionals can play in digital transformation initiatives. Present statistical evidence of low-code's market growth and its direct correlation to enhanced compensation and new opportunities.

Securing buy-in from IT professionals, particularly system administrators, is a strategic imperative for successful Power Platform adoption. By showcasing the platform's potential to drive career projection and growth, supported by compelling salary statistics and growth trends in the low-code development market, organizations can ignite the enthusiasm and commitment of their technology experts. Empowering these professionals to leverage Power Platform not only amplifies their individual career journeys but also contributes to the organization's overall digital transformation success.

Microsoft Power Platform admin team – enabling transformational capabilities

In the ever-evolving landscape of digital transformation, organizations are increasingly turning to the Microsoft Power Platform to drive innovation, streamline processes, and enhance collaboration. As organizations embrace this platform, the role of the Microsoft Power Platform admin team becomes pivotal. Let's take a look into the crucial responsibilities of the admin team, focusing on secure user enablement and how their actions align with different maturity levels of the organization, as defined by the CMMI.

Initial maturity level – setting the foundation

At the initial maturity level, organizations might have pockets of success with the Power Platform but lack a comprehensive approach to governance and strategy. The Microsoft Power Platform admin team takes the lead in establishing the foundation for secure user enablement. This includes defining an environment strategy that outlines the structure and scope of environments for development, testing, and production.

Additionally, the admin team sets the groundwork for DLP policies. These policies are designed to safeguard sensitive information and maintain compliance with data protection regulations. The team's actions ensure that users are enabled to explore Power Platform capabilities while adhering to security best practices.

Repeatable maturity level – implementing control and guidance

As organizations progress to the repeatable maturity level, they begin to implement controls and identify widely used applications. The Microsoft Power Platform admin team steps in to provide the necessary guidance for secure user enablement. They establish guidelines for makers to follow, ensuring that solutions are developed within the boundaries of compliance and security.

At this stage, the admin team takes a proactive role in managing users, capacity, and licensing. By effectively managing these aspects, they ensure that the organization optimizes its resources while adhering to licensing agreements. The admin team's actions lay the groundwork for a structured approach to Power Platform usage that is both controlled and productive.

Defined maturity level – standardizing for success

Organizations at the defined maturity level have achieved measurable success in their digital transformation journey. The Microsoft Power Platform admin team's role now shifts towards standardizing practices for secure user enablement. They collaborate closely with makers to establish guidelines and best practices that align with the organization's goals and compliance requirements.

To ensure data availability, the admin team leverages connectors, integrations, or migration strategies to make relevant data accessible to makers. By effectively managing data integration, they empower makers to create solutions that are well-informed and data-driven. This collaborative approach fosters a culture of responsible and effective solution development.

Capable maturity level – enabling enterprise transformation

Reaching the capable level signifies that the Power Platform is driving a broader-scale transformation. The admin team's role evolves to support enterprise-critical applications and integrations. This includes deploying advanced governance mechanisms, such as advanced DLP policies, conditional access, and multi-factor authentication. Additionally, the admin team establishes communication channels with Platform Champions to address concerns and share best practices, ensuring that secure user enablement is aligned with organizational goals.

Efficient maturity level – orchestrating mission-critical functions

At the efficient level, the Power Platform has proven its capabilities in transforming mission-critical functions. The admin team now focuses on fostering an established community of experts. They facilitate the utilization of legacy capabilities and modern cloud architecture to achieve seamless data access and integration. The admin team works in harmony with fusion teams, comprising business and IT experts, to enable secure, high-impact solutions that drive innovation and efficiency across the organization.

In the journey of digital transformation, the role of the Microsoft Power Platform admin team cannot be understated. As organizations progress through the different levels of maturity, from initial to efficient, the admin team evolves from laying the foundation to orchestrating mission-critical functions. By enabling secure user enablement, aligning with the organization's goals, and establishing robust governance mechanisms, the admin team empowers the Power Platform to drive transformational capabilities. In essence, the admin team serves as the backbone that supports innovation, efficiency, and the realization of the organization's digital transformation aspirations.

Action plan for forming, nurturing, and empowering Power Platform admin teams

Forming, nurturing, and empowering an effective Power Platform Admin team is crucial to ensure the successful implementation, governance, and security of Microsoft Power Platform environments. Follow this action plan to guide your team through the process:

Step 1: Build a solid foundation

Start by establishing a strong foundational knowledge base within your Power Platform Admin team. These initial steps will provide team members with essential insights into the platform's core principles and best practices for secure, effective governance:

- **PL-900 exam**: Encourage team members to complete the PL-900 Power Platform Fundamentals exam. This will provide them with a comprehensive understanding of Power Platform's core concepts, capabilities, and components.

- **Learning path**: Have team members take the Microsoft learning path focused on identifying best practices for securing and governing Power Platform environments. This path will equip them with the knowledge required to establish robust governance measures.

Step 2: Implement best practices

With foundational knowledge in place, the next step is to implement proven best practices to enhance the security, governance, and efficiency of your Power Platform environment. These resources will equip your team with practical tools and in-depth strategies tailored to your organization's needs:

- **Admin and governance best practices checklist**: Guide your team to use the admin and governance best practices checklist provided by Microsoft. This checklist will help them apply their learning to your organization's specific Power Platform environment. Encourage them to follow guidelines for data loss prevention, role-based access control, and secure sharing.

- **Deep dive whitepaper**: Encourage your team to read the Power Platform admin whitepaper. This resource will provide them with a deeper understanding of advanced admin strategies, governance frameworks, and security considerations.

Step 3: Formation and nurturing

To establish a cohesive and effective Power Platform admin team, focus on gathering individuals with complementary skills and clear role assignments. This structure, combined with regular meetings, will foster collaboration, enhance knowledge-sharing, and drive continuous improvement:

- **Form the admin team**: Assemble a dedicated Power Platform admin team comprising individuals with diverse skill sets, including technical knowledge, data management, and communication skills.

- **Assign roles**: Designate specific roles within the admin team, such as governance lead, security lead, integration lead, and so on. Each role should align with the team members' strengths and expertise.

- **Regular meetings**: Schedule regular meetings for the admin team to discuss ongoing projects, challenges, and updates. This will foster collaboration, knowledge sharing, and continuous improvement.

Step 4: Empowerment and growth

Fostering a culture of growth and empowerment within the admin team is key to sustaining long-term success. By encouraging continuous learning, skill development, and leadership opportunities, you enable team members to stay current, tackle challenges effectively, and contribute to the team's overall impact:

- **Encourage continuous learning**: Promote a culture of continuous learning within the admin team. Encourage team members to stay updated with the latest Power Platform features, security enhancements, and industry trends.

- **Skill enhancement**: Support team members in enhancing their technical skills through workshops, online courses, and hands-on labs. This will enable them to tackle complex challenges with confidence.

- **Leadership opportunities**: Provide opportunities for team members to take leadership roles in managing specific aspects of the Power Platform environment. This not only empowers them but also enhances the team's effectiveness.

Step 5: Monitor and adapt

Maintaining alignment and adaptability within the Power Platform environment requires ongoing evaluation. Regular audits and a strong feedback loop empower the admin team to ensure compliance, refine strategies, and foster continuous improvement in governance practices:

- **Regular audits**: Conduct regular audits of the Power Platform environment to ensure compliance with governance policies. Use this as an opportunity for the admin team to assess their strategies and make necessary adjustments.

- **Feedback loop**: Establish a feedback loop where team members can openly share their insights, concerns, and suggestions. This collaborative approach will lead to continuous improvement in admin practices.

Forming, nurturing, and empowering a Power Platform admin team is a strategic investment that pays off in terms of enhanced security, effective governance, and successful digital transformation initiatives. By following this action plan, your team will be well-equipped to manage Power Platform environments, address challenges proactively, and drive continuous innovation within your organization.

Empowering citizen developers – fusion team collaboration and beyond

Organizations are increasingly recognizing the transformative potential of the Microsoft Power Platform. This suite of tools empowers individuals across organizations to become citizen developers—non-technical personnel who can create, deploy, and manage applications and workflows. This section explores the rise of citizen developers, the growing demand in the job market, the required skills in Power Platform, and the imperative need for upskilling.

The emergence of citizen developers

Traditionally, software development was confined to IT departments, often leading to bottlenecks, delays, and missed opportunities for innovation. The Power Platform, however, democratizes application development, enabling employees with domain expertise to take charge. Citizen developers leverage low-code and no-code tools to create solutions that address specific business challenges, fostering agility and enhancing efficiency.

Job market demand for citizen developers

The demand for citizen developers is on the rise as organizations realize the value of distributing application development capabilities. Companies are actively seeking individuals who can bridge the gap between business needs and technical solutions. The job market is evolving to embrace these new roles, offering positions such as business analyst developer or low-code application specialist.

Required skills in Power Platform

While being a citizen developer doesn't necessitate extensive coding knowledge, a certain skill set is still crucial:

- **Domain expertise**: Citizen developers need to intimately understand their department's processes and requirements to create tailored solutions
- **Problem-solving**: The ability to dissect challenges and envision innovative solutions is essential
- **Data literacy**: Proficiency in understanding and manipulating data is crucial, especially with Power BI
- **Visual thinking**: Creating intuitive interfaces requires a knack for designing user-friendly experiences
- **Basic logical thinking**: Even though it's not complex coding, understanding basic logic helps streamline processes

Upskilling for citizen developers

For employees willing to step into the role of citizen developer, upskilling is a must:

- **Power Platform training**: Comprehensive training in Power Apps, Power BI, and Power Automate provides a solid foundation

- **Best practices**: Learning how to design effective solutions and following best practices ensures efficiency

- **Data manipulation**: Mastering data transformations, cleansing, and modeling is crucial for accurate insights

- **Security and compliance**: Understanding how to build secure applications while adhering to data protection regulations is paramount

- **Problem-solving workshops**: Participating in hackathons or problem-solving workshops hones practical skills

Benefits of citizen development

The rise of citizen developers offers numerous benefits to organizations:

- **Faster innovation**: Empowering non-technical employees to create solutions accelerates innovation cycles

- **Reduced IT bottlenecks**: Offloading development tasks from IT departments frees them to focus on more complex projects

- **Tailored solutions**: Domain experts craft solutions precisely aligned with business needs

- **Cost efficiency**: Developing applications in-house reduces dependency on external development teams

The emergence of citizen developers is reshaping how organizations approach application development and digital transformation. Leveraging the Power Platform, individuals with domain expertise are driving innovation, streamlining processes, and enhancing efficiency. As the demand for these roles continues to grow, individuals who embrace upskilling and hone the necessary skills will be well-positioned to shape the future of business application development.

Fusion development teams – unleashing synergy in Power Platform adoption

In the landscape of Power Platform adoption and digital transformation, the concept of fusion development teams emerges as a dynamic force that catalyzes innovation, optimizes legacy capabilities, and fuses modern cloud architecture. These teams play a pivotal role in organizations that have reached the advanced "efficient" level of the CMMI, where the capabilities of the Power Platform are harnessed to transform mission-critical functions. This section explores the essence of fusion development teams and the potential job titles, roles, and responsibilities within the context of Power Platform adoption.

Understanding fusion development teams

Fusion development teams are multidisciplinary groups that unite individuals from various domains, combining diverse expertise to maximize the potential of the Power Platform. These teams serve as innovation catalysts, orchestrating the integration of legacy systems and modern cloud architecture. They bridge the gap between traditional applications and cutting-edge solutions, facilitating seamless interactions and driving the transformation of core business functions.

Potential job titles and roles

Building a robust fusion development team for Power Platform success involves selecting roles that cover a range of specialized skills. The following roles contribute unique expertise, from solution design and integration to user experience and change management, ensuring that Power Platform implementations are well-aligned, scalable, and user-centric:

- **Solution architects**: Solution architects within a fusion development team possess a panoramic view of the organization's technology landscape. They design the blueprint for integrating Power Platform solutions with legacy systems, ensuring scalability, security, and alignment with strategic objectives.

- **Power Platform experts**: These individuals are proficient in Power BI, Power Apps, and Power Automate. They are responsible for creating, customizing, and optimizing applications that enhance efficiency, automation, and decision-making across various departments.

- **Legacy system integration specialists**: These specialists focus on integrating existing legacy systems with modern Power Platform solutions. They ensure data consistency, seamless communication, and optimal performance between legacy and contemporary components.

- **Cloud architects**: Cloud architects play a crucial role in designing the cloud infrastructure that supports Power Platform applications. They optimize cloud resources, security measures, and scalability to meet the evolving needs of the organization.

- **Data engineers**: Data engineers are tasked with data management, integration, and transformation. They ensure that data flows smoothly between systems, enabling accurate analytics and informed decision-making.

- **User Experience (UX) designers**: UX designers enhance the user experience of Power Platform applications, ensuring they are intuitive, user-friendly, and aligned with user expectations.

- **Change management specialists**: Change management specialists guide stakeholders through the adoption of new solutions, facilitating smooth transitions and minimizing disruptions.

Roles and responsibilities

A fusion development team within the Power Platform ecosystem brings a broad scope of responsibilities that drive organizational modernization, collaboration, and innovation. From seamless integration and cross-departmental collaboration to security, training, and continuous improvement, these roles and responsibilities ensure the Power Platform solutions are effective, secure, and adaptable to changing business needs:

- **Integration and modernization**: Fusion development teams take the lead in integrating legacy systems with modern Power Platform solutions. They design connectors, APIs, and workflows that enable seamless data flow and functionality between diverse applications.

- **Collaboration**: These teams facilitate collaboration between departments, breaking down silos and enabling cross-functional synergies through integrated solutions.

- **Innovation**: Fusion development teams drive innovation by leveraging the Power Platform's capabilities to create new ways of doing business, optimizing processes, and delivering value to end users.

- **Security and compliance**: Ensuring data security and compliance with industry regulations is a paramount responsibility of these teams. They implement necessary controls and measures to protect sensitive information.

- **Training and support**: Fusion development teams provide training and support to end users, ensuring they are equipped to utilize Power Platform solutions effectively.

- **Continuous improvement**: These teams engage in continuous improvement efforts, refining solutions based on user feedback, performance metrics, and evolving business needs.

Fusion development teams represent the vanguard of innovation, adeptly merging legacy systems and modern technology to drive digital transformation. In the "Efficient" stage of Power Platform adoption, these teams exemplify the organization's ability to harness the platform's capabilities for mission-critical functions. Through collaboration, integration, and expertise, fusion development teams empower organizations to achieve optimal synergy between traditional and cutting-edge technologies, propelling them into the forefront of digital advancement.

Building a digital culture – collaboration, learning, and exploration for transformation (capability building – crawl, walk, run)

The true catalyst for transformation lies within the development of a vibrant digital culture—a culture that fosters collaboration, continuous learning, and fearless exploration. Let's explore the vital components of building a digital culture, emphasizing the creation of a Champions Community and the incremental journey of capability building, aligning with the CMMI framework.

The essence of the champions community

At the heart of organizational growth and transformation is the champions community—a dynamic ecosystem that nurtures collaboration, knowledge sharing, and innovative thinking. This community serves as a platform where individuals can congregate, irrespective of their geographic or departmental boundaries, to collaborate, seek answers, and exchange ideas. It is a safe haven for inquisitive minds, a place where knowledge knows no bounds.

Within the champions community, the essence of digital culture flourishes. It's a culture that embraces diversity of thought, encourages open dialogue, and recognizes that every individual can contribute to the journey of transformation. This community is not just a platform; it's a mindset—a mindset that believes in the collective power of exploration, learning, and innovation.

Crawl – laying the foundation

In the realm of capability building, the "Crawl" phase represents the initial step toward establishing a robust digital culture. Organizations embark on this journey by recognizing the value of collaboration and learning. Early adopters and enthusiasts become the pioneers of the champions community, creating a space for dialogue, knowledge exchange, and camaraderie.

During this phase, organizations set up forums, virtual spaces, and communication channels that facilitate interaction. Regular events, such as webinars, workshops, and meetups, become the pulse of the community. The objective is to foster a sense of belonging and to encourage individuals to step forward and share their experiences and insights.

Walk – nurturing growth

As the digital culture evolves, the organization moves from the "Crawl" phase to the "Walk" phase of capability building. During this stage, the champions community gains momentum and expands its reach. The focus shifts from sporadic interactions to intentional engagement. Regular events become a staple, and the community's impact starts to permeate across departments and regions.

In the "Walk" phase, leaders play a pivotal role in amplifying the culture's influence. They promote and encourage participation, recognize contributions, and provide platforms for emerging voices. Collaboration becomes ingrained in the organization's DNA, and the champions community evolves into a go-to hub for seeking expertise, sharing success stories, and igniting innovative discussions.

Run – empowering transformation

The pinnacle of capability building is the "Run" phase, where the champions community becomes a driving force for transformation. The digital culture has matured into a way of life, transcending hierarchies and organizational divisions. Individuals from all corners of the organization actively engage, contributing to the collective intelligence and fueling innovation.

In the "Run" phase, the champions community is not limited to virtual spaces—it thrives in physical events, hackathons, and innovation showcases. Leaders recognize that transformation is not limited to technology; it's a mindset shift that requires continuous learning and an insatiable curiosity. The community empowers individuals to step into leadership roles, advocate for change, and champion new initiatives. A champions community shouldn't be limited to the enterprise employees work for. It can transcend company boundaries fostering collaboration between parties across different organizations, including vendors, customers, and known specialists including Microsoft Most Valuable Professionals.

Building a digital culture that thrives on collaboration, learning, and exploration is not a luxury; it's a necessity for organizations striving for meaningful digital transformation. The champions community stands as a testament to the power of collective intelligence, transcending boundaries and fostering a culture that celebrates innovation. As organizations progress through the phases of capability building—Crawl, Walk, Run—they solidify a foundation that nurtures a spirit of transformation, empowers individuals, and propels the organization toward a future of limitless possibilities.

Identifying potential champions

Embracing the Power Platform is a crucial step for organizations embarking on the journey of digital transformation. A key factor in driving the successful adoption of the platform is identifying and nurturing Power Platform champions within the organization. These individuals are not only passionate about the technology but also have the innate ability to inspire, guide, and encourage their peers to explore and harness the potential of the Power Platform. This section delves into the process of discovering these champions, providing them with the right training, and empowering them to become evangelists for driving transformative change.

Champions are often individuals who have already exhibited an interest in and aptitude for exploring technology. If your organization utilizes Microsoft 365, it's likely that some employees have already encountered Power Apps through its integration with Microsoft Teams, SharePoint, and OneDrive. These early adopters are the ones who gravitate towards tools that facilitate innovation and improved efficiency.

While organic adoption might already be occurring, it's essential to proactively identify these potential champions and provide them with a structured role in your adoption strategy. They might be individuals who are proficient in Excel, Access, or SharePoint, or those who are known for pushing boundaries and exploring new tools. Identifying these individuals allows you to build a foundation for cultivating a culture of innovation.

Training and mentoring

Once potential champions are identified, the next step is to provide them with comprehensive training that empowers them to fully understand and effectively use the Power Platform. The Microsoft Learn portal serves as an invaluable resource in this regard. The portal offers a wealth of tutorials, courses, and resources that cover various aspects of the Power Platform. From building apps to automating workflows and creating insightful reports, the portal caters to different learning styles and skill levels.

As part of the training process, encourage champions to explore the Microsoft Learn portal to gain a solid understanding of the platform's capabilities. This self-paced learning allows champions to dive deep into the areas that resonate with their interests and expertise. Furthermore, it's important to provide specialized training sessions that cater to the specific needs of your organization. These sessions can be led by in-house experts or external trainers with proficiency in the Power Platform.

Empowering champions as evangelists

Training is just the first step; true champions are those who not only excel in using the platform but also willingly share their knowledge and experiences with their peers. Empower these champions to become evangelists for the Power Platform. Encourage them to conduct knowledge-sharing sessions, workshops, and presentations to showcase the platform's potential and demonstrate how it can drive innovation in various business processes.

Utilize platforms such as internal collaboration tools, company newsletters, and town hall meetings to provide champions with opportunities to share their insights. By highlighting their successes and contributions, you not only recognize their efforts but also motivate others to explore the Power Platform.

Leveraging Microsoft MVPs and communities

In addition to internal champions, consider leveraging external resources. The Microsoft **Most Valuable Professional** (**MVP**) program recognizes individuals who have demonstrated exceptional expertise in Microsoft technologies. The MVP website can help you identify specialists who excel in Power Platform-related areas. Connecting with these MVPs can provide your champions with insights from industry experts and access to a broader community that shares experiences and best practices.

Power Platform champions are the driving force behind successful adoption and transformation within an organization. By identifying individuals with a natural inclination towards technology, training them comprehensively, and empowering them to become evangelists, organizations can foster a culture of innovation and efficient use of the Power Platform. As these champions share their knowledge and experiences, they inspire their peers, build momentum, and contribute significantly to the organization's digital transformation journey.

Summary

In this chapter, you have gained insights into the importance of stakeholder analysis and alignment for driving the successful adoption of the Power Platform. You've learned about the significance of understanding stakeholders' roles, interests, and organizational maturity levels, as assessed through the **Capability Maturity Model Integration** (**CMMI**).

The information presented in this chapter is valuable to you as it equips you with strategic approaches to identify stakeholders, analyze their alignment with organizational goals, and tailor adoption strategies accordingly. Understanding the maturity levels of the organization enables you to implement effective alignment strategies, facilitating smoother navigation through different stages of adoption.

In the next chapter, you will delve into the topic of *Streamlining Operations: Automating Processes with Solutions Built with Power Platform*. There, you will learn about leveraging the Power Platform to automate processes and streamline operations, further enhancing organizational efficiency and effectiveness.

Q&A

1. How does stakeholder analysis contribute to successful Power Platform adoption?

    Stakeholder analysis helps identify key individuals and their roles, enabling targeted engagement and alignment with organizational goals.

2. What is the Capability Maturity Model Integration (CMMI), and how does it apply to Power Platform adoption?

    CMMI is a framework for assessing organizational maturity levels. In the context of Power Platform adoption, it helps organizations understand their readiness and tailor adoption strategies accordingly.

3. What are some alignment strategies for different maturity levels?

    Alignment strategies vary based on maturity levels but may include executive sponsorship, training initiatives, and fostering a culture of innovation and collaboration.

4. What roles are included in the Power Platform dream team?

    The Power Platform dream team comprises roles such as executive sponsor, success owner, champions, training lead, department leads, communication lead, Power Platform admin team, and Power Platform nurture team.

9

Streamlining Operations: Automating Processes with Solutions Built with Power Platform

In today's rapidly evolving business landscape, optimizing operations through automation is paramount for achieving heightened efficiency and productivity. Power Platform stands as a robust arsenal, offering a spectrum of tools to construct solutions capable of automating an array of tasks and workflows. However, embarking on this journey necessitates the strategic selection of **proof of concept (POC)** candidates tailored to address specific organizational needs and pain points. This introductory segment underscores the importance of identifying processes characterized by repetition, time inefficiency, or error susceptibility as ideal contenders for automation leveraging Power Platform. Furthermore, to ensure seamless implementation and scalability, a foundational understanding of **application lifecycle management (ALM)** principles is indispensable.

Here is what you will learn about in this chapter:

- Identifying suitable POC candidates for Power Platform automation
- Analyzing processes to find automation opportunities
- Accelerating solution development with ALM and the Creator Kit
- Using the Creator Kit for hands-on experience

Identifying suitable POC candidates

In the realm of digital transformation, identifying suitable POC candidates is a crucial initial step toward leveraging Power Platform for organizational enhancement. Power Platform offers a versatile suite of tools designed to empower users to automate processes, analyze data, and build applications without extensive coding knowledge. However, before diving into full-scale implementation, organizations must strategically select POC candidates that align with their specific needs, objectives, and digital transformation initiatives. There are two main areas to understand before POC candidates are identified and selected, as we will discuss next.

Understanding organizational pain points

Before proceeding with the selection of POC candidates, organizations need to conduct a thorough analysis of their current operational landscape and identify the areas that require improvement. This means carefully reviewing their processes, workflows, and pain points, and evaluating them for potential opportunities to enhance efficiency, productivity, and quality. To achieve this, they need to engage with key stakeholders from various departments and encourage them to share their perspectives and experiences. Through these collaborative dialogues, they can gain a deeper understanding of the challenges that different segments of the organization face, such as inefficiencies, manual work, data silos, and duplicate tasks. With this comprehensive and nuanced understanding, they can effectively determine which processes are most suitable for transformation, optimization, or enhancement through the innovative capabilities of Power Platform. This proactive approach enables organizations to identify promising POC candidates and fosters a culture of continuous improvement and digital innovation.

Criteria for POC selection

Several criteria guide the selection of POC candidates for Power Platform implementation, including their potential impact on organizational efficiency, productivity, cost savings, or customer satisfaction, alongside technical feasibility within existing infrastructure. Opting for manageable complexity ensures quick wins without risking intricate or mission-critical projects; ensuring access to necessary data sources is crucial for analysis and automation within the Power Platform environment. Additionally, involving end users and stakeholders from the outset ensures alignment, relevance, and buy-in, fostering smoother adoption and integration of Power Platform solutions. Let us dive into the specific criteria in the following figure and the list that follows:

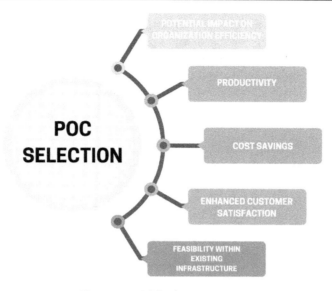

Figure 9.1 – POC selection criteria

- **Impact on organizational efficiency**: This criterion assesses the potential of a POC candidate to streamline processes, reduce manual effort, and optimize resource utilization within the organization. It involves analyzing **key performance indicators** (**KPIs**) related to efficiency, such as cycle time, throughput, and resource utilization rates. By implementing Power Platform solutions, organizations aim to automate repetitive tasks, eliminate bottlenecks, and enhance workflow efficiency, ultimately driving productivity and reducing operational costs.

- **Productivity**: Productivity measures the output generated from input resources, including time, labor, and materials. POC candidates with high productivity potential demonstrate the ability to automate manual tasks, streamline workflows, and empower employees to focus on value-added activities. Through Power Platform implementation, organizations can equip employees with tools to automate routine processes, collaborate more efficiently, and make data-driven decisions, leading to increased productivity across departments.

- **Cost savings**: Cost savings are a critical consideration for organizations seeking to optimize their operations. POC candidates with potential cost-saving benefits demonstrate the ability to reduce operational expenses, eliminate waste, and optimize resource allocation. This criterion involves conducting a cost-benefit analysis to evaluate the potential **return on investment** (**ROI**) associated with implementing Power Platform solutions. By automating manual tasks, reducing errors, and improving operational efficiency, organizations can achieve significant cost savings in areas such as labor, materials, and time.

- **Enhanced customer satisfaction**: Customer satisfaction is a key driver of organizational success and growth. POC candidates that can enhance customer satisfaction demonstrate the ability to improve service quality, responsiveness, and overall customer experience. This criterion involves assessing how Power Platform solutions can enable organizations to better understand customer needs, deliver personalized experiences, and address inquiries and issues more effectively. By implementing solutions that streamline customer-facing processes, organizations can enhance customer satisfaction, loyalty, and retention.

- **Feasibility within existing infrastructure**: Feasibility within existing infrastructure assesses the compatibility of POC candidates with the organization's current technology stack, systems, and architecture. This criterion involves evaluating factors such as integration capabilities, scalability, security, and compliance requirements. Organizations must ensure that Power Platform solutions can seamlessly integrate with existing systems and workflows while meeting security and compliance standards. By selecting POC candidates that align with the organization's technology roadmap and infrastructure capabilities, organizations can minimize implementation risks and ensure the successful adoption and integration of Power Platform solutions.

Selecting the right POC candidates is the first step toward leveraging Power Platform for digital transformation. This involves analyzing organizational processes to identify areas for improvement. Identifying pain points helps highlight areas where automation can have the greatest impact. Engaging with stakeholders across departments provides a comprehensive view of these challenges. Let's revisit key aspects associated with POC selection.

Key criteria for selecting POC candidates include the following:

- **Organizational efficiency**: Streamlining processes and optimizing resource utilization
- **Productivity**: Automating tasks and improving workflow efficiency
- **Cost savings**: Reducing operational expenses and improving ROI
- **Customer satisfaction**: Enhancing service quality and responsiveness
- **Feasibility**: Ensuring compatibility with existing infrastructure and systems

By strategically selecting suitable POC candidates, organizations can effectively use Power Platform to automate processes and achieve their digital transformation goals. This proactive approach not only identifies the right candidates but also lays a strong foundation for continuous improvement and innovation.

In the next section, we will dive deeper into the methods for examining your current workflows and processes. This will help you identify additional opportunities for automation, further optimizing your operations with Power Platform. Understanding the intricacies of your operational landscape is crucial for uncovering hidden inefficiencies and maximizing the potential of your automation efforts.

Analyzing processes to find automation opportunities

In the quest for efficiency and optimization, organizations often turn to automation as a means to streamline operational processes. However, before diving into automation initiatives, a thorough analysis of existing processes is essential to identify areas ripe for improvement. This analysis involves delving into the intricacies of organizational workflows and scrutinizing each step for inefficiencies, bottlenecks, and opportunities for enhancement. By leveraging both general principles of business analysis and specific tools within the Power Platform ecosystem, such as process mining and task mining in Power Automate, organizations can gain valuable insights and pinpoint areas for automation that yield maximum impact.

General business analysis techniques

Business analysis, drawing from both **Capability Maturity Model Integration (CMMI)** and the **Business Analysis Body of Knowledge (BABOK)**, lays the groundwork for identifying areas ripe for automation within operational processes. Integrating principles from CMMI and BABOK enhances the effectiveness and comprehensiveness of the analysis, providing organizations with a robust framework to identify and address process inefficiencies:

- CMMI emphasizes the importance of process improvement and maturity in achieving organizational goals. By aligning with CMMI principles, business analysis endeavors to assess the maturity of operational processes and identify opportunities for enhancement. Techniques such as process mapping and value stream mapping, central to CMMI's process improvement approach, enable organizations to visualize and analyze workflows comprehensively. Process mapping entails the meticulous documentation of each step in a process, capturing inputs, outputs, and dependencies to uncover redundancies and inefficiencies. Similarly, value stream mapping focuses on the end-to-end flow of activities, shedding light on areas of waste and non-value-added activities that impede process efficiency.

- BABOK, on the other hand, provides a comprehensive guide to business analysis practices, offering techniques and methodologies to analyze and improve business processes. Root cause analysis, a fundamental technique within BABOK, plays a pivotal role in identifying the underlying factors contributing to process inefficiencies. By delving deep into the root causes of issues, organizations can address the underlying problems rather than merely treating the symptoms. This approach aligns closely with CMMI's emphasis on continuous improvement, enabling organizations to enhance process maturity and drive operational excellence.

By integrating principles from both CMMI and BABOK, organizations can conduct a holistic analysis of operational processes to identify areas for automation effectively. This combined approach enables organizations to leverage the strengths of each framework, ensuring a thorough understanding of process inefficiencies and paving the way for targeted automation initiatives. Ultimately, by aligning business analysis practices with principles from CMMI and BABOK, organizations can drive significant improvements in operational efficiency, productivity, and overall business performance.

For example, through process mapping, leaders can visually document each step of a process, identifying inefficiencies, redundancies, and bottlenecks that could be addressed through automation. Similarly, value stream mapping helps to highlight end-to-end process flows, enabling leaders to identify areas of waste and non-value-added activities ripe for automation.

Specific Power Platform tools

Within the Power Platform ecosystem, tools such as process mining and task mining in Power Automate offer specialized capabilities for analyzing operational processes and identifying automation opportunities. Process mining involves analyzing event logs and data from IT systems to visualize and understand the actual flow of processes within an organization. By examining timestamps, user interactions, and system activities, process mining tools can uncover deviations, bottlenecks, and variations in process execution, providing insights into areas for improvement and automation.

Task mining, a feature within Power Automate, focuses on analyzing user interactions and behaviors within digital systems to identify repetitive tasks and inefficiencies. By recording and analyzing user interactions with applications and systems, task-mining tools can identify patterns, bottlenecks, and opportunities for automation. This granular understanding of user behavior enables organizations to prioritize automation initiatives that directly impact productivity and efficiency.

Exploring how process mining and low-code development team up

Businesses seeking faster results are adopting low-code development, avoiding complex coding and large developer teams. Process mining identifies which business processes are best suited for low-code methods.

Low-code development simplified

Low-code development allows software creation without extensive coding knowledge, enabling both developers and non-developers to quickly build apps and products using pre-made parts, templates, drag-and-drop tools, and automation. This accelerates the production of websites, apps, and other digital solutions.

Role of process mining

Process mining helps companies determine which processes can be quickly adapted to low-code, guiding them on where to focus their efforts, whether on low-code or more code-heavy projects. It ensures a smooth transition to low-code, avoiding bottlenecks and optimizing workflows with clear, data-driven plans.

Practical application

Organizations can combine general business analysis techniques with Power Platform tools to comprehensively analyze operational processes, starting with process and value stream mapping to visualize workflows. Process mining tools analyze event logs to uncover inefficiencies, while task mining in Power Automate provides insights into user behaviors and automation opportunities. This integrated approach offers a holistic view of operations, identifying areas for automation that streamline tasks, optimize workflows, and drive digital transformation.

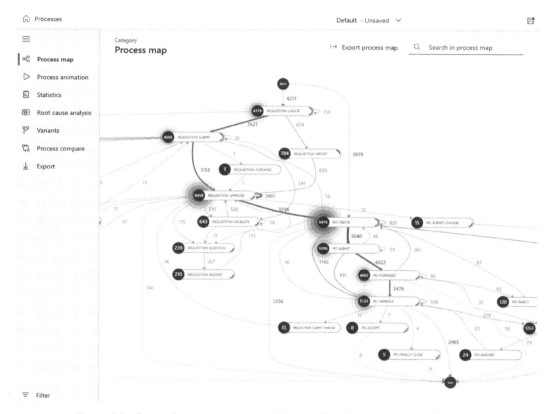

Figure 9.2 – Power Automate process mining accelerating solution development with Power Platform: leveraging the ALM Accelerator and Creator Kit

In the fast-paced world of modern business, agility and innovation are the keys to staying ahead of the curve. Organizations are constantly seeking ways to accelerate the development of solutions that address their evolving needs, while also maintaining high standards of quality and reliability. Enter Microsoft Power Platform – a suite of low-code tools that empower users to build custom applications, automate workflows, analyze data, and create chatbots with ease.

> **Note**
>
> Before you download and install the Creator Kit, ensure that you enable code components in your environment first to enable an environment to use code components inside its apps.

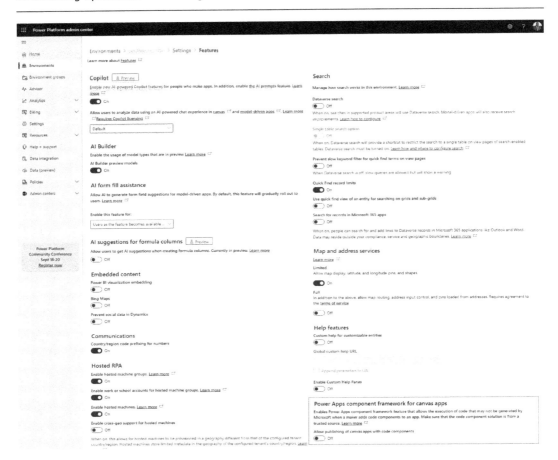

Figure 9.3 – Enabling controls at the environment level

These tools and features are designed to simplify and streamline the ALM process for Power Platform users, regardless of their skill level or role. By leveraging these tools and features, organizations can accelerate their solution development and achieve better outcomes with Power Platform. The following sections will help us understand the concept of ALM and how we can apply it to our own organizations.

What is ALM?

ALM is a strategic approach encompassing the governance, development, and maintenance of applications, critical for ensuring operational excellence and alignment with organizational objectives. ALM integrates a spectrum of disciplines including requirements management, software architecture, development, testing, maintenance, change management, support, continuous integration, project management, deployment, release management, and governance.

ALM tools, available in the ALM Accelerator and Creator Kit, serve as pivotal assets, fostering a standardized framework for seamless communication and collaboration among cross-functional teams, including software development, quality assurance, and operational departments. These tools are designed to streamline processes, enhance productivity, and mitigate risks by automating key aspects of software development and delivery. Governance, a cornerstone of ALM, involves managing requirements, resources, and system administration tasks such as data security, user access, change tracking, review, audit, deployment control, and rollback. This ensures regulatory compliance, risk mitigation, and optimized resource allocation.

Application development within the ALM framework entails a strategic approach to identify current challenges, meticulously plan, architect, design, develop, and rigorously test applications. This encompasses both traditional developer and app maker roles, fostering innovation and agility in solution delivery. Maintenance, another crucial facet of ALM, involves the seamless deployment of applications and the ongoing management of optional and dependent technologies. This ensures the longevity, performance optimization, and scalability of applications throughout their lifecycle.

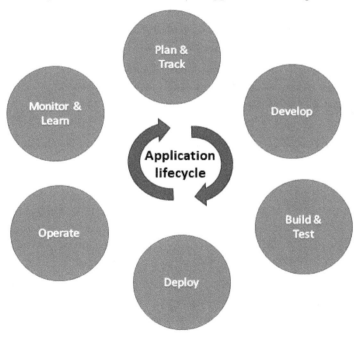

Figure 9.4 – ALM overview

The application lifecycle, as governed by ALM principles, follows a cyclical software development process encompassing phases such as planning and tracking, development, building and testing, deployment, operation, monitoring, and continuous improvement. By adhering to ALM best practices, organizations can drive efficiency, enhance agility, and achieve sustainable success in their digital transformation journey.

ALM within Power Platform

In Microsoft Power Platform, Dataverse serves as a robust repository for securely managing data and processes utilized by business applications. Integration with Dataverse is essential for leveraging the full suite of Power Platform features and tools for ALM.

Key concepts crucial for comprehending ALM within Microsoft Power Platform include the following:

- **Environments**: These are dedicated areas designed for storing, managing, and sharing your organization's business data, applications, and workflows. These environments function as containers that segregate apps based on varying roles, security requirements, or intended user groups. Each environment is capable of hosting a single Microsoft Dataverse database, ensuring organized and secure data management within distinct operational contexts.

- **Solutions**: These serve as the cornerstone for implementing ALM, enabling the distribution of components across environments via export and import functionalities. Components represent various artifacts utilized within applications, ranging from tables, columns, canvas and model-driven apps, Power Automate flows, chatbots, and charts to plugins.

- **Automation**: This plays a pivotal role in the application lifecycle, enhancing productivity, reliability, quality, and efficiency within ALM processes. Employing automation tools and tasks facilitates the validation, exporting, packaging, unpacking, and deployment of solutions, while also enabling the creation and resetting of sandbox environments. Microsoft has made available a set of tools to enable automation of various functions. Microsoft Power Platform Build Tools can be used to synchronize solution metadata, generate build artifacts, deploy solutions to downstream environments, provision or deprovision environments, and perform analysis checks against solutions.

- **Source control**: It's crucial to consider collaboration within your development team when undertaking a project. By breaking down silos and encouraging open communication, your team can enhance software delivery. Tools and workflows such as Git, GitHub, and Azure DevOps are specifically designed to facilitate communication and improve software quality. However, managing configurations in a solution system can pose challenges for team development. Organizations must carefully coordinate changes from multiple developers to minimize merge conflicts, as source control systems have limitations on how merges are handled. It's advisable to avoid situations where multiple individuals make simultaneous changes to complex components, such as forms, flows, and canvas apps.

- **Continuous integration and continuous delivery (CI/CD)**: This is a software development practice aimed at improving the efficiency, reliability, and speed of delivering applications. It involves automating various stages of the development lifecycle, from code integration and testing to deployment and delivery. CI involves frequently integrating code changes into a shared repository, typically multiple times a day. Each integration triggers automated builds and tests to validate the changes. By continuously integrating code, developers can quickly identify and address integration errors, ensuring that the software remains functional and stable throughout the development process. CD extends the principles of CI by automating the deployment process, enabling teams to reliably and efficiently deliver software updates to production environments. With CD, every successful build is potentially deployable to production, reducing the time and effort required to release new features or fixes.

Within the realm of Power Platform development, two primary types of DevOps pipelines are available: Azure DevOps pipelines and in-product pipelines. Additionally, GitHub Actions serves as a flexible option, enabling teams to automate build, test, and deployment tasks directly from their repositories:

- **Azure DevOps pipelines**: These provide a robust platform for orchestrating CI/CD pipelines tailored to Power Platform solutions. With Azure DevOps pipelines, developers can automate the build, test, and deployment processes, ensuring efficient and consistent delivery of applications. These pipelines seamlessly integrate with Power Platform environments, enabling teams to streamline development workflows and accelerate time-to-market. Azure DevOps offers extensive customization options, allowing teams to configure pipelines to suit their specific requirements and preferences.

- **In-product pipelines**: In addition to Azure DevOps pipelines, Power Platform also offers built-in, or in-product, pipelines that are tightly integrated within the Power Platform environment. These in-product pipelines enable users to automate deployment tasks directly from within Power Apps, Power Automate, and Power BI. Leveraging in-product pipelines, developers can automate the deployment of solutions, flows, and reports without the need for external tools or platforms. This native integration simplifies the deployment process and enhances the agility of development teams by eliminating the need to switch between different environments.

- **GitHub Actions**: GitHub Actions provides a flexible, workflow automation tool that supports CI/CD pipelines for Power Platform. By integrating with Power Platform environments, GitHub Actions allows developers to automate build, test, and deployment tasks directly from their repositories. This tool's open source nature and extensive community support make it adaptable and ideal for teams looking to streamline development and collaborate efficiently across projects.

ALM strategy

In adhering to ALM principles, it's essential to establish distinct environments for both application development and production. While basic ALM practices can be achieved with only separate development and production environments, it's advisable to also maintain at least one separate test environment. This additional test environment facilitates comprehensive end-to-end validation, encompassing solution deployment and application testing. Depending on the organization's requirements, additional environments such as **user acceptance testing** (**UAT**), **systems integration testing** (**SIT**), and training environments may also be necessary.

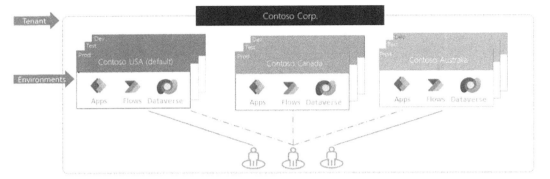

Figure 9.5 – ALM strategy (Microsoft Learn)

Separate development environments serve to isolate changes from ongoing work efforts, preventing unfinished changes from impacting the development process. Moreover, distinct development environments help mitigate instances where one individual's modifications negatively affect others' work.

Given the unique requirements of each organization, it's crucial to carefully assess and determine the specific environment needs to effectively support ALM practices.

Common questions to ask when setting up an ALM strategy for Power Platform include the following:

1. **What types of environments should I use? And how many?**

    - **Production environment**: These are intended for permanent organizational use. They can be created and managed by an administrator or any user with a Power Apps license, requiring at least 1 GB of available database capacity. These environments are also automatically generated for upgraded Dataverse databases. They serve as the primary platform for essential organizational operations.

    - **Sandbox environment**: These are non-production environments, which offer features such as copy and reset. Sandbox environments are used for development and testing, separate from production.

- **Developer environment**: Developer environments are created by users who have the Developer Plan license. They're special environments intended only for use by the owner, for development purposes.

- **Default environment**: This is a special type of production environment. Each tenant has a default environment that's created automatically. They are not recommended for production features.

- **Trial environment**: These are designed to accommodate short-term testing requirements and are automatically cleared after a brief duration. They have a 30-day expiration period and are restricted to one per user.

- **Microsoft Dataverse for Teams environment**: When you initiate the creation of an app within Teams or install an app from the app catalog for the first time, a Dataverse for Teams environment is automatically generated for the corresponding team.

2. **How can I automatically provision environments from the source code?**

   Does the ALM strategy necessitate automating the provisioning of different types of environments to fulfill the organization's needs? If so, the strategy must outline the necessary automation tasks and how the **Microsoft Power Platform Build Tools** (**PPBT**) can facilitate this process. Should PPBT offer the required automation capabilities, Azure DevOps can aid in orchestrating the environment setup.

3. **What are the dependencies on my environments?**

   When importing various solutions into your target environment, you're essentially building layers, with the existing solution serving as the foundation for the imported one. It's crucial to avoid cross-solution dependencies to ensure smooth solution layering. Having multiple solutions in the same environment that utilize the same component, particularly tables, should be circumvented. To mitigate cross-dependency risks, it's advisable to segment your solutions based on component type.

Solution concepts

Solutions in Power Platform are packaged sets of components that are used to build, customize, and deploy business applications. They serve as containers for organizing and managing various elements such as tables, columns, views, forms, workflows, and other resources within the Power Platform ecosystem. Solutions allow users to package and distribute their customizations, configurations, and applications across different environments, facilitating collaboration, version control, and deployment management. They play a pivotal role in ALM by providing a structured approach to building and managing applications within the Power Platform environment.

Unmanaged and managed solutions

Solutions are essential for organizing, transporting, and managing app components across different environments. There are two types of solutions: managed and unmanaged.

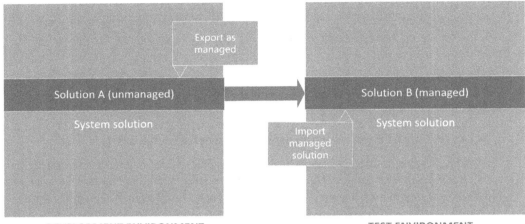

Figure 9.6 – Solution types

- **Unmanaged solutions**: These are crafted during the development phase. These solutions are utilized exclusively within development environments while modifications to applications are made. Unmanaged solutions can be exported in either an unmanaged or managed state. It's advisable to export unmanaged versions of solutions and then store them in your source control system. Unmanaged solutions should be regarded as the primary source for Microsoft Power Platform assets. When an unmanaged solution is deleted, only the solution container containing any customizations included within it is removed; all unmanaged customizations persist and remain associated with the default solution.

- **Managed solutions**: These, on the other hand, are deployed to environments other than development environments specific to that solution. This encompasses test, UAT, SIT, and production environments. Managed solutions can be independently serviced from other managed solutions within an environment. As a best practice in ALM, managed solutions should be generated by exporting an unmanaged solution as managed and treated as a build artifact.

> **Note**
>
> When you customize within the development environment, you operate within the unmanaged layer. Subsequently, when exporting the customized solution from the unmanaged layer to distribute it to another environment, the solution is imported into the managed layer of that environment.

Solution lifecycle

Solutions provide essential functionalities that support various actions crucial for application lifecycle processes:

- **Create**: This allows users to author and export unmanaged solutions, providing the initial framework for customization and development.

- **Update**: This facilitates the creation of updates to a managed solution that are then deployed to the parent managed solution. It's important to note that components cannot be deleted with an update.

- **Upgrade**: This enables the importation of a solution as an upgrade to an existing managed solution. This process involves removing unused components, implementing upgrade logic, and rolling up all patches into a new version of the solution. During upgrades, components that are no longer included in the upgraded version may be deleted. Users have the option to perform the upgrade immediately or stage it for additional actions before completion.

- **Patch**: This allows users to create patches containing only the changes for a parent managed solution, such as adding or editing components and assets. Patches are typically utilized for making small updates, similar to hotfixes. When imported, patches are layered on top of the parent solution, and components cannot be deleted with a patch.

Solution publisher

Every app and other components within a solution, such as tables and customizations, are associated with a solution publisher. It's recommended to create your own publisher instead of using the default one. You specify the publisher when initially creating a solution.

The solution publisher, acting as the component owner, governs changes allowed by other solution publishers. While ownership transfers within the same publisher are feasible, they aren't possible across publishers. Once assigned to a managed solution, altering the publisher becomes impractical, emphasizing the need for a single publisher for potential layering adjustments. Choose a meaningful solution publisher name for clarity.

Publishers also include a prefix to prevent naming conflicts, allowing solutions from different publishers to coexist smoothly in an environment. For instance, Contoso's solution uses the prefix `contoso`.

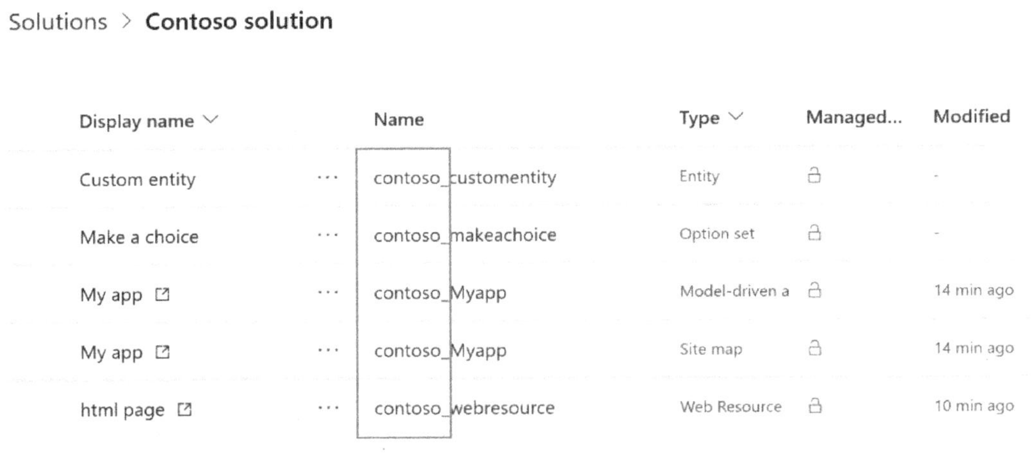

Solutions > **Contoso solution**

Display name ∨		Name	Type ∨	Managed...	Modified
Custom entity	···	contoso_customentity	Entity	🔒	-
Make a choice	···	contoso_makeachoice	Option set	🔒	-
My app ☐	···	contoso_Myapp	Model-driven a	🔒	14 min ago
My app ☐	···	contoso_Myapp	Site map	🔒	14 min ago
html page ☐	···	contoso_webresource	Web Resource	🔒	10 min ago

Figure 9.7 – Solution publisher prefix

> **Note**
>
> When changing a solution publisher prefix, ensure you do it before creating any new apps or metadata items, as the names of metadata items cannot be altered once they are created. Refer to https://learn.microsoft.com/en-us/power-platform/alm/solution-concepts-alm.

Solution dependencies

Due to the hierarchical nature of managed solutions, certain managed solutions may rely on components from other managed solutions. Some solution publishers leverage this to create modular solutions. In such cases, you may need to install a foundational "base" managed solution before installing a secondary solution that further customizes its components. The secondary solution is reliant on components from the first solution.

The system actively tracks these inter-solution dependencies. Attempting to install a solution requiring an absent base solution will result in installation failure, accompanied by a message prompting the installation of the prerequisite solution first. Similarly, due to these dependencies, the uninstallation of the base solution is prohibited while a dependent solution remains installed. To uninstall the base solution, you must first remove any dependent solutions.

ALM Accelerator for Power Platform

The ALM Accelerator for Power Platform serves as a canvas app that offers a streamlined interface to Azure Pipelines and Git source control, facilitating ALM. It represents a reference implementation of ALM methodologies, leveraging Power Platform's inherent capabilities to initiate ALM processes efficiently. Utilizing a combination of low-code canvas apps tailored for makers and administrators, alongside Azure Pipelines YAML and PowerShell templates, the ALM Accelerator simplifies the ALM adoption process.

Through the ALM Accelerator for Power Platform, makers gain the ability to conduct source control, maintain version history, and deploy solutions within the Power Platform environment. Utilizing the ALM Accelerator mandates that all Power Platform components – such as apps, flows, and customizations – be encapsulated within a solution.

While the ALM Accelerator doesn't demand advanced ALM proficiency, users should possess a basic understanding of utilizing solutions within the Power Platform ecosystem, as explained in this book.

Who should utilize the ALM Accelerator?

The ALM Accelerator caters to Power Platform makers and maker teams:

- Makers who are new to ALM concepts but desire the ability to preserve their work, track changes, and collaborate with other users.

- Makers proficient in advanced Git concepts, such as pull requests, branching, and merging, seeking to leverage familiar Git workflows for source control and deployment automation

> **Note**
>
> Configuring and implementing the ALM Accelerator requires administrator-level expertise in Power Platform environments, solutions, and Azure Pipelines. Additionally, familiarity with Microsoft Power Platform and Dataverse administration is essential. Refer to `https://learn.microsoft.com/en-us/power-platform/guidance/alm-accelerator/overview`.

The following diagram illustrates how the ALM Accelerator facilitates collaboration between maker teams and various environments, including development, validation, testing, and production.

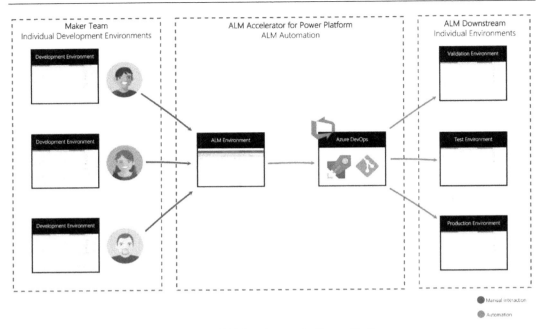

Figure 9.8 – ALM Accelerator for Power Platform

The ALM Accelerator for Power Platform streamlines ALM by automating and enhancing processes such as version control, CI, and deployment. When used in conjunction with the Creator Kit, which offers pre-built components and templates, the ALM Accelerator enables developers to build high-quality apps more quickly and reliably. In the following section, we will explore the components available within the Creator Kit.

Creator Kit

The Creator Kit represents an invaluable resource in crafting Power Apps experiences tailored for both web and mobile platforms, leveraging an array of convenient components essential in contemporary software design. Within this kit lies a rich repository encompassing a diverse component library, comprising numerous widely-used Power Apps component framework controls meticulously curated to streamline development processes. Additionally, developers benefit from a selection of pre-designed templates and supplementary utilities meticulously crafted to enhance productivity and efficiency.

Integral to the Creator Kit's offerings is the adoption of the Fluent UI framework, ensuring a seamless integration of controls and components. This framework plays a pivotal role in facilitating the creation of user experiences characterized by consistency, aesthetic appeal, and functionality across various devices and platforms. By harnessing the capabilities of the Fluent UI framework, developers can effortlessly craft captivating, intuitive, and effective interfaces for custom business applications, aligning seamlessly with modern design principles and user expectations.

Implementing the Creator Kit

Before integrating the components provided by the Creator Kit into your applications, it is advisable to utilize the reference app to familiarize yourself with the behavior and implementation patterns of these components. Through the reference app, you will gain insights into the nuances of component usage and learn effective methods for incorporating them into your applications.

The Creator Kit comprises a comprehensive set of assets, meticulously organized and distributed across three distinct solutions. These solutions encapsulate a diverse range of components, controls, templates, and utilities aimed at enhancing developer productivity and facilitating the creation of compelling user experiences. The kit includes the following solutions:

Solution Name	Contents
CreatorKitCore	24 Power Apps component framework and canvas components
CreatorKitReference (Model Driven apps)	A reference app (Model Driven with custom pages) to interactively learn with A canvas page template
CreatorKitReference (Canvas)	Interactive learning app: A reference app (Canvas) that allows users to learn interactively without needing a standalone Power Apps license Canvas template app: A pre-built template app to streamline the creation of new applications Theme editor: A tool that generates Theme JSON, enabling easy and consistent styling of components

Table 9.1 – Creator Kit component details

Reference App

Once the Creator Kit is installed, you will have access to a sample app called **Reference App**. Utilize this application to gain insights into each component's functionality, receive recommended best practices for achieving an optimal user experience, interact with the components firsthand, and delve into the implementation code that drives their behavior. We highly advise exploring the components within the reference application before integrating them into your live applications.

Observe how each component behaves and renders data, and access the **Code** tab to examine the underlying Power Fx formulas responsible for their functionality. Additionally, you can benefit from the inline guidance provided within the application, offering valuable insights into best practices associated with each control.

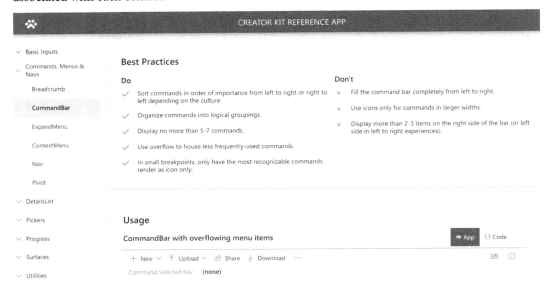

Figure 9.9 – Reference App

Templates

The templates are crafted to assist you in swiftly initiating the creation of responsive apps using Fluent UI. They come preloaded with custom components and are linked to a Theme JSON variable, simplifying the development startup process. These templates are essential for streamlining the development of Canvas apps and custom pages.

Fluent Theme Designer app

Theming is a mechanism by which a consistent look and feel can be applied to all the components on a page. For now, this means sharing a color scheme across the entire page. The Fluent Theme Designer app brings significant enhancements that cater to Power Platform makers, users, and administrators:

- **Makers** can now channel their efforts toward building the core features of an application, thanks to the cohesive Fluent UI design. This design coherence simplifies the process of creating custom pages, making them appear more consistent and akin to Model-Driven apps. With the assistance of the kit, even those without advanced frontend skills or access to design resources can craft stunning apps with contemporary designs effortlessly.

- **Users** will benefit from interacting with a unified set of components that are intuitive and familiar, as they are consistent with those found in all modern Microsoft applications. Notably, these components deliver a performance boost, contributing to a smoother user experience that enhances productivity during app usage.

- **Administrators** responsible for ensuring UI consistency across their organization will find value in the modern theming architecture inherent in Fluent UI's components. These components, developed and supported by dedicated engineering teams at Microsoft, offer a reliable solution for maintaining UI consistency. As a result, companies can confidently deploy apps featuring Creator Kit components into production environments.

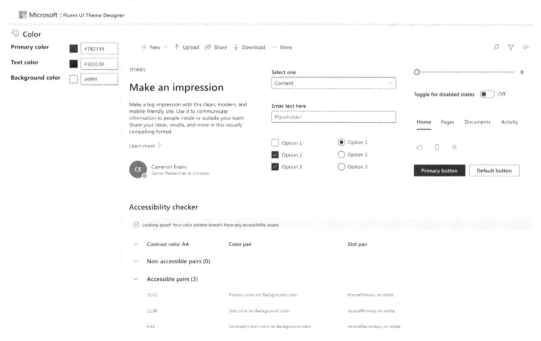

Figure 9.10 – Fluent Theme Designer app

The Fluent Theme Designer app in the Creator Kit enables developers to easily customize and apply consistent themes to Power Platform applications. It streamlines the process of adjusting colors, fonts, and other visual elements, ensuring a cohesive and professional look that aligns with organizational branding.

A practical example of POC selection and development using Power Platform

An online retailer wants to use Power Platform to improve its customer service operations, which face several challenges, such as lack of unified customer view, high manual effort, long wait times, inconsistent service quality, and low customer satisfaction. The retailer identifies four potential POC candidates:

- A Power Apps solution for a single interface to access and update customer data and order details
- A Power Automate solution for automating customer service workflows and tasks
- A Power BI solution for analyzing and visualizing customer service data and metrics
- A custom Copilots (formerly known as Power Virtual Agents) solution for creating a chatbot for common customer questions and self-service

The retailer evaluates each POC candidate based on impact and feasibility criteria. The following table shows the evaluation results:

POC Candidate	Impact on Efficiency	Impact on Productivity	Impact on Cost Savings	Impact on Customer Satisfaction	Feasibility within Infrastructure
Power Apps	High: Streamlines processes and reduces manual effort	High: Increases output and quality of service	Medium: Reduces operational expenses and errors	High: Improves responsiveness and accuracy of service	High: Integrates easily with existing systems and data sources
Power Automate	High: Eliminates bottlenecks and optimizes resource utilization	High: Empowers agents to focus on value-added activities	High: Achieves significant cost savings in labor, time, and materials	Medium: Enhances service speed and consistency	High: Integrates easily with existing systems and workflows
Power BI	Medium: Provides insights and recommendations for efficiency improvement	Medium: Enables data-driven decision-making and performance management	Low: Requires minimal investment and maintenance costs	Low: Indirectly affects customer satisfaction through improved service quality	Medium: Integrates with existing data sources but requires data preparation and transformation

Custom Copilot	Low: Requires human intervention for complex issues	Low: Reduces workload for simple inquiries but increases complexity for escalated issues	Medium: Reduces labor costs for basic inquiries but increases development and maintenance costs for chatbot	Medium: Improves self-service options and availability but may reduce personalization and empathy	Low: Requires integration with existing systems and data sources as well as security and compliance considerations

Table 9.2 – POC candidate evaluation cheat sheet

Based on the evaluation results, the organization decides to prioritize the Power Apps and Power Automate solutions as the most promising POC candidates, as they have the highest potential impact on organizational efficiency, productivity, cost savings, and customer satisfaction, as well as high feasibility within existing infrastructure. The organization then proceeds to plan and execute the POCs for these two solutions, involving end users and stakeholders throughout the process to ensure alignment, relevance, and buy-in.

Summary

In conclusion, this chapter has explored essential strategies for streamlining operations and accelerating solution development using Power Platform. We began by discussing the importance of identifying suitable POC candidates, emphasizing the need to select initiatives that align with organizational goals and demonstrate potential for tangible benefits. Next, we delved into the process of analyzing operational processes to identify areas ripe for automation, highlighting the significance of optimizing efficiency and productivity through targeted automation efforts.

You can leverage the insights gained from POC selection and operational process analysis to effectively utilize the Creator Kit, including the reference app and Fluent Theme Designer app, for creating POCs and MVPs.

- **POC selection**: Utilize the criteria established during POC selection to identify specific areas within operational processes that can benefit from automation or enhancement. Focus on processes with high potential for improvement or those aligned with strategic objectives.

- **Operational process analysis**: Conduct a thorough analysis of identified processes to understand their intricacies, pain points, and potential areas for optimization. Use this analysis to prioritize which processes are most suitable for POC development and MVP creation.

- **Utilizing Creator Kit features**: Leverage the reference app within the Creator Kit to explore and experiment with various components and design patterns. This hands-on experience will enable users to visualize how these components can be integrated into their applications to address specific process challenges.

- **Fluent Theme Designer app**: Utilize the Fluent Theme Designer app to create cohesive and visually appealing themes for POCs and MVPs. By customizing the color schemes and visual elements, users can enhance the user experience and ensure consistency across their applications.

- **Creating POCs and MVPs**: With insights from POC selection and operational process analysis, use the Creator Kit's resources to develop POCs and MVPs that address identified process challenges or automation opportunities. Iterate on these prototypes based on feedback and testing results to refine and validate their effectiveness.

By integrating POC selection, operational process analysis, and utilization of Creator Kit features, you can effectively leverage Power Platform to create impactful POCs and MVPs that drive innovation and operational excellence within your organization.

In the next chapter, you will learn how to establish a solid security framework to protect your data and applications. You will discover strategies to promote a security-first mindset throughout your organization. Additionally, you will understand the importance of ongoing monitoring and risk management to safeguard your operations and explore methods to continually improve and innovate while maintaining security and compliance.

Get This Book's PDF Version and Exclusive Extras

Scan the QR code (or go to `packtpub.com/unlock`). Search for this book by name, confirm the edition, and then follow the steps on the page.

Note: Keep your invoice handy. Purchases made directly from Packt don't require one.

10

Fortifying the Foundation: Integrating Systems, Ensuring Governance, and Security

As technology advances rapidly, organizations need to build a solid foundation that can integrate systems, enforce governance, and enhance security. This requires a **Center of Excellence (CoE)** journey that consists of four key stages: Secure, Evangelize, Monitor, and Evolve. The Secure stage establishes a comprehensive security framework based on industry standards and best practices. The Evangelize stage spreads the knowledge and adoption of best practices across the workforce. The Monitor stage continuously monitors and manages risks using advanced tools and technologies. The Evolve stage adopts a culture of continuous improvement and innovation using the insights and feedback from monitoring and other sources.

This chapter will explain how organizations can fortify their foundation through a CoE journey that covers the preceding states. By doing so, they can create a robust and secure technological ecosystem that can navigate the dynamic landscape of technology and protect their valuable assets and data. Here is what we will explore as part of this chapter:

- Establishing a solid security framework (Secure)
- Cultivating a security-centric culture (Evangelize)
- Continuous monitoring and proactive risk management (Monitor)
- Embracing continuous improvement and innovation (Evolve)

Establishing a solid security framework (Secure)

The Microsoft Power Platform is a suite of low-code tools that enable anyone to build apps, automate workflows, analyze data, and create chatbots. It empowers users to solve business problems and innovate faster, without depending on IT or developers. However, this also introduces some challenges for governance, security, and compliance. How can you ensure that your users are following best practices, protecting sensitive data, and using the right licenses and connectors?

That's where the CoE strategy comes in. A CoE is a team or a function that provides leadership, guidance, and support for the adoption and governance of Power Platform in your organization. A CoE can help you balance the benefits of self-service and citizen development with the risks of data loss, security breaches, and license violations.

A CoE can start off quite simply with a single individual using the provided tools and best practices to get a view of their Power Platform adoption in their organization and might grow into a more mature investment with multiple functions and roles to manage multiple aspects of governance, training, support, and automated app deployment across the organization. We encourage you to understand where you are in your adoption journey and invest accordingly, as described in previous chapters of this book. We recommend you start your governance journey by establishing **data loss prevention (DLP)** policies and managing licenses and access to data sources. Let's start with a definition of DLP policies, how they can help you prevent data leakage and unauthorized access, and how you can create and manage them using the Power Platform admin center. We will also cover how you can manage licenses and access to data sources for your Power Platform users, and how you can use the CoE Starter Kit to automate and simplify some of these tasks.

Data loss prevention policies

To control which connectors can be used together in Power Platform, you can create DLP policies. Connectors are the components that enable apps, flows, and chatbots to access data and services from various sources, such as SharePoint, Outlook, X (formerly Twitter), or Salesforce. Depending on the sensitivity and confidentiality of the data, you can classify connectors as business data only, no business data allowed, or blocked. For example, you might want to prevent users from creating an app that connects to a SharePoint site with sensitive customer information and an X account, and posts tweets with that information. By creating DLP policies, you can avoid data leakage and unauthorized access to your data.

You can use the Power Platform admin center to create and manage DLP policies. These policies can be created at the tenant level, which applies to all environments in your organization, or at the environment level, which applies to a specific environment. You can also add policies for specific security groups, which apply to the users who are members of those groups. You can assign connectors to one of the three groups: business data only, non-business data, or blocked. You can also use the default policies provided by Microsoft, which are based on the connector classifications and the connector certification status.

When you create or edit a DLP policy, you can choose when to enforce it and how to apply it. You can enforce it immediately or on a future date, by applying the policy to specific environments as your organization may see fit. You can view the impact of your policy on the apps and flows in your organization and see whether any of them will be affected or blocked by the policy. You can also view the policy violations and take actions to resolve them, such as notifying the app or flow owner or deleting the app or flow.

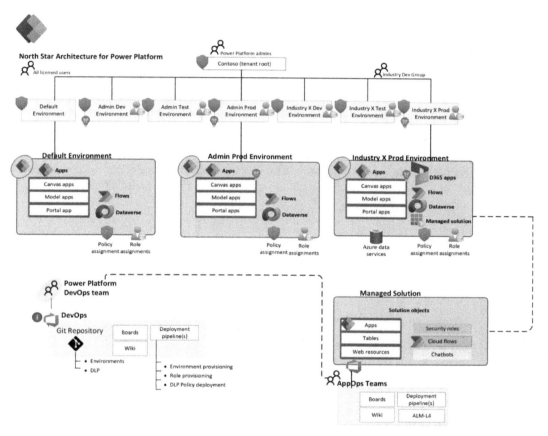

Figure 10.1 – Power Platform DLP levels

Licenses and access to data sources

Another aspect of securing your Power Platform adoption is managing the licenses and access to data sources for your users. Licenses determine what features and capabilities your users can access in Power Platform, such as the number of apps, flows, and chatbots they can create and run, the types of connectors they can use, and the storage and capacity limits they have. Access to data sources determines what data and services your users can connect to and use in their apps, flows, and chatbots, such as SharePoint, Outlook, SQL Server, or Salesforce.

You can manage licenses and access to data sources using the Power Platform admin center, the Microsoft 365 admin center, or the Microsoft Entra ID admin center. You can assign licenses to users individually or in bulk or use group-based licensing to automatically assign licenses to users who are members of a security group. You can also view the license usage and consumption in your organization, and see how many licenses are assigned, used, and available.

You can grant or revoke access to data sources for users individually or in bulk or use Conditional Access policies to enforce rules and conditions for accessing data sources, such as requiring multi-factor authentication, device compliance, or location-based restrictions. You can also view the data source usage and connections in your organization and see which data sources are used, by whom, and for what purpose.

CoE Starter Kit

One of the challenges of managing licenses and access to data sources is that it can be time-consuming and tedious, especially if you have many users, environments, apps, flows, and chatbots in your organization. That's why we recommend using the CoE Starter Kit, a set of tools and templates that can help you automate and simplify tasks, especially when it comes to security.

The CoE Starter Kit consists of four components:

- Core component
- Governance component
- Nurture component
- Audit component

Each component contains a set of apps, flows, and dashboards that you can install and customize for your organization. The Core component provides you with a holistic view of your Power Platform inventory, usage, and performance. The Governance component helps you enforce DLP policies, manage orphaned apps and flows, and archive unused apps and flows. The Nurture component helps you create a community of practice, provide training and support, and showcase success stories. The Audit component helps you monitor and audit the actions and activities of your Power Platform users.

> **Note**
>
> You can download and install the CoE Starter Kit from the GitHub repository: `https://github.com/microsoft/coe-starter-kit`. You can also find the documentation, tutorials, and videos on how to use and customize the CoE Starter Kit for your organization.

Having established a solid security framework, the next step is to ensure that your organization cultivates a security-centric culture. In the next section, you will learn how to promote a security-first mindset throughout your organization. This involves the following:

- Building awareness and understanding of security practices among all users

- Providing ongoing training and resources to keep security at the forefront

- Encouraging collaboration and communication to maintain a vigilant security posture

By focusing on these aspects, you can ensure that security is embedded into the fabric of your organization, creating a proactive and resilient approach to protecting your data and applications. This will build upon the foundation laid in the current chapter and further enhance your organization's governance and security practices.

Cultivating a security-centric culture (Evangelize)

A security-centric culture is essential for ensuring that security practices are ingrained in the daily operations of an organization. This culture ensures that security considerations are deeply embedded in the organizational ethos, decision-making processes, and daily practices of all employees. Within the context of Power Platform and the CoE, fostering this culture involves promoting security awareness, encouraging security best practices, and utilizing specific tools to reinforce these principles. Let's explore how to create such a culture in your organization using Power Platform and the CoE framework.

Promoting security awareness

Promoting security awareness ensures that all employees understand the importance of security and their role in maintaining it. This is crucial for preventing security breaches and ensuring compliance.

Some of the ways to promote security awareness among employees are the following:

- **Conduct regular security awareness campaigns**: Security awareness campaigns are initiatives that aim to educate and inform employees about the latest security threats, best practices, and policies. Security awareness campaigns can be delivered through various methods, such as posters, videos, quizzes, games, or newsletters. They should be tailored to the audience, relevant to the context, and engaging for the participants. Organizations can also measure the effectiveness of their campaigns by tracking metrics, such as participation rates, feedback scores, or knowledge retention.

- **Implement a security awareness training program**: Security awareness training is a formal and structured way of teaching employees the skills and behaviors they need to protect the organization's data and assets. Security awareness training should cover topics such as password management, phishing prevention, device security, data protection, and incident reporting. Security awareness training should be mandatory for all employees and updated regularly to reflect the changing security landscape. Organizations can also use gamification, simulations, or scenarios to make the training more interactive and realistic.

Facilitating training and education

To cultivate a security-centric culture effectively, it is imperative to invest in comprehensive training and education initiatives. These initiatives should be designed to enhance the security acumen of all employees, ensuring they are well-equipped to handle potential threats and understand the importance of their roles in maintaining the organization's security posture. Here are some strategies to consider:

- **Regular training sessions**: Conduct regular training sessions that cover both general security best practices and specific guidelines for using Power Platform securely. These sessions should be mandatory for all employees, with additional, more in-depth training for those involved in development and IT.

- **Role-based training**: Provide specialized training tailored to different user roles within Power Platform. For instance, makers should be trained in secure app development, while IT administrators should focus on managing security configurations and monitoring.

- **Certification programs**: Encourage employees to pursue certifications relevant to Power Platform and security, such as Microsoft Certified: Power Platform Fundamentals and Microsoft Certified: Security, Compliance, and Identity Fundamentals.

Using clear communication

Effective communication is a cornerstone of fostering a secure environment within an organization. By ensuring that employees are well-informed and continually updated, organizations can significantly enhance their security posture. Here are some methods to achieve this:

- **Security policies and guidelines**: Develop and distribute clear, concise security policies and guidelines specific to Power Platform usage. Ensure these documents are easily accessible through the CoE portal or intranet.

- **Regular updates**: Keep employees informed about new security threats, policy updates, and best practices through newsletters, webinars, and intranet postings.

- **Visual aids and reminders**: Use visual aids such as posters, infographics, and digital signage within office spaces and online platforms to reinforce key security messages and reminders.

Encouraging security best practices

Encouraging security best practices involves empowering individuals and teams to take ownership of security within their areas of responsibility. The following are a few suggestions.

Identify and promote security champions

To foster a culture of security awareness and proactive engagement, organizations must take deliberate steps to empower their employees and provide ongoing support:

- **Role definition**: Clearly define the responsibilities of security champions within each team. Their role is to advocate for security practices, assist in enforcing policies, and act as liaisons between their teams and the CoE.

- **Empowerment**: Provide security champions with advanced training, access to security tools, and the authority to influence security decisions within their teams. Regularly update them on new security trends and practices.

- **Recognition**: Recognize and reward the efforts of security champions through incentives such as awards, bonuses, or public acknowledgment. This motivation can drive continuous engagement and commitment to security.

Establish a feedback loop

To effectively address security concerns and enhance the organization's security posture, consider implementing the following strategies:

- **Reporting mechanisms**: Establish simple, straightforward mechanisms for reporting security concerns, such as dedicated email addresses, chat channels, or intranet forms. Ensure these channels are well publicized and easily accessible.

- **Anonymous feedback**: Enable anonymous reporting to encourage employees to report security issues without fear of retribution.

- **Continuous improvement**: Regularly review the feedback received and implement changes to address security concerns. Communicate back to the organization on how their feedback is driving improvements to foster a sense of involvement and ownership.

- **Action plans**: Develop action plans based on Secure Score recommendations to address identified security gaps. Secure Score in Microsoft Defender for Cloud is a numerical value that summarizes an organization's security posture. Prioritize actions based on their potential impact and ease of implementation.

- **Progress tracking**: Regularly monitor Secure Score to track progress and adjust strategies as needed. Use the score as a benchmark to measure the effectiveness of your security initiatives over time.

Plan phishing simulations

To enhance security awareness and improve employees' ability to recognize and respond to phishing attacks, organizations can implement the following comprehensive strategies:

- **Simulation campaigns**: Conduct regular phishing simulation campaigns to test employee awareness and readiness in identifying and responding to phishing attacks. Use realistic scenarios to create impactful learning experiences.

- **Training follow-up**: Follow up phishing simulations with targeted training for employees who failed the test. Provide feedback and resources to help them improve their skills.

- **Metrics and reporting**: Analyze the results of phishing simulations to identify trends and areas for improvement. Use this data to refine your training programs and increase overall security awareness.

Integrating security culture with CoE

The CoE plays a pivotal role in embedding a security-centric culture within an organization. The CoE can provide the structure, resources, and governance needed to ensure security is a priority across all Power Platform initiatives.

CoE responsibilities in cultivating a security-centric culture

- **Governance framework**: Establish and maintain a governance framework that includes security policies, standards, and best practices specific to Power Platform. Ensure these are communicated and enforced across the organization.

- **Knowledge sharing**: Use the CoE to facilitate knowledge sharing and collaboration on security topics. This can include creating a central repository of security resources, hosting webinars, and organizing workshops.

- **Innovation and best practices**: Promote innovation in security practices by encouraging the exploration of new tools and techniques. Share success stories and best practices across teams to foster a culture of continuous improvement.

- **Monitoring and reporting**: Leverage the CoE to monitor compliance with security policies and track key security metrics. Regularly report on the organization's security posture to senior leadership and stakeholders.

Security-Centric Culture

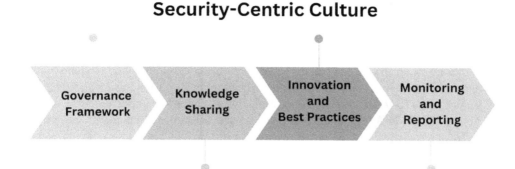

Figure 10.2 – Key elements for security-centric culture

Sharing success stories

Sharing success stories can inspire and motivate makers and users to adopt security best practices and learn from the experiences of others. It can also showcase the value and impact of Power Platform solutions on the organization's security posture and performance.

Some of the methods your organization can use to share success stories are the following:

- **Organize show-and-tell sessions**, where makers or users can present their Power Platform solutions and demonstrate how they have implemented security features and followed security guidelines. Show-and-tell sessions can be an interactive and engaging way to share knowledge, tips, and lessons learned, as well as to solicit feedback and suggestions from the audience.

- **Publish case studies as a newsletter**, where the CoE can highlight the security aspects and outcomes of Power Platform solutions that have been deployed or used in the organization. Case studies can provide a detailed and comprehensive overview of the security challenges, solutions, results, and benefits of Power Platform projects, as well as the best practices and recommendations that can be applied to similar scenarios.

As we establish a security-centric culture, it's equally important to ensure that security measures are continually monitored and managed. In the next section, we will explore strategies for ongoing security monitoring and risk management to protect your organization proactively. This includes implementing continuous monitoring systems, setting up proactive risk management protocols, and ensuring real-time responses to potential threats.

This approach will build upon the security culture you've cultivated, ensuring that your organization remains vigilant and responsive to emerging security challenges.

Continuous monitoring and proactive risk management (Monitor)

The Microsoft Power Platform CoE and admin center emphasize continuous monitoring and proactive risk management to maintain secure and efficient environments. By leveraging advanced tools and technologies, such as the Power Platform admin center and CoE, Power BI dashboards, Power Automate flows, and Starter Kit Power Apps, organizations can track usage and performance, identifying and mitigating potential risks early to ensure compliance with governance policies. Additionally, management and admin connectors within Power Platform allow for automated monitoring and administrative tasks. These connectors, along with PowerShell cmdlets, facilitate efficient risk management and operational oversight, ensuring a resilient technological environment.

The role of monitoring in the CoE

The CoE acts as the central hub for overseeing the deployment, maintenance, and governance of Power Platform within an organization. Effective monitoring by the CoE involves a comprehensive approach to observe and assess the performance of various components continuously. This ensures alignment with organizational standards and regulatory requirements, preventing risks from escalating into significant problems.

Key metrics and performance indicators

To establish a robust monitoring framework, it is essential to identify and track key metrics and performance indicators. These include the following:

- **Resource usage**: Monitor the consumption of resources such as data storage, compute power, and API calls to optimize usage and prevent bottlenecks
- **Access and usage patterns**: Track user activity to identify unusual patterns or unauthorized access attempts
- **Dataverse utilization**: Assess the health and performance of CDS environments to ensure data integrity and efficient operations
- **Connector management**: Monitor the usage of connectors, especially new or custom connectors, to maintain security and compliance
- **Sharing and alerts**: Implement sharing policies and alert mechanisms to detect and respond to unauthorized data sharing or policy violations

Tools and technologies for monitoring

Several tools and technologies can assist the CoE in implementing effective monitoring practices:

- **Power Platform admin center**: Provides a centralized dashboard to monitor the health, usage, and security of Power Platform components

- **Azure Monitor**: Offers comprehensive monitoring for applications, infrastructure, and networks, integrating seamlessly with Power Platform

- **Power BI**: Enables advanced data visualization and analysis, helping to identify trends and insights from monitoring data

- **Security Information and Event Management (SIEM) systems**: Integrates with Power Platform to detect and respond to security threats in real time

Proactive risk management

Proactive risk management involves anticipating potential risks and implementing measures to mitigate them before they impact the organization. Key strategies include the following:

- **Risk assessment and analysis**: Regularly conduct risk assessments to identify potential vulnerabilities and threats. Use this analysis to prioritize mitigation efforts.

- **Policy development and enforcement**: Develop and enforce security policies that govern the use of Power Platform. Ensure all users are aware of these policies and their responsibilities.

- **Incident response planning**: Create and maintain an incident response plan outlining procedures for addressing security incidents and breaches. Regularly test and update this plan to ensure its effectiveness.

- **User training and awareness**: Educate users on best practices for security and compliance. Regular training sessions can help reinforce the importance of these practices.

Governance and compliance

Governance and compliance are integral to the management and monitoring framework within Power Platform. The admin center and CoE Starter Kit provide robust features to ensure that all activities within the platform align with organizational policies and regulatory standards. Administrators can define and enforce governance rules, monitor adherence to these rules, and take corrective actions when necessary.

Compliance monitoring is facilitated through detailed audit logs and activity reports, which provide a comprehensive view of user interactions and system changes. These logs are crucial for conducting audits, investigating incidents, and demonstrating compliance with industry regulations. The CoE Starter Kit's analytics tools further aid in compliance management by highlighting areas of concern and suggesting improvements.

Continuous monitoring and proactive risk management are indispensable pillars for safeguarding the Microsoft Power Platform environment. Leveraging advanced tools such as the Power Platform admin center, CoE Power BI dashboards, Power Automate flows, and Starter Kit Power Apps enables organizations to monitor usage, track performance metrics, and identify potential risks early on. This proactive approach ensures compliance with governance policies and minimizes disruptions to operations. Here's what you can expect:

- **Continuous improvement strategies**: Implementing iterative approaches to enhance security measures over time
- **Encouraging innovation**: Fostering a culture that embraces creativity while maintaining rigorous security standards
- **Adapting to technological changes**: Staying ahead by adapting to evolving technologies and industry trends

We will explore strategies to continually improve security measures, encourage innovative solutions, and adapt to changing technological landscapes, ensuring that your organization remains at the forefront of operational excellence and security.

Embracing continuous improvement and innovation (Evolve)

Continuous improvement and innovation are key objectives of the management and monitoring processes within Power Platform. By leveraging the insights gained from continuous monitoring and proactive risk management, organizations can identify opportunities for optimization and innovation. The CoE Starter Kit's feedback mechanisms enable administrators to gather user feedback and performance data, which can be used to enhance existing solutions and develop new ones. Establishing a culture of continuous improvement ensures that the Power Platform environment remains agile, responsive, and aligned with the evolving needs of the organization. The tools available within the CoE can help maintain a culture of innovation, ensure that solutions are constantly refined, and align development with business needs and user expectations.

The role of continuous improvement and innovation

Continuous improvement and innovation are crucial for sustaining a competitive advantage and operational efficiency. In the context of the Power Platform CoE, these concepts involve the following:

- **Regularly assessing and enhancing solutions**: Ensuring that Power Platform applications and workflows are consistently optimized for performance and user experience

- **Encouraging innovation**: Promoting a culture where employees are motivated to propose new ideas and improvements

- **Aligning with business goals**: Ensuring that innovations and improvements align with the strategic objectives of the organization

CoE Starter Kit dashboards

The dashboards within the CoE Starter Kit provide key support for policy enforcement and procedural enhancements within your organization. These visual tools primarily serve the purpose of monitoring for potential security issues. Additionally, they help identify the most frequently used apps, their authors (makers), and the connectors being utilized. The information provided by these dashboards assists businesses in deciding who, what, and which aspects of the platform need attention and improvement.

Maker dashboard

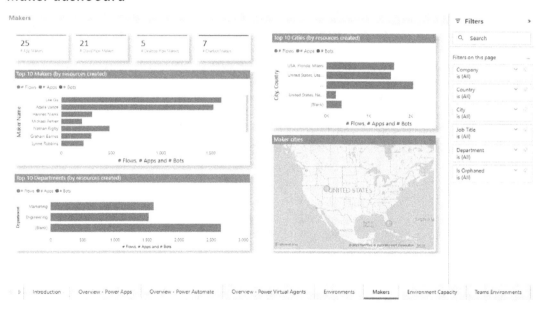

Figure 10.3 – Maker dashboard

This dashboard page provides a comprehensive view of maker activities and contributions within the organization. Its main features include the number of active makers, trends in maker activity over time, top makers based on app and flow creation, and a detailed list of apps and flows created by each maker.

App Usage dashboard

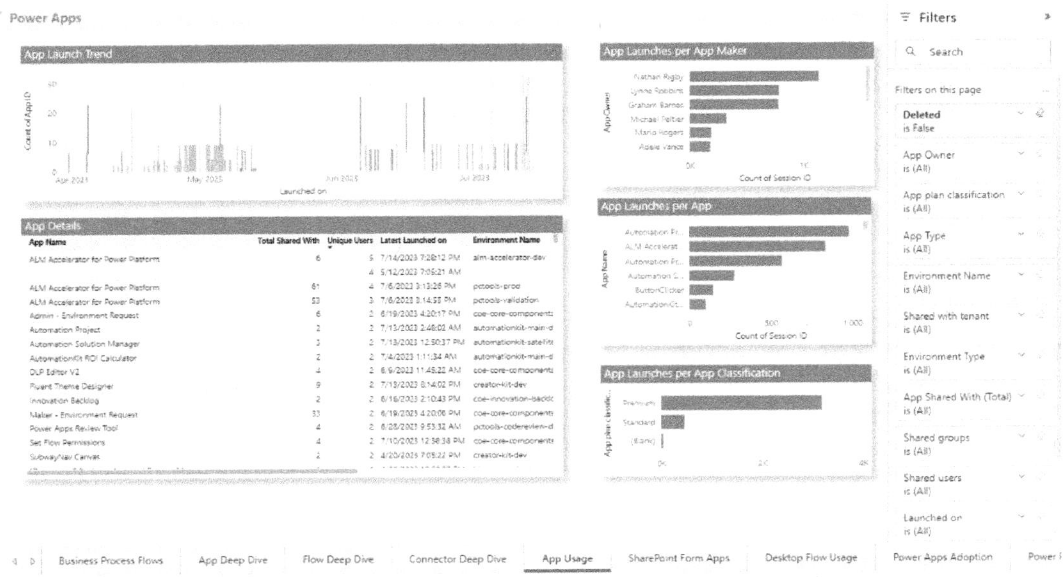

Figure 10.4 – App Usage dashboard

The App Usage dashboard tracks and analyzes the usage patterns of apps within the organization. Key data highlighted on this dashboard includes metrics on app launches and active users, usage trends over time, and the identification of the most used apps.

Year-over-year (YoY) adoption

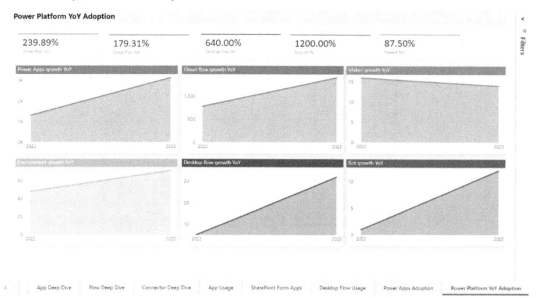

Figure 10.5 –YoY dashboard

This visualization compares adoption metrics year over year to identify growth and trends. The data presented includes a comparison of apps and flows creation and usage. This information assists leaders in deciding which areas require additional attention.

Innovation Backlog app

Figure 10.6 – Innovation Backlog app

The Innovation Backlog app is designed to manage and prioritize new ideas and innovations proposed by employees and stakeholders. It helps ensure that innovative ideas are captured, evaluated, and implemented systematically.

The following are some of the key features of the Innovation Backlog app.

- **Idea submission**: Employees can submit their innovative ideas through a user-friendly interface. Submissions can include detailed descriptions, expected benefits, and any relevant documentation.

- **Evaluation and scoring**: Ideas are evaluated based on criteria such as feasibility, potential impact, alignment with business goals, and resource requirements. Scoring mechanisms can be used to rank ideas.

- **Tracking and management**: Once approved, ideas are tracked through various stages of implementation. This includes resource allocation, development, testing, and deployment.

- **Collaboration and communication**: The app facilitates collaboration among stakeholders, ensuring that ideas are refined and developed effectively.

Integration and synergy

Both the feedback and Innovation Backlog apps are integral to a holistic approach to continuous improvement and innovation within the Power Platform CoE. Their integration provides several synergies:

- **Unified platform for improvement and innovation**: By combining feedback management and innovation tracking, the CoE can ensure that both incremental improvements and breakthrough innovations are handled efficiently

- **Data-driven decision-making**: Insights from feedback analytics can inform the evaluation of new ideas, ensuring that innovations address actual user needs and pain points

- **Enhanced collaboration**: A unified approach facilitates better communication and collaboration among different teams, including development, operations, and business stakeholders

Implementation best practices

To maximize the benefits of the feedback and Innovation Backlog apps, organizations should consider the following best practices:

- **Promote adoption**: Encourage employees to use these tools regularly. This can be achieved through training, awareness campaigns, and by demonstrating the impact of user contributions.

- **Define clear processes**: Establish clear processes for feedback collection, idea evaluation, and innovation implementation. This includes setting criteria for prioritization and decision-making.

- **Leverage analytics**: Use the analytics capabilities of these apps to identify trends, measure impact, and make informed decisions.

- **Regular reviews**: Conduct regular reviews of the feedback and innovation backlog to ensure that the most critical issues and valuable ideas are addressed promptly.

- **Align with business strategy**: Ensure that the continuous improvement and innovation efforts are closely aligned with the organization's strategic objectives and goals.

Summary

This chapter focused on building a robust, secure, and well-governed Power Platform environment through a structured CoE approach. It introduced four key stages of the CoE journey: Secure, Evangelize, Monitor, and Evolve, each playing a critical role in establishing a solid foundation for Power Platform adoption.

The Secure stage emphasizes creating a comprehensive security framework, including implementing DLP policies, managing licenses, and using the CoE Starter Kit to automate security tasks. The Evangelize stage focuses on fostering a security-centric culture through awareness, training, and clear communication, ensuring that security is integrated into everyday practices across the organization. The Monitor stage involves continuous monitoring of the platform's performance, user activity, and compliance with governance policies, leveraging tools such as the Power Platform admin center, CoE dashboards, and advanced risk management strategies. Finally, the Evolve stage highlights the importance of continuous improvement and innovation, utilizing insights from monitoring and feedback to refine existing solutions and drive new developments.

By adopting this structured approach, organizations can ensure that their Power Platform initiatives are secure, well governed, and continuously optimized, laying the groundwork for sustained success and innovation.

In the next chapter, you will learn how to build strong foundations for your Power Platform solutions by applying governance and security principles and practices. You will see how to define and enforce policies and standards, how to monitor and audit your environment, and how to manage risks and compliance issues. By doing so, you will ensure that your Power Platform solutions are secure, reliable, and trustworthy.

Join our community on Discord

Join our community's Discord space for discussions with the authors and other readers:

`https://packt.link/powerusers`

11

Establishing Strong Foundations: Governance and Security in Power Platform Solutions

Foundations of governance and security in Power Platform offer a comprehensive solution for governance and security, enabling users to create compelling apps and workflows while safeguarding their data and information. In this chapter, you will learn how to leverage the following features and functionalities of the Power Platform ecosystem:

- Data loss prevention (DLP) policies: safeguarding organizational data

- Tenant isolation: ensuring safe and secure utilization of Power Platform connectors

- Specialized security roles

By establishing strong foundations in governance and security, you will be able to leverage the full potential of the Power Platform ecosystem while protecting your valuable data and information.

Data loss prevention policies: safeguarding organizational data

DLP policies are one of the key features of the Power Platform ecosystem that enable users to safeguard their organizational data and uphold information security standards. DLP policies serve as guardrails, preventing inadvertent exposure of sensitive data across different connectors and environments. In this section, you will learn how to implement data protection measures, define connector usage rules, prevent inadvertent data exposure, and assess the impact of DLP policies on canvas apps and cloud flows in tenants.

Connectors

A **connector** is a component that enables users to connect to a data source or service and perform various actions within Power Platform. Connectors, at their most basic level, are strongly typed representations of restful **application programming interfaces**, also known as **APIs**. Connectors can be classified into three categories:

- **Business**: Connectors that access sensitive or confidential data, such as SharePoint, Dynamics 365, or SQL Server
- **Non-business**: Connectors that access public or non-sensitive data, such as Twitter, YouTube, or Weather
- **Blocked**: Connectors that are prohibited from being used in the tenant, such as Dropbox, Gmail, or Facebook

Besides organization data categories, connectors can be grouped by design and industry maturity into three categories: **certified connectors**, **custom connectors**, and **virtual connectors**.

Figure 11.1 lists connectors available within Power Platform, showcasing the range of options that users have at their disposal to integrate with various services and applications seamlessly.

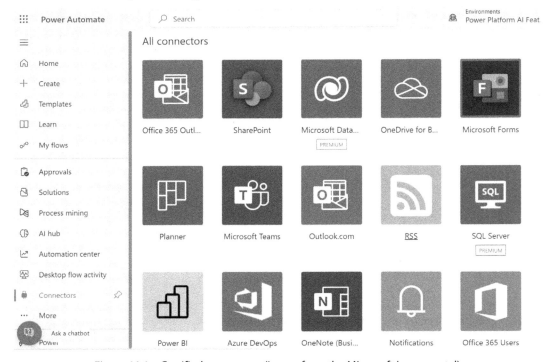

Figure 11.1 – Certified connectors (image from the Microsoft Learn portal)

Certified connectors refer to connectors that have undergone rigorous testing and certification processes to ensure they meet Microsoft's standards for security, reliability, and compliance. These connectors provide users with a reliable means of integrating with other Microsoft services and external services, all while maintaining data integrity and security.

Custom connectors allow makers to create their own connectors to integrate with external systems or services not covered by the standard set of certified connectors. While offering flexibility and customization options, custom connectors require careful consideration to ensure that they comply with data policies and don't compromise data security. *Figure 11.2* illustrates how makers can design their own connectors, enabling seamless integration with external systems and services beyond the standard certified options.

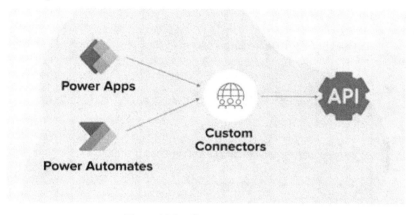

Figure 11.2 – Custom connectors

Virtual connectors are connectors that appear in data policies for administrators to control; however, they're not based on a restful API. The proliferation of virtual connectors has stemmed from data policies being one of the most popular governance controls in Power Platform (e.g. Copilot Studio connectors). *Figure 11.3* highlights how virtual connectors are listed in the data policies area, enabling administrators to effectively manage their tenants and environments.

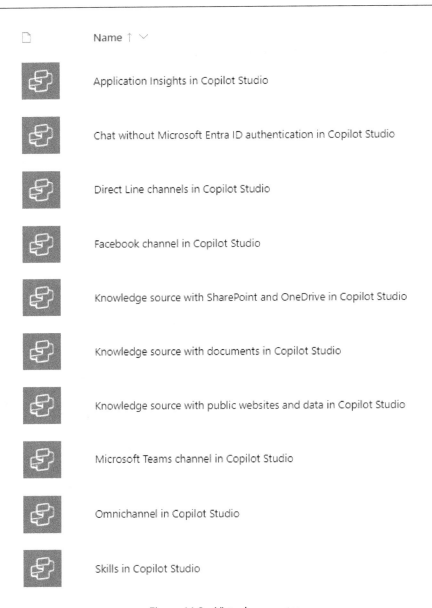

Figure 11.3 – Virtual connectors

Virtual connectors, like Copilot Studio, show the range of integration options in Power Platform. The next section covers their pros and cons to help you make the most of them.

Pros and cons of Power Platform connectors

Power Platform connectors offer several advantages that make them a valuable tool for integrating various services and applications. One of the primary benefits is the ease of integration they provide. These connectors simplify the process of connecting different services without requiring extensive coding knowledge, making them accessible to non-developers. Additionally, the platform boasts a wide range of connectors for popular services such as Microsoft 365, Azure, Salesforce, and many more, which offers extensive integration options. This facilitates seamless data flow between different systems, enabling real-time data synchronization and the automation of workflows.

The pre-built connectors save time by reducing the time needed to create integrations, thus allowing for faster deployment of solutions. They are also part of Power Platform's low-code/no-code approach, which lowers the barrier to entry for users with minimal coding experience. Security and compliance are also key advantages, as connectors are designed with enterprise-grade security features to ensure data privacy and protection. Moreover, connectors can scale with your business needs, supporting projects of varying sizes, from small to large enterprise-level applications. Lastly, the large user community and extensive documentation provide valuable support and resources to help troubleshoot and optimize the use of connectors.

Despite these benefits, there are some downsides to using Power Platform connectors. One major drawback is the limited customization they offer, which might not meet the needs of more complex or unique integration scenarios. Furthermore, since connectors often rely on cloud services, a stable internet connection is necessary for them to function properly. Performance issues can also arise, particularly when dealing with large volumes of data or frequent operations. Another consideration is licensing costs, as some connectors, especially premium ones, may require additional fees that can accumulate based on the number of users and services integrated. Moreover, connectors might not always support the latest features or updates of the integrated services immediately, leading to potential delays in leveraging new functionalities. Although they are user-friendly, there is still a learning curve associated with effectively using and troubleshooting connectors, particularly for users with no technical background.

Given the potential risks and limitations, it is crucial to control the access and execution of connectors through well-established governance strategies. Implementing governance ensures that the use of connectors aligns with organizational policies and compliance requirements. A key aspect of governance is managing DLP policies. Let's explore DLP further.

Understanding DLP in Power Platform

Protecting your organization's data is crucial, especially in a world where data breaches and cyber-attacks happen frequently. You need to have effective ways to prevent data loss in Power Platform, a set of tools that help you create business solutions. This chapter explains how to secure your corporate data with DLP in Power Platform. It also covers the importance of having good governance strategies, and how to set up DLP policies and follow best practices to ensure data security.

A well-established DLP strategy within Power Platform offers significant advantages for **makers**, **administrators**, and **developers**, closely tying into the broader goals defined in the Power Platform **Center of Excellence (CoE)**. For makers, a robust DLP strategy provides a secure framework within which they can innovate confidently, knowing that the data they handle is protected, thus fostering creativity without compromising security. Administrators benefit from streamlined governance, as clear DLP policies reduce the risk of data breaches and ensure compliance with regulatory standards, making it easier to manage and monitor data usage across the organization. For developers, well-defined DLP policies simplify the integration of various services and connectors, as they have clear guidelines on data handling and can focus on building effective solutions rather than worrying about security loopholes.

Aligning these DLP strategies with the principles of a CoE, organizations can standardize best practices, promote a culture of continuous improvement, and ensure that all stakeholders are aligned in their approach to data security and governance. This holistic approach enhances collaboration, drives efficiency, and ultimately contributes to the organization's overall success. Following are examples of major data breaches in organizations that failed to implement security measures and incorporate a solid DLP strategy.

Major data breaches through a fragile DLP strategy

Data breaches continue to highlight the critical importance of robust DLP strategies. Major incidents have stemmed from vulnerabilities that could have been mitigated by stronger DLP measures. These significant data breaches, affecting millions of individuals, highlight the critical need for robust DLP policies, effective patch management, and continuous monitoring to safeguard sensitive information and prevent unauthorized access:

- **Equifax data breach (2017)**: One of the most infamous breaches occurred when a vulnerability in a web application framework led to the exposure of personal information for approximately 147 million people. This incident was attributed to inadequate patch management and a lack of effective DLP policies that could have prevented unauthorized access. According to the Bank Info Security magazine, the 2017 Equifax data breach resulted in financial losses exceeding $1.4 billion, including fines, legal settlements, and remediation expenses.

- **Target data breach (2013)**: Attackers gained access to the personal and credit card information of over 40 million customers. The breach was facilitated by weak DLP measures and insufficient monitoring of data flow between systems, emphasizing the need for comprehensive DLP strategies. The 2013 Target data breach cost the company over $202 million, covering legal fees, settlements, security upgrades, and lost revenue, as reported by Breach Sense.

- **Capital One data breach (2019)**: A misconfigured firewall resulted in the exposure of personal information for over 100 million customers. This breach underscored the importance of stringent DLP policies and continuous monitoring to mitigate unauthorized access to sensitive data. The Capital One data breach cost the company hundreds of millions, including an $80 million regulatory fine, a $190 million class-action settlement, and extensive remediation efforts, as reported by CBS News.

The concept of DLP

DLP involves a collection of tools and processes aimed at ensuring sensitive data is not lost, misused, or accessed by unauthorized users. DLP strategies are designed to prevent data breaches by monitoring, detecting, and blocking the transfer of critical information.

In the context of Power Platform, DLP is particularly important because the platform integrates and automates various business processes, often handling sensitive data. Without proper DLP measures, organizations risk exposing confidential information, potentially resulting in significant financial losses, reputational harm, and regulatory penalties.

Components of DLP

A comprehensive DLP strategy typically includes the following:

- **Identification of sensitive data**: Recognizing what constitutes sensitive information within the organization
- **Enumeration of certified connectors**: Identifying and listing all connectors that are required by solutions within the organization and evaluating the connectors' access to information
- **Policy creation**: Establishing rules and policies for handling sensitive data
- **Monitoring and detection**: Continuously monitoring data flow to detect potential violations of DLP policies
- **Response and mitigation**: Implementing measures to block or remediate unauthorized access or data breaches

Setting up DLP in Power Platform

Implementing a DLP policy in Power Platform is essential for safeguarding your organization's data and ensuring compliance with regulatory requirements. By following a structured process within the Power Platform admin center, you can define how data moves between different connectors, control access, and protect sensitive information. This proactive approach helps to mitigate risks and reinforces your organization's data security framework. Following are the steps involved in setting up DLP policies:

1. **Identify sensitive data**: Determine what data within your organization is sensitive and requires protection. This includes personal information, financial data, intellectual property, and any other data that is critical to the organization.

2. **Create DLP policies**: In Power Platform, DLP policies are created in the Power Platform admin center. These policies define which connectors can be used together in apps and flows, and which data can be shared between services.

3. **Configure connectors**: Classify connectors as either "Business" or "Non-Business." Business connectors are those that handle sensitive data, while Non-Business connectors are used for general data. This classification helps control data flow and prevents the inadvertent sharing of sensitive information.

4. **Enforce policies**: Apply DLP policies to environments within Power Platform to ensure compliance. This enforcement can be tailored to specific environments, ensuring that different departments or projects adhere to relevant data protection rules.

5. **Monitor and audit**: Continuously monitor the usage of connectors and data flows within Power Platform. Regular audits help identify potential policy violations and areas where policies may need to be adjusted.

Step-by-step guide

1. Access the Power Platform admin center:

    I.   Navigate to the Power Platform admin center and sign in with admin credentials.

2. Create a new DLP policy:

    I.   In the admin center, go to the **Data policies** section.

    II.   Click on **New policy** to create a new DLP policy.

    III. Provide a name and description for the policy.

3. Classify connectors:

    I.   Select the connectors you want to classify as Business or Non-Business.

    II.   For example, classify connectors such as SharePoint, Dynamics 365, and SQL Server as Business connectors, and connectors such as Twitter and RSS as Non-Business connectors.

4. Apply the policy:

    I.   Choose the environments where the policy should be applied.

    II.   Save and publish the policy to enforce it across the selected environments.

5. Monitor and adjust:

    I.   Regularly review the policy's effectiveness through the admin center.

    II.   Adjust it as needed based on usage patterns and new data protection requirements.

Figure 11.4 presents a view of the DLP setup wizard.

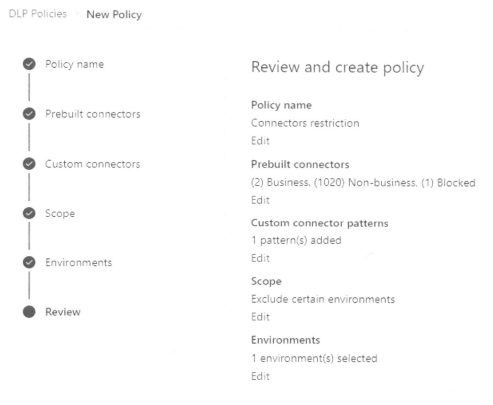

Figure 11.4 – DLP setup

Setting up a DLP policy in Power Platform is a vital measure to protect your organization's data by controlling how it flows between connectors. However, creating a policy is just the first step; ongoing assessment and monitoring are essential to ensure compliance and to identify any potential breaches. Regularly reviewing these policies and adjusting them as needed will help maintain the integrity of your data and prevent unauthorized access, ultimately fortifying your organization's overall security posture.

Tenant isolation: ensuring safe and secure utilization of Power Platform connectors

Companies increasingly adopt cloud services and platforms to streamline operations and enhance productivity. The importance of ensuring secure and isolated environments within these platforms is paramount. Tenant isolation in Power Platform is a critical strategy for ensuring that data and resources are securely segregated, preventing unauthorized access and minimizing the risk of data breaches.

This section explores the concept of tenant isolation, its importance, implementation strategies, and best practices for utilizing Power Platform connectors securely within isolated environments.

Understanding tenant isolation

Tenant isolation refers to the practice of segregating resources and data within a multi-tenant environment to ensure that each tenant's data and activities are isolated from others. In the context of Power Platform, this means creating separate environments for different departments, projects, or clients, ensuring that data and workflows within one environment do not interfere with or access those in another.

Figure 11.5 underscores the importance of Power Platform environment isolation in enhancing security, ensuring compliance, optimizing performance, and enabling tailored customizations.

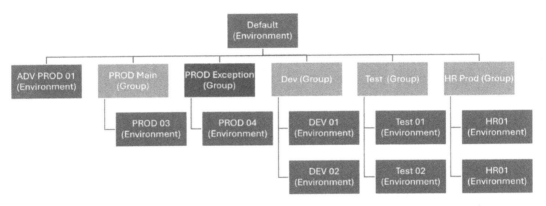

Figure 11.5 – Environment isolation strategy in Power Platform

The importance of tenant isolation cannot be overstated. It serves multiple purposes:

- **Security**: Prevents unauthorized access to sensitive data
- **Compliance:** Ensures adherence to regulatory requirements by isolating data based on geographical or departmental boundaries
- **Performance**: Reduces the risk of performance degradation caused by resource contention between different tenants
- **Customization**: Allows for environment-specific customizations without affecting other tenants

Key components of tenant isolation

Effective tenant isolation involves several key components:

- **Environments**: Separate environments within Power Platform that serve as isolated containers for resources and data.
- **Security groups**: Microsoft Entra security groups to control access to environments.
- **Data policies**: DLP policies that govern data sharing and connector usage within and across environments.
- **Role-Based Access Control (RBAC)**: Fine-grained access control based on user roles to enforce least privilege access. We will expand on this subject in *Chapter 12*.

Implementing tenant isolation in Power Platform

Implementing tenant isolation in Microsoft Power Platform is essential for safeguarding data and ensuring secure collaboration across different organizational units or external partners. Tenant isolation allows administrators to control cross-tenant connections, thereby minimizing the risk of unauthorized data access or exfiltration.

Understanding tenant isolation

Tenant isolation in Power Platform refers to the ability to restrict or allow connections between your tenant and external tenants. By default, cross-tenant connections are permitted, enabling users to establish connections to external data sources if they possess valid Microsoft Entra credentials. However, enabling tenant isolation allows administrators to block these connections, ensuring that data remains within the organization's boundaries unless explicitly permitted.

Configuring tenant isolation

To set up tenant isolation, follow these steps:

1. **Access the Power Platform admin center**: Navigate to the Power Platform admin center and sign in with administrative credentials.
2. **Enable tenant isolation**: Within the admin center, locate the tenant isolation setting. Toggle the setting to **On** to activate tenant isolation. This action will block all inbound and outbound cross-tenant connections by default.
3. **Define allowlist rules**: To permit specific cross-tenant connections, create allowlist rules. These rules specify which external tenants are allowed to connect to your tenant (inbound) and which external tenants your users can connect to (outbound). You can configure these rules to allow all tenants in a specific direction by using the wildcard pattern "*".

While tenant isolation focuses on securing data flow and restricting external access across tenants, environment isolation takes this a step further by creating distinct environments within a single tenant, ensuring data and resources are securely segmented at an internal level.

Environment isolation

Environment isolation is a cornerstone of information segregation throughout the **application lifecycle management (ALM)** cycle. By creating distinct environments for each stage – such as development, testing, and production – organizations can maintain clear boundaries for data, applications, and resources. This segmentation minimizes the risk of accidental data exposure, ensures controlled access at every phase, and supports a streamlined workflow where changes can be developed and tested without impacting live production systems. Such an approach is critical for maintaining compliance, improving collaboration, and safeguarding the integrity of solutions as they progress through the ALM cycle. Creating environments in Power Platform is a straightforward process that helps you organize and manage your apps and data. In the Power Platform admin center, you start by selecting the option to create a new environment.

Setting up isolated environments

Setting up isolated environments in Power Platform involves creating separate workspaces to keep your data and applications distinct and secure. By defining different environments, you can ensure that each project or team operates independently, with its own set of resources and configurations. This isolation helps protect sensitive information, simplifies management, and reduces the risk of conflicts between different projects. It's a key step in maintaining a well-organized and secure platform where each environment can be tailored to specific needs or compliance requirements. The following are key points to cover when designing an environment strategy and creating specific environments:

1. **Create environments**:

    I.　In the Power Platform admin center, create separate environments for different departments, projects, or clients.

    II.　Each environment should be configured with specific resources and settings tailored to its purpose.

2. **Configure security groups**:

    I.　Use Microsoft Entra to create security groups for each environment.

    II.　Assign users to security groups based on their roles and responsibilities.

3. **Apply DLP policies**:

    I.　Define and enforce DLP policies that control which connectors can be used within each environment.

    II.　Ensure that sensitive data is only accessible through approved connectors.

Figure 11.6 shows the main settings associated with Power Platform environment creation.

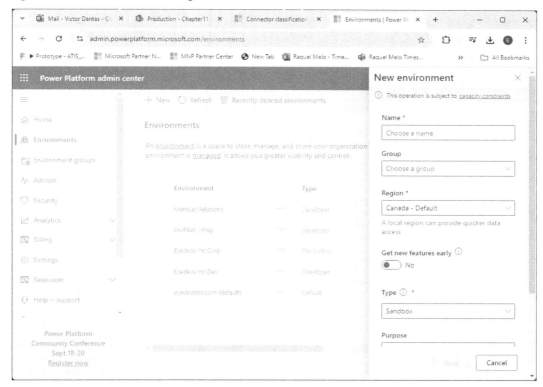

Figure 11.6 – Create a new environment

In addition to configuring environments and applying DLP policies, it is imperative to establish specialized security roles to enhance governance and control. These roles play a significant role in managing access and permissions within Power Platform and Dataverse environments, contributing to a robust security framework.

Specialized security roles

As digital transformation progresses rapidly, it is essential to have strong governance and control over data and applications. Power Platform enables you to build, automate, and analyze business solutions, but it also requires a solid security framework. Security roles are a key component of Power Platform and Dataverse environments, as they help you manage access and permissions. In this section, you will learn about the different types of security roles, data access levels, **out-of-the-box (OOB)** security roles, field-based security, and how to integrate Microsoft Entra groups with these roles to create a comprehensive security strategy.

Security roles in Power Platform/Dataverse environments

Security roles in Power Platform and Dataverse environments define what actions users can perform and what data they can access. These roles are essential for maintaining a secure environment by ensuring that users have the appropriate permissions based on their responsibilities. Security roles encompass various aspects of data and application security, including access control, data modification, and user management.

Figure 11.7 shows the security role setup interface in Dataverse, featuring a grid where rows represent entities and columns display permission levels, with circular icons indicating access scope.

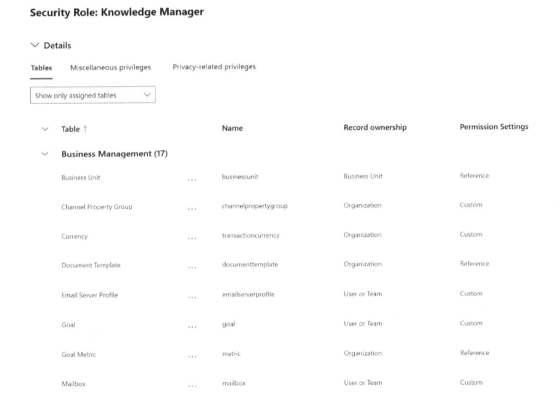

Figure 11.7 – Dataverse security roles

Security roles in Power Platform and Dataverse are crucial for defining the actions users can perform and the data they can access, ensuring a secure environment tailored to their responsibilities. These roles are vital for managing access control, data modification, and user management, safeguarding the integrity of the system. Understanding these roles sets the foundation for exploring data access levels, which will be discussed in the next section.

Data access levels

Data access levels in Dataverse security roles define the scope of data users can access based on their roles, ranging from their own records to the entire organization. This ensures users have the right level of visibility and control, aligning with their job functions and maintaining data security.

Data access levels in Power Platform determine the extent to which users can view or modify data. These levels include the following:

- **None**: No access to data
- **User**: Access to data owned by the user
- **Business Unit**: Access to data within the user's business unit
- **Parent: Child Business Units**: Access to data within the user's business unit and its child business units.
- **Organization**: Access to all data within the organization.

Figure 11.8 displays a key for Dataverse data access levels, using circular icons from **None** (empty) to **Organization** (fully filled). Each level, such as **User** and **Business Unit**, is color-coded and labeled for easy reference.

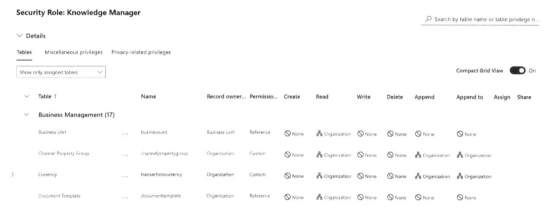

Figure 11.8 – Data access levels

These access levels ensure that data is only accessible to those who need it, thereby minimizing the risk of unauthorized access and data breaches.

Out-of-the-box (OOB) security roles

Power Platform and Dataverse provide several OOB security roles that simplify the management of user permissions. Some of the key OOB security roles include the following:

- **System Administrator**: Full access to all data and configuration settings. This role can perform any action within the environment.

- **System Customizer**: Access to customize the system but limited data access.

- **Environment Maker**: Can create apps, flows, and other resources within an environment.

- **Basic User**: Access to use apps and data that they own or that is shared with them.

- **Basic User**: Basic access to Dataverse data and apps.

These roles provide a foundation for managing security within Power Platform and can be customized to fit organizational needs. Administrators can create custom roles to define specific permissions, granting users access only to the data and tools required for their roles. Custom security roles can be scoped to tables and combined with Microsoft Entra security groups for streamlined management.

Column-level security

Field-based security in Dataverse allows for granular control over access to specific fields within an entity. This is particularly useful when sensitive information needs to be protected even from users who have access to other parts of the record. Field-based security settings determine whether a user can read, update, or create specific fields based on their security role.

Field security in Dataverse involves defining permissions for individual fields and grouping them into field security profiles, which are then assigned to specific security roles:

- **Field-level permissions**: Define read, update, and create permissions for individual fields

- **Field security profiles**: Group field-level permissions and assign them to security roles

Field-based security features ensure that sensitive information remains protected while still allowing users to perform their necessary tasks.

Figure 11.9 shows the Dataverse field security setup, listing fields with toggles to enable security and set **Read**, **Update**, and **Create** permissions.

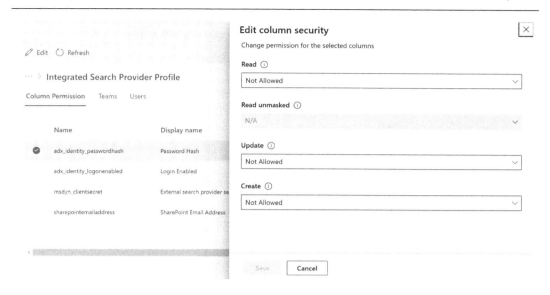

Figure 11.9 – Field-level security

The screenshot illustrates how column-level security in Dataverse protects sensitive data. Next, we'll explore how to streamline security by integrating Microsoft Entra groups with Power Platform security roles.

Integrating Microsoft Entra groups with security roles

Integrating Microsoft Entra groups with security roles in Power Platform enhances user management by simplifying the assignment of permissions, ensuring consistency across applications, and providing scalability for large organizations.

Benefits of integration

Integrating Microsoft Entra groups with security roles in Power Platform offers several benefits:

- **Simplified user management**: Streamlines the process of assigning and managing user permissions by leveraging existing Microsoft Entra groups

- **Consistency**: Ensures that users have consistent access across various applications and services

- **Scalability**: Facilitates the management of permissions for large numbers of users, especially in dynamic and growing organizations

Steps to integrate Microsoft Entra groups with security roles

Integrating Microsoft Entra groups with security roles in Dataverse involves a series of steps to align your organization's structure with user access needs:

1. **Create Microsoft Entra groups**: In Microsoft Entra, create groups that reflect the organizational structure and access needs.

2. **Add users to Microsoft Entra groups**: Manage user memberships within Microsoft Entra groups to control access.

3. **Create a team in Dataverse**: Create a Dataverse team of type Microsoft Entra Security Group.

4. **Assign security roles to Microsoft Entra groups**: In the Power Platform admin center, assign the appropriate security roles to the Microsoft Entra groups.

Figure 11.10 depicts the steps to integrate Microsoft Entra groups with security roles in Dataverse.

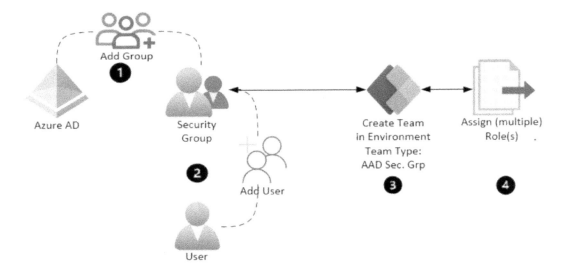

Figure 11.10 – AAD group and Dataverse team integration

This section outlined the process of integrating Microsoft Entra groups with security roles in Dataverse, which includes creating Microsoft Entra groups, managing user memberships, forming corresponding teams in Dataverse, and assigning security roles through the Power Platform admin center. Let us explore a real-life scenario demonstrating how these steps are applied in practice, highlighting the practical benefits of this integration.

Example scenario

Consider a scenario where a marketing department requires access to specific datasets and apps within Power Platform. The steps to integrate Microsoft Entra groups with security roles would be the following:

1. Create a marketing AAD group: Create a Microsoft Entra group named `Marketing Department`.

2. Assign roles: In the Power Platform admin center, assign the **Environment Maker** and **Basic User** security roles to the **Marketing Department** group.

3. Add users: Add all marketing team members to the **Marketing Department** AAD group.

By following these steps, all users in the marketing department automatically receive the necessary permissions based on their group membership, simplifying the management of security roles and ensuring consistent access control.

Best practices for managing security roles

Effective security management in Dataverse relies on key practices such as enforcing the principle of least privilege, conducting regular audits, customizing roles to fit business needs, and providing user training to ensure a secure and compliant environment. Let us explore the details of each practice:

- **Principle of least privilege**: Grant users only the minimum permissions required to perform their tasks. Regularly review and update security roles to align with changes in responsibilities and organizational structure.

- **Regular audits**: Perform regular audits of security roles and permissions to identify and mitigate discrepancies or potential security risks. This ensures a secure and compliant environment.

- **Role customization**: While OOB security roles provide a solid foundation, customize roles to suit specific business needs. Tailoring these roles helps ensure that users have appropriate permissions, reducing the risk of unauthorized access.

- **User training**: Educate users about the importance of security roles and the appropriate use of permissions. Training helps users understand their responsibilities and the impact of their actions on data security.

These best practices will help you define and maintain security by managing roles effectively and ensuring proper implementation.

Summary

In this chapter, we explored the foundational aspects of governance and security within Power Platform, focusing on key areas that ensure data protection and compliance. We began by delving into DLP policies, understanding their importance in safeguarding organizational data and preventing inadvertent exposure across various connectors and environments. We then discussed the concept of tenant isolation, highlighting its role in securing data flow and minimizing risks associated with multi-tenant environments. Finally, we examined specialized security roles, emphasizing their significance in enhancing governance and control by providing granular access to data and functionalities within Power Platform.

We detailed how to implement data protection measures, define connector usage rules, and assess the impact of DLP policies on canvas apps and cloud flows.

We explored how to manage secure data flows, govern tenant connectivity, and minimize data exfiltration risks by implementing isolated environments within Power Platform.

We discussed how to assign role-based access, control platform functionalities, and integrate Microsoft Entra groups with security roles to enhance governance and control.

By establishing these strong foundations in governance and security, you are better equipped to leverage the full potential of the Power Platform ecosystem while protecting your valuable data and information.

In the next chapter, we will shift our focus to understanding how we can ensure Power Platform solutions comply with industry-specific regulations and standards. We will explore the various compliance requirements, best practices for meeting these standards, and how to leverage Power Platform tools and features to maintain regulatory compliance. This will include discussions on GDPR, and other key regulatory frameworks, providing you with a comprehensive guide to navigating compliance in your Power Platform environment.

12

Navigating Compliance: Meeting Industry Regulations in Power Platform Deployments

Ensuring compliance with industry regulations is paramount for organizations of all sizes. As data breaches and privacy concerns become increasingly prevalent, adhering to regulatory requirements not only protects sensitive information but also helps maintain customer trust and avoid hefty fines. **Power Platform**, with its robust capabilities for developing and automating business solutions, is a powerful tool for organizations striving to meet these compliance demands. However, leveraging this platform effectively requires a deep understanding of the regulatory landscape and the specific compliance measures that need to be implemented.

In this chapter, we will show you how to make sure your Power Platform solutions follow the key industry regulations. We will start by explaining why compliance is important and what can happen if you don't follow it. We will then look at specific regulations, such as the **General Data Protection Regulation (GDPR)**, **Health Insurance Portability and Accountability Act (HIPAA)**, and **California Consumer Privacy Act (CCPA)**, and tell you what they mean for your organization. Here are the topics we will explore further:

- Security compliance and regulations
- Establishing geographical locations and environments in Power Platform deployments
- The Microsoft Trust Center – your resource for compliance and transparency
- Securing data transmission and API access in Power Platform deployments

Security compliance and regulations

In this section, we will explore the intricate relationship between global information security regulations and Power Platform. We provide a comprehensive overview of key regulatory frameworks, such as GDPR, HIPAA, and CCPA, and examine how these frameworks impact the development and deployment of solutions on Power Platform. By detailing specific compliance requirements and best practices, we demonstrate how to align your Power Platform initiatives with these regulations, ensuring that your organization's data-handling processes are secure and legally compliant. Understanding this context is critical as businesses navigate an increasingly complex regulatory environment, where the ability to adapt and adhere to stringent security standards is essential for safeguarding sensitive information and maintaining operational integrity. Additionally, we will examine IT compliance and regulations across major global geographical regions and discuss Microsoft's strategy for providing support and guidelines to address them.

Europe

In Europe, regulations such as GDPR impose strict requirements on data handling and protection, influencing how businesses develop and manage applications on Power Platform. Compliance with GDPR is crucial, particularly regarding user consent, data minimization, and cross-border data transfers:

- **GDPR**: GDPR sets a high standard for data protection across the **European Union** (**EU**). Power Platform users in Europe must ensure that personal data is processed lawfully, transparently, and for a specific purpose. Solutions must include features for data anonymization, encryption, and secure data transfers to comply with GDPR.

- **ePrivacy Directive**: Also known as the "Cookie Law," the ePrivacy Directive complements GDPR by focusing on electronic communications. Power Platform solutions that utilize cookies or similar technologies must obtain user consent and ensure the confidentiality of communications.

North America

In North America, several key information security regulations govern how organizations must handle and protect data. These regulations impact the development and use of business applications within Power Platform, necessitating specific compliance measures to ensure data security and privacy:

- **GDPR**: Though an EU regulation, GDPR affects many North American companies that handle the data of EU citizens. GDPR mandates strict data protection measures, including data minimization, consent for data processing, and the right to be forgotten. Power Platform solutions must incorporate these principles, ensuring data encryption, secure data storage, and robust access controls.

- **HIPAA**: HIPAA is critical for organizations handling **protected health information** (**PHI**) in the **United States** (**US**). Power Platform solutions used in healthcare must ensure compliance with HIPAA's requirements for data confidentiality, integrity, and availability. This includes implementing encryption, access controls, and audit logging to track data access and modifications.

- **CCPA**: The CCPA enhances privacy rights and consumer protection for residents of California. Organizations using Power Platform must provide transparency regarding data collection practices, allow consumers to opt out of data selling, and ensure the secure handling of personal information. Compliance with CCPA in Power Platform solutions involves rigorous data protection policies and user rights management.

- **Sarbanes-Oxley Act (SOX)**: SOX impacts publicly traded companies in the US, requiring stringent controls over financial data to prevent fraud. Power Platform solutions that manage financial data must include audit trails, data integrity checks, and access controls to comply with SOX requirements.

Asia-Pacific

In the Asia-Pacific region, countries such as Australia and Singapore have implemented their own data protection laws, such as the Australian Privacy Act and Singapore's **Personal Data Protection Act (PDPA)**. These regulations require organizations to implement robust security measures when using platforms such as Power Platform to ensure that personal data is handled securely and in compliance with local laws:

- **PDPA – Singapore**: The PDPA governs the collection, use, and disclosure of personal data in Singapore. Power Platform solutions must adhere to PDPA by implementing data protection policies, ensuring data accuracy, and securing consent for data processing.

- **Privacy Act 1988 – Australia**: This act regulates the handling of personal information in Australia. Power Platform users must comply by safeguarding data, providing access to personal information upon request, and implementing policies for data correction and breach notifications.

- **China's Cybersecurity Law**: This law imposes strict data localization requirements and security measures for personal information and important data. Power Platform solutions in China must ensure data is stored locally and implement robust cybersecurity measures.

Middle East

UAE, Saudi Arabia, and other countries in the Middle East have introduced data protection regulations, such as the UAE Data Protection Law and Saudi Arabia's **Personal Data Protection Law (PDPL)**. These regulations mandate specific security practices and compliance measures to protect data privacy, impacting the way business applications are developed and used on Power Platform in the region:

- **Data Protection Law Dubai International Financial Centre (DIFC)– UAE**: This law governs data protection within the DIFC. Power Platform solutions used in DIFC must ensure data processing transparency, obtain user consent, and implement data security measures.

- **PDPL – Saudi Arabia**: Effective from 2022, this law regulates the processing of personal data in Saudi Arabia. Power Platform users must comply by securing personal data, ensuring data accuracy, and providing individuals with access to their data.

Across these regions, adherence to local regulations is critical to ensuring that the use of Power Platform aligns with global standards for data security and privacy.

Establishing geographical locations and environments in Power Platform deployments

Organizations must navigate a complex web of data privacy and regulatory requirements. Establishing geographical locations and environments in Power Platform deployments is crucial to ensure compliance with these regulations across different regions. This section explores how to strategically set up geographical environments within Power Platform to meet compliance and regulatory standards, focusing on key regions around the world.

Importance of geographical locations in compliance

The geographical location of data storage and processing can significantly impact compliance with local and international regulations. Various regulations, such as the GDPR in Europe and the CCPA in California, impose strict requirements on how and where data can be stored and processed. By strategically deploying environments in specific geographical locations, organizations can better manage data sovereignty, privacy, and security.

Power Platform environment strategy

- **Regional Data Centers**: Microsoft's Power Platform offers data centers in multiple regions worldwide, allowing organizations to choose where their data is stored and processed. This capability is essential for complying with data residency requirements, such as those imposed by GDPR, which mandates that the personal data of EU citizens must be processed within the EU unless certain conditions are met.

- **Multi-Region Deployment**: Organizations can deploy environments in multiple regions to ensure compliance with local laws and regulations. This approach helps in addressing data residency requirements and provides redundancy and disaster recovery capabilities. For example, a multinational corporation may set up environments in Europe, North America, and Asia to serve its global operations while ensuring data compliance in each region.

- **Environment Types**: Power Platform allows the creation of various environment types, such as production, sandbox, and trial. Each environment type can be deployed in specific regions to segregate data and applications based on compliance needs. Production environments can be in regions with stringent data protection laws, while sandbox environments used for development and testing can be placed in regions with more flexible regulations.

Implementing compliance in Power Platform

To ensure compliance with various regional regulations, organizations should consider the following best practices:

- **Data Residency and Sovereignty**: Select appropriate geographical locations for deploying Power Platform environments to comply with data residency requirements. Use Microsoft's regional data centers to ensure data remains within specified regions.

- **Data Protection and Privacy**: Implement comprehensive data protection measures, including encryption, access controls, and **data loss prevention** (**DLP**) policies. Ensure Power Platform solutions are configured to support user consent management and data subject rights.

- **Regular Audits and Assessments**: Conduct regular compliance audits and assessments to ensure that Power Platform environments adhere to relevant regulations. Use Microsoft's compliance tools and resources to monitor and report on compliance status.

- **Documentation and Transparency**: Maintain thorough documentation of data protection policies, procedures, and compliance measures. Ensure transparency with stakeholders regarding data processing practices and compliance efforts.

Microsoft Government Cloud and Power Platform – ensuring global infosec compliance

Microsoft Government Cloud offers a robust and secure cloud environment designed to meet the stringent compliance and security requirements of government agencies around the world. Integrating Power Platform with Microsoft Government Cloud provides organizations with powerful tools for building applications, automating workflows, and gaining insights from data, all while ensuring adherence to various infosec compliance policies. This section explores the capabilities of Microsoft Government Cloud, its relationship with Power Platform, and how it addresses compliance needs across different regions.

Microsoft Government Cloud overview

Microsoft Government Cloud is tailored to meet the specific regulatory and security requirements of government entities. It includes Azure Government, Microsoft 365 Government, and Dynamics 365 Government, each offering a comprehensive suite of services designed to support the unique needs of public sector organizations. Key features of Microsoft Government Cloud include the following:

- **Enhanced Security and Compliance**: Built-in security controls and compliance certifications to meet government standards

- **Data Residency and Sovereignty**: Ensuring data is stored and processed within specific geographic boundaries to comply with local regulations

- **Isolation and Dedicated Infrastructure**: Physical and logical isolation from commercial cloud instances to provide higher levels of security and compliance

Power Platform on Microsoft Government Cloud

Power Platform, consisting of Power BI, Power Apps, Power Automate, Power Pages, and Copilot Studio, can be deployed on Microsoft Government Cloud to leverage its secure and compliant environment. This integration offers several benefits:

- **Compliance with Government Regulations**: By deploying Power Platform solutions on Microsoft Government Cloud, organizations can ensure that their applications and workflows meet the stringent regulatory requirements imposed by government bodies. This is particularly crucial for handling sensitive government data and personal information.

- **Enhanced Security Measures**: Power Platform on Microsoft Government Cloud inherits the robust security features of the cloud environment, including advanced threat protection, data encryption, and identity management. These measures help safeguard data and maintain the integrity and confidentiality of government information.

- **Seamless Integration with Government Services**: Power Platform's ability to integrate with other Microsoft Government Cloud services, such as Azure Government and Dynamics 365 Government, enables seamless data sharing and collaboration across different government systems, enhancing operational efficiency and decision-making.

Compliance coverage across regions

Microsoft Government Cloud is designed to meet the compliance needs of various regions around the world. The following sections include some examples of how it aligns with specific infosec compliance policies in different countries.

US (FedRAMP, CJIS, and DoD SRG)

- **Federal Risk and Authorization Management Program (FedRAMP)**: Microsoft Government Cloud complies with FedRAMP, which sets rigorous security standards for cloud services used by federal agencies. This includes maintaining high levels of data protection and continuous monitoring.

- **Criminal Justice Information Services (CJIS)**: For law enforcement agencies, compliance with the CJIS Security Policy is critical. Microsoft Government Cloud meets CJIS requirements, ensuring secure handling of criminal justice information.

- **Department of Defense (DoD) Security Requirements Guide (SRG)**: The DoD SRG mandates strict security controls for handling DoD data. Microsoft Government Cloud achieves the necessary compliance levels to support DoD missions.

United Kingdom (G-Cloud)

- **G-Cloud**: The UK government's G-Cloud framework provides a compliant cloud services marketplace for public sector organizations. Microsoft Government Cloud is part of this framework, ensuring it meets the UK government's security and compliance standards, such as GDPR and other local data protection laws.

United Arab Emirates (UAE)

- **UAE Dubai Electronic Security Center (DESC)**: DESC sets forth security requirements for government entities in Dubai. Microsoft Government Cloud complies with DESC regulations, providing a secure and compliant environment for processing and storing data in the UAE.

EU (GDPR)

- **GDPR**: GDPR imposes strict data protection requirements on organizations handling EU citizens' data. Microsoft Government Cloud ensures compliance with GDPR by providing data residency options within the EU, robust data protection measures, and support for data subject rights.

Australia (IRAP)

- **Information Security Registered Assessors Program (IRAP)**: IRAP sets security standards for Australian government agencies. Microsoft Government Cloud meets IRAP requirements, offering a secure environment for storing and processing government data in Australia.

Implementing Power Platform on Microsoft Government Cloud

To leverage the benefits of Power Platform on Microsoft Government Cloud, organizations should consider the following steps:

1. **Assess Compliance Requirements**: Understand the specific compliance requirements for your region and industry. This includes local data protection laws, security standards, and government regulations.
2. **Choose the Right Environment**: Select the appropriate Microsoft Government Cloud environment (e.g., Azure Government, Microsoft 365 Government) that aligns with your compliance needs. Ensure the environment provides the necessary certifications and compliance assurances.
3. **Configure Security Controls**: Implement security controls and configurations in Power Platform to enhance data protection. This includes setting up encryption, access controls, and compliance policies tailored to your organization's requirements.
4. **Regular Compliance Audits**: Conduct regular audits and assessments to ensure ongoing compliance with relevant regulations. Use Microsoft's compliance tools and resources to monitor and report on compliance status.

5. **Training and Awareness**: Educate employees and stakeholders on compliance requirements and best practices for using Power Platform in a secure and compliant manner. This includes training on data handling, security protocols, and regulatory obligations.

Overview of Microsoft compliance offerings

Here is a summary of the compliance offerings for various industries and global regions:

Category	Compliance Standards
Global	CIS Benchmark, CSA-STAR Attestation, CSA-STAR Certification, CSA-STAR Self-Assessment, CyberGRX, ISO 20000-1:2011, ISO 22301, ISO 27001, ISO 27017, ISO 27018, ISO 27701, ISO 9001, SOC 1, SOC 2, SOC 3, WCAG
US Government	CJIS, CNSSI 1253, DFARS, DoD IL2, DoD IL5, DoE 10 CFR Part 810, EAR, FedRAMP, FIPS 140-2, IRS 1075, ITAR, NIST 800-171, NIST CSF, Section 508 VPATS
Industry	23 NYCRR Part 500, AFM + DNB (Netherlands), APRA (Australia), AMF and ACPR (France), CDSA, DPP (UK), EBA (EU), FACT (UK), FCA + PRA (UK), FDA CFR Title 21 Part 11, FERPA, FFIEC (US), FINMA (Switzerland), FISC (Japan), FSA (Denmark), GLBA (US), GSMA, GxP, HDS (France), HIPAA / HITECH, HITRUST, KNF (Poland), Know Your Third Party (KY3P), MARS-E (US), MAS + ABS (Singapore), MPA, NBB + FSMA (Belgium), NEN-7510 (Netherlands), NERC, OSFI (Canada), PCI-3DS, PCI-DSS, RBI + IRDAI (India), SEC 17a-4, SEC 18a-6, FINRA 4511, & CFTC 1.31, SEC Regulation SCI (US), Shared Assessments, SOX, TISAX
Regional	ABS OSPAR (Singapore), BIR 2012 (Netherlands), C5 (Germany), Canadian Privacy Laws, CCCS Medium (Canada), CCPA (US-California), Cyber Essentials Plus (UK), IRAP (Australia), DJCP (China), EN 301 549 (EU), ENISA IAF (EU), ENS (Spain), EU Model Clauses, GB 18030 (China), GDPR (EU), G-Cloud (UK), IDW PS 951 (Germany), ISMAP (Japan), ISMS (Korea), IT-Grundschutz workbook (Germany), LOPD (Spain), MeitY (India), MTCS (Singapore), My Number (Japan), National Information Assurance (Qatar), NZ CC Framework (New Zealand), PASF (UK), PDPA (Argentina), Personal Data Localization (Russia), TRUCS (China), VCDPA (US-Virginia)

Table 12.1 – Compliance standards per category

This comprehensive compliance coverage makes Power Platform a versatile and secure tool for organizations navigating complex regulatory landscapes. For more details, refer to https://learn. microsoft.com/en-us/compliance/regulatory/offering-home.

The Microsoft Trust Center – your resource for compliance and transparency

The **Microsoft Trust Center** serves as a vital resource for organizations seeking to ensure compliance and maintain transparency in their use of Power Platform. As regulatory requirements evolve and become more stringent, the Trust Center provides essential tools and information to help businesses navigate these complexities.

Overview of the Microsoft Trust Center

The Microsoft Trust Center is designed to be a comprehensive hub for information on Microsoft's security, privacy, and compliance practices. It offers detailed documentation, compliance guides, and certification information that cover a wide array of global standards and regulations. This centralized resource is invaluable for organizations aiming to meet industry-specific compliance requirements while leveraging Microsoft's cloud services.

Key features and offerings

- **Compliance Documentation**: The Trust Center provides extensive documentation on how Microsoft products and services comply with various regulatory standards, such as GDPR, HIPAA, and ISO/IEC 27001. This includes detailed white papers, audit reports, and FAQs that help organizations understand the measures Microsoft has implemented to ensure compliance. The Power Platform admin guide on compliance and data privacy further details how the platform supports compliance efforts across various jurisdictions.

- **Certifications and Attestations**: Organizations can access up-to-date information on Microsoft's certifications and attestations. This includes independent third-party audit reports that verify Microsoft's adherence to international standards and regulatory requirements. These certifications can be used to support your organization's compliance claims and demonstrate due diligence to auditors and stakeholders.

- **Privacy and Data Protection**: The Trust Center outlines Microsoft's commitment to privacy and data protection. It provides insights into how Microsoft handles data, including data residency, data transfer mechanisms, and data processing agreements. This transparency helps organizations ensure that their data is managed in accordance with regulatory expectations. For Power Platform, specific measures include data encryption, access control, and compliance with data protection laws, such as GDPR and CCPA.

- **Security Practices**: Detailed information on Microsoft's security practices, including threat management, security monitoring, and incident response, is available through the Trust Center. Understanding these practices can help organizations align their own security measures with Microsoft's, creating a cohesive and robust security posture. Power Platform adheres to Microsoft's comprehensive security framework, ensuring that solutions are built on a secure foundation.

- **Compliance Manager:** The Microsoft Compliance Manager is an essential tool provided through the Trust Center. It offers a comprehensive compliance score and actionable insights to help organizations manage and improve their compliance posture. The tool provides a detailed assessment of your compliance with various standards and regulations, offering guidance on how to address gaps and enhance your compliance efforts.

The Microsoft Trust Center is an essential resource for organizations aiming to ensure compliance and maintain transparency when using Power Platform. As regulatory requirements grow increasingly complex, the Trust Center offers the necessary tools and information to help businesses navigate these challenges effectively. Understanding how to leverage this resource is key to staying compliant. Next, we will explore securing data transmission and API access in Power Platform deployments, crucial aspects of maintaining data integrity and security.

Securing data transmission and API access in Power Platform deployments

Power Platform enables rapid application development, data analysis, and business process automation. However, these capabilities also pose significant risks if the data transmission and API access are not properly secured. In today's digital landscape, attackers can exploit vulnerabilities in these areas to compromise the integrity and confidentiality of sensitive information within Power Platform deployments. Therefore, it is essential for technical authorities in Power Platform and information security to follow the best practices and essential strategies outlined in this section. This section will help you to implement robust security measures to protect your data and applications from unauthorized access and manipulation.

At-rest data protection

One way to protect your data from unauthorized access, even if someone breaches your firewalls, penetrates your network, gains physical access to your devices, or overrides the permissions on your local machine, is to encrypt it. This makes it unreadable to anyone who does not have the proper key. Power Platform uses various storage types to store the data. The data is distributed across different storage types:

- Azure SQL Database for relational data
- Azure Blob Storage for binary data, such as images and documents
- Azure Search for search indexing
- Microsoft 365 Activity Log and Azure Cosmos DB for audit data
- Azure Data Lake for analytics

Power Platform databases, also known as Dataverse, utilize SQL **transparent data encryption** (TDE) compliant with FIPS 140-2 standards to provide real-time encryption and decryption for data and log files, ensuring data encryption at rest. For data stored in Azure Blob Storage, Azure Storage Encryption is used, employing 256-bit AES encryption that is also FIPS 140-2 compliant. By default, Microsoft manages the database encryption key for environments using a Microsoft-managed key. However, for those seeking greater control over data protection, Power Platform offers the option of using a **customer-managed encryption key** (CMK). This option allows you to manage your encryption key within your Azure key vault, giving you the ability to rotate or change the key as needed and revoke Microsoft's access to your data by restricting key access at any time.

In-transit data protection

Power Platform leverages Azure's capabilities to protect data in transit, both externally and internally. Data in transit refers to data that is moving from one location to another, such as from a user device to a data center, or from one virtual network to another. Power Platform uses industry-standard transport protocols, such as TLS, to encrypt data in transit and prevent unauthorized access or interception. It also makes use of industry-standard protocols, such as **Transport Layer Security** (**TLS**), to encrypt data in transit. This ensures that any data exchanged between clients and servers, or between different services, is protected from interception and eavesdropping. Additionally, Power Platform uses Microsoft's own backbone network for internal communication between Microsoft services, which reduces the exposure of data to the public internet.

Microsoft utilizes a variety of encryption methods, protocols, and algorithms to secure data at rest – data that is stored within the infrastructure. Power Platform employs industry-leading encryption protocols, such as **AES**, **RSA**, and **SHA**, to ensure the confidentiality and integrity of data at rest. Additionally, Power Platform follows best practices for key management, which include the generation, storage, and use of encryption keys. The platform ensures that encryption keys are properly secured, rotated, and audited, with access limited to authorized entities only.

Figure 12.1 shows the levels of security within different storage or transport states.

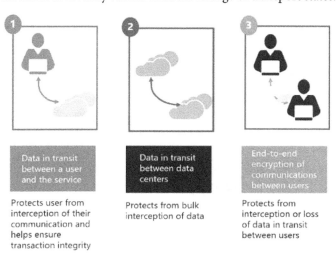

Figure 12.1 – Data encryption per state

Figure 12.1 illustrates the levels of security applied to data across various states, including data at rest, data in transit, and data in use. Each state represents a critical phase in the data life cycle, requiring tailored security measures to protect sensitive information.

API access through connectors

Power Platform services and data sources use different authentication methods to ensure security. First, let's investigate how Power Platform services access external data sources. The general process is similar for all data sources. Next, we'll dive into how the authentication credentials are determined. They may vary depending on the app and the data sources. Power Platform's main data source is called **Dataverse**, which is a cloud-based data platform that provides secure and scalable storage for Power Platform and other applications.

Connecting to Microsoft Dataverse

Power Apps and Power Automate are two of the main components of Power Platform that enable users to create and automate business processes. They can access Dataverse data in different ways, depending on the type of app and the connector used.

Power Apps and Dataverse

Power Apps enables users to build two kinds of applications: canvas apps and model-driven apps. Canvas apps offer a drag-and-drop interface, allowing users to design from the ground up, while model-driven apps are structured around the underlying data model and business logic provided by Dataverse. Both app types can connect directly to Dataverse without the need for an additional connector. However, canvas apps require storing consent for interaction with other environments within the Power Apps **resource provider** (**RP**), a service responsible for managing permissions and resources in Power Apps. The following diagram provides a visual overview of how canvas apps integrate with Dataverse:

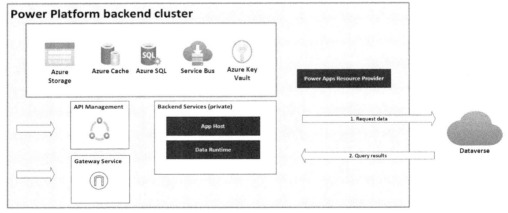

Figure 12.2 – Power Apps connection to Dataverse (reference: https://learn.
microsoft.com/en-us/power-platform/admin/security/overview)

With an understanding of how canvas and model-driven apps integrate with Dataverse, we can now explore how Power Automate interacts with Dataverse to streamline workflows and automate business processes.

Power Automate and Dataverse

Power Automate is a service that enables users to create workflows and automate tasks across different applications and services. Power Automate can access Dataverse data using two methods: the API Hub and the legacy connectors. The API Hub is a service that provides a unified authentication and discovery mechanism for Power Platform and other Microsoft services. Power Automate uses the API Hub to authenticate with Dataverse, but after that, it communicates directly with Dataverse for data operations. The legacy connectors are older connectors that use the **Common Data Service** (**CDS**) endpoint to access Dataverse data. They are still supported, but they have some limitations and drawbacks compared to the API Hub method.

Connecting to other data sources

Power Platform services leverage connectors to interface with external data sources beyond Dataverse. The following diagram depicts a typical architecture where an Azure **API Management** (**APIM**) connector is utilized.

Figure 12.3 illustrates how Power Platform backend services communicate with an API Hub / APIM connector to access external data sources.

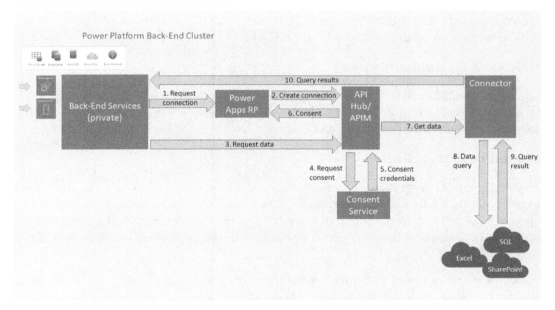

Figure 12.3 – Power Platform connector execution

- **Power Platform Service**: This initiates a connection request to the Power Apps RP.

- **Power Apps RP**: This requests the API Hub to establish a connection and manage authentication token exchange.

- **Power Platform Service**: This sends a data query request to the APIM connector.

- **APIM Connector**: This requests authorization from the consent service to access the data source.

- **Consent Service**: This provides authorization credentials to the APIM connector.

- **APIM Connector**: This forwards consent credentials to the Power Apps RP, which stores them for future data requests to bypass re-consent.

- **APIM Connector**: This relays the data query to the external connector.

- **External Connector**: This sends the query to the data source.

- **Data Source**: This returns the requested data to the external connector.

- **External Connector**: This passes the data back to the Power Platform backend cluster.

The APIM connector sends consent credentials to the Power Apps RP. These credentials are stored in the RP, ensuring that Power Apps doesn't prompt for consent again the next time data is accessed.

Authenticating data sources

Power Platform connects to various data sources through connectors, which are pre-built or custom-made interfaces that facilitate data exchange. To ensure data security and compliance, Power Platform and its connectors require different levels of authentication.

Power Platform authentication

The first level of authentication is between the user and the Power Platform service. The user needs to sign in to the Power Platform service with a valid Microsoft account or a Microsoft Entra account. This authentication verifies the user's identity and grants access to the Power Platform tools and features.

Data source authentication

The second level of authentication is between the user and the data source. The user needs to provide the credentials that the connector requires to access the data source. These credentials are stored and managed by the API Hub credentials service, which is a secure vault that encrypts and protects the credentials. The user can manage the credentials through the Power Platform portal or the Power Apps app.

Some connectors support more than one authentication method. For example, the SharePoint connector supports OAuth 2.0, Windows, and basic authentication methods. The authentication method determines how the credentials are obtained and used by the connector. The authentication method is specific to each data source instance and is based on the choice of the app maker when creating the connection.

Explicit and implicit authentication

In Power Apps, there are two primary methods for authenticating data sources: explicit and implicit authentication. They are as follows:

- **Explicit authentication** involves using the credentials of the app user to access the data source. This approach ensures that data access aligns with the user's specific permissions and roles. For instance, if a user has read-only permissions for a SharePoint list, the app will restrict them from editing or deleting any data.

- **Implicit authentication** uses the credentials provided by the app creator during the connection setup. In this case, the data access permissions are based on the app creator's roles. For example, if the app creator has full control over a SharePoint list, the app will permit any user to view, edit, or delete data.

Whenever possible, it is recommended to use explicit authentication, as it is more secure and adheres to the principle of least privilege, ensuring users have only the access necessary for their tasks.

Data source permissions

Even in the case of explicit authentication, it's important to remember that it's the user's rights on a data source that determines what the user can see and edit. The app interface does not override or restrict the data source permissions that the user has.

For example, suppose you have a SharePoint list that includes Name and Salary columns. You then build an app that exposes only the Name column. This means that users have access only to the Name column in your app.

However, suppose your users have SharePoint list permissions that allow them to view and edit both the Name and Salary columns. Now, suppose a specific user has Power Apps maker rights to that SharePoint list. In this case, nothing prevents that user from creating a new app that accesses the Salary column. The permissions that you grant through the user interface of your app don't deny the data source permissions that the user has.

Therefore, you should always ensure that the data source permissions are aligned with the business requirements and the app functionality. You should also educate your users about the data security and compliance policies and best practices.

Summary

As we wrap up our discussion on navigating compliance in Power Platform deployments, it's clear that adhering to industry regulations is fundamental to maintaining trust, security, and operational integrity. This chapter has provided a comprehensive overview of the regulatory landscape and compliance standards across industries and regions, emphasizing strategies to ensure Power Platform solutions meet requirements for data classification, protection, retention, and governance. It covered authentication levels for accessing data sources, highlighting their impact on security and compliance. The difference between explicit and implicit authentication in Power Apps was explained, with guidance on selecting the right approach. Finally, it outlined the role of APIM in monitoring and controlling data access within Power Platform. In the next chapter, we will explore how to measure the success of your Power Platform initiatives. We will discuss how to define and track **key performance indicators** (**KPIs**) that align with your business goals and outcomes. We will also introduce you to the tools and resources available in Power Platform to help you monitor and improve your app performance, user adoption, and return on investment. You will learn how to use Power Platform Starter Kit and the Center of Excellence to create dashboards, reports, and alerts that provide actionable insights into your Power Platform environment.

Join our community on Discord

Join our community's Discord space for discussions with the authors and other readers:

`https://packt.link/powerusers`

13

From Metrics to Milestones: Measuring Success in Power Platform Initiatives

This chapter will guide you in defining and measuring the success of your Power Platform initiatives. Power Platform is a low-code platform that enables you to create solutions for your organization's needs. You will learn how to use the **Center of Excellence (CoE)** Starter Kit to create a strategic roadmap for your Power Platform transformation. You will also learn how to select and align **key performance indicators (KPIs)** to track the adoption and impact of your Power Platform solutions.

In this chapter, you will learn how to define and measure success in Power Platform initiatives. You will explore the following topics:

- Strategy and vision
- Identifying and measuring success
- SMART goals and KPI benchmarks

By the end of this chapter, you will be able to demonstrate your progress and the value of your Power Platform initiatives to your organization and beyond.

Defining a strategic roadmap using the CoE Starter Kit

A well-defined strategy is essential for driving the successful adoption and implementation of digital transformation using Power Platform within your organization. Establishing a clear vision and strategic roadmap ensures that your Power Platform implementation initiatives align with broader business objectives and deliver measurable value. The CoE Starter Kit provides the necessary tools and frameworks to support this process, enabling you to create a robust governance model and foster a culture of innovation. Before we dive into tools to enable a successful Power Platform implementation, let's investigate key concepts associated with defining strategy and vision for adoption.

The role of strategy in Power Platform adoption

A clear strategy is the foundation for successful Power Platform adoption. Organizations must develop a roadmap that outlines both short-term and long-term goals. These goals should align with overall business objectives, ensuring that Power Platform adoption supports digital transformation across the enterprise.

The strategic roadmap should cover the following:

- **Business alignment**: How Power Platform will solve key business challenges and support organizational goals

- **Technology readiness**: Evaluating existing systems and how they can be integrated with Power Platform

- **People and culture**: Identifying the skills and capabilities needed within the organization for a smooth transition

- **Investment planning**: Setting realistic budgets for software, training, and change management

Vision maturity levels

The maturity model for Power Platform adoption includes five distinct stages: Initial, Repeatable, Defined, Capable, and Efficient. Focusing on the **strategy** and **vision** aspects, we'll assess maturity at different levels.

Initial (level 100)

At the Initial level, organizations are experimenting with Power Platform in a decentralized manner. The adoption may be driven by individual departments or teams with no centralized vision or strategy. There's little to no alignment with enterprise-wide business goals, and as a result, Power Platform projects may lack consistency:

- **Strategy**: There's minimal formal strategy. Individual efforts are not coordinated, resulting in isolated and often under-optimized solutions.

- **Vision**: The long-term potential of Power Platform is not fully understood or articulated. The vision is limited to solving immediate problems without understanding the broader business context.

Repeatable (level 200)

At the Repeatable level, organizations begin to recognize the importance of a cohesive Power Platform strategy. Teams may start to share successful practices, and a clearer roadmap begins to emerge:

- **Strategy**: The organization acknowledges the need for alignment between business objectives and technology solutions. Some efforts are made to prioritize Power Platform projects that support key business outcomes.

- **Vision**: A broader vision starts to develop, with a focus on enabling innovation across departments. The organization realizes that Power Platform can streamline processes and create efficiencies but is still limited in scope.

Defined (level 300)

The Defined level signifies that the organization has developed a clear, organization-wide strategy for Power Platform adoption. Teams are empowered with governance models and resources to implement Power Platform solutions aligned with the business strategy:

- **Strategy**: The strategic roadmap is formally documented, outlining how Power Platform initiatives will support both current and future business goals. Cross-functional teams collaborate to ensure Power Platform solutions align with larger digital transformation efforts.

- **Vision**: The organization's vision for Power Platform is holistic. The goal is to create scalable, reusable solutions that foster innovation and provide competitive advantages. Leaders articulate a long-term plan for expanding the platform's use, including citizen development, automation, and AI integration.

Capable (level 400)

At the Capable level, organizations fully integrate Power Platform into their digital transformation strategy. Solutions are scalable and integrated across business units. The strategy is continuously refined based on performance metrics and evolving business needs:

- **Strategy**: The roadmap includes continuous optimization, driven by data and feedback. Power Platform is seen as a critical component of the business's IT infrastructure, and investments in governance, security, and scalability ensure its long-term success.

- **Vision**: The vision extends beyond operational improvements. Power Platform is viewed as a key enabler of innovation and competitive differentiation. Organizations at this level explore advanced capabilities such as AI, machine learning, and predictive analytics within the platform.

Efficient (level 500)

At the Efficient level, organizations have fully operationalized Power Platform as part of their digital ecosystem. The platform not only drives efficiency and innovation but also opens new business opportunities:

- **Strategy**: Power Platform is fully integrated with other core business systems. The strategic roadmap focuses on ongoing innovation, continuous improvement, and unlocking new revenue streams.

- **Vision**: Power Platform is seen as an essential driver of business strategy. Leaders consistently refine their vision to include emerging technologies, keeping the organization at the forefront of digital innovation.

Figure 13.1 illustrates the Power Platform adoption levels, represented as a stairwell leading to greater maturity and innovation. Each step marks a distinct level, starting from the Initial stage at the bottom and ascending through Repeatable, Defined, and Capable, and finally reaching Efficient at the top. Brief descriptions accompany each level, providing insights into the characteristics and strategic focus of organizations at that stage. The stairwell analogy reflects the journey toward a fully operational and innovative digital ecosystem, where Power Platform drives not only efficiency but also new business opportunities and competitive differentiation.

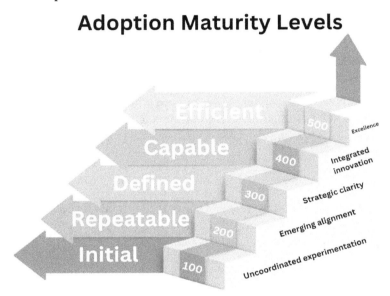

Figure 13.1 – Power Platform vision maturity levels

Leveraging the CoE Starter Kit to assess Power Platform vision maturity

The CoE Starter Kit helps organizations identify their Power Platform vision maturity level by providing tools and insights that assess the current state of their platform usage, governance, and innovation capabilities.

It begins with an assessment of your current environment, helping you understand your organization's maturity in using Power Platform and identifying key areas for improvement. This assessment allows you to define clear objectives that guide your Power Platform journey, ensuring that each step is aligned with your organization's long-term goals.

One of the primary benefits of using the CoE Starter Kit is its ability to integrate strategic planning with operational execution. It allows you to establish governance structures, set up monitoring and reporting mechanisms, and define KPIs that track progress and success. By leveraging these capabilities, you can create a strategic roadmap that not only outlines the path to achieving your vision but also provides the tools to measure and adjust your approach as needed.

In essence, the CoE Starter Kit enhances your organization's ability to define and execute a strategic roadmap for Power Platform transformation. By following best practices and leveraging the tools provided by the CoE Starter Kit, you can ensure that your Power Platform strategy is well aligned with your organization's broader vision, effectively managed, and capable of delivering sustained business value. As we move to the next section, we will explore how to identify and measure success through KPIs to track the impact of your Power Platform initiatives.

Here are practical examples of how the CoE Starter Kit can be used to assess an organization's Power Platform vision maturity:

- **Tracking platform usage and adoption**: Using the Power BI adoption dashboard within the CoE Starter Kit, you can monitor the number of active makers, apps, and flows. If the data shows limited use across only a few departments, it indicates that the organization may be at the Initial or Repeatable stage. Conversely, widespread usage across multiple departments suggests higher maturity, such as the Defined or Capable level.

- **Monitoring solution scalability**: By analyzing the App and Flow Inventory feature in the CoE Starter Kit, organizations can assess whether their solutions are scalable and reused across departments. If most apps are built to solve isolated, department-specific problems without broader scalability, it signals a lower maturity level. Higher maturity is indicated by solutions designed for enterprise-wide use, reflecting alignment with long-term strategy and innovation.

- **Evaluating governance structures**: The CoE Starter Kit's governance dashboard helps track the implementation of policies, security, and compliance across the organization. For example, organizations at the Defined or Capable stage will have more structured governance in place, ensuring that Power Platform aligns with company-wide business objectives and follows a unified strategy.

- **Tracking citizen developer engagement**: The CoE Starter Kit provides insights into citizen development activity – showing who is creating apps, their frequency, and the complexity of solutions. If there's limited citizen development, the organization might be at the Repeatable or Defined stage. The higher involvement of business users in creating apps and automation indicates a more mature level, such as Capable or Efficient, where the Power Platform vision includes a robust citizen developer program.

- **Measuring innovation through advanced features**: The CoE Starter Kit can track the usage of advanced Power Platform features such as AI Builder or Power Automate's **robotic process automation (RPA)**. Organizations using these capabilities extensively are likely at the Capable or Efficient level, where innovation and advanced technologies are central to their Power Platform vision and strategy.

- **Reviewing change management and training initiatives**: Through the CoE Starter Kit's insights, organizations can assess the extent of their training and change management efforts. If only basic training has been conducted or limited resources are available to help users, the organization might be at the Repeatable stage. However, if comprehensive, ongoing training programs are in place, they're likely at a more advanced maturity level, such as Capable or Efficient, with a long-term vision for fostering a Power Platform culture.

These examples demonstrate how the CoE Starter Kit can provide actionable insights to help organizations evaluate their current Power Platform vision maturity level and identify areas for strategic improvement.

Identifying and measuring success

Effectively measuring the success of Power Platform initiatives hinges on identifying and aligning KPIs that align with your organization's goals. By leveraging these KPIs, you can track Power Platform adoption and its impact, ensuring that it drives the intended business outcomes. In this section, we will explore how to define and align KPIs to effectively measure the success of Power Platform adoption while maintaining strategic alignment between business objectives and technology solutions.

Understanding the role of KPIs in Power Platform adoption

KPIs serve as the measurable values that demonstrate how effectively an organization is achieving its business objectives through Power Platform adoption. Identifying the right KPIs ensures that an organization can continuously monitor progress, optimize resources, and adapt its strategy as needed. Without defined KPIs, measuring the **return on investment** (**ROI**) for Power Platform initiatives becomes challenging.

Effective KPIs should do the following:

- Align with broader business goals
- Be **specific**, **measurable**, **achievable**, **relevant**, and **time-bound** (**SMART**)
- Provide both quantitative and qualitative insights into adoption progress

Identifying key metrics

The first step in measuring success is identifying KPIs that align with your organization's strategic goals and business objectives. These KPIs should be tailored to the specific outcomes you seek through Power Platform adoption, such as improved efficiency, cost reduction, or enhanced customer engagement. Common metrics include the time saved through automation, reduction in operational costs, and user adoption rates.

Take these examples:

- **Operational efficiency**: KPIs might measure time saved by automating manual processes or reducing dependency on traditional IT development cycles

- **Cost reduction**: KPIs could track reductions in IT costs or third-party app expenditures by using Power Platform to build in-house solutions

- **Customer satisfaction**: KPIs might include customer satisfaction scores or the speed of responding to customer inquiries via Power Apps or Power Automate workflows

By linking Power Platform adoption KPIs directly to these business goals, organizations ensure that every initiative drives meaningful value and contributes to strategic success.

Key categories of KPIs for Power Platform adoption

To effectively measure Power Platform adoption, organizations should focus on KPIs in several key categories, including user engagement, solution impact, innovation, and governance. Each of these categories provides unique insights into how Power Platform is delivering value across the business:

- **User engagement KPIs**: These KPIs help organizations assess the extent of Power Platform adoption by tracking how users and teams are engaging with the platform:

  - **Number of active makers and users**: Measures how many individuals are actively building apps or flows or leveraging Power BI within the platform

  - **App usage**: Tracks the frequency and volume of usage for specific apps, showing how much value they provide to users

  - **Citizen developer participation**: Measures the number of non-IT employees creating solutions, indicating how effectively Power Platform is fostering a culture of innovation

- **Solution impact KPIs**: These KPIs evaluate how well Power Platform solutions are addressing specific business needs and delivering measurable results:

  - **Time saved from automation**: Quantifies the hours saved by automating manual processes with Power Automate or custom apps, showcasing operational efficiency gains

  - **Error reduction**: Measures the reduction in errors or inconsistencies in processes that were previously manual, highlighting improvements in accuracy

  - **Cost savings from internal app development**: Tracks the cost saved by building custom solutions in-house instead of purchasing third-party applications or services

- **Innovation and transformation KPIs**: Innovation-focused KPIs measure how Power Platform is contributing to broader organizational transformation and the development of new capabilities:

  - **Number of new business processes digitized**: Tracks how many processes have been digitized using Power Platform, signaling the organization's commitment to digital transformation

  - **New services or offerings enabled by Power Platform**: Measures how many new customer-facing services or products have been launched using the platform, indicating its role in driving innovation

  - **Rate of innovation adoption**: Tracks how quickly new Power Platform features or updates are integrated into organizational workflows

- **Governance and compliance KPIs**: These KPIs assess how well the organization is managing the governance and security aspects of Power Platform adoption:

  - **Adherence to governance policies**: Measures the compliance rate with established governance frameworks, indicating how well the platform is controlled and monitored

  - **Data security incidents**: Tracks the number of security breaches or compliance issues related to Power Platform solutions, ensuring that risks are minimized

  - **Audit trail and monitoring efficiency**: Measures how effectively Power Platform activities are monitored and audited to maintain compliance with internal and external regulations

Building an effective KPI framework for Power Platform adoption

To ensure that KPIs effectively measure Power Platform adoption success, organizations must build a robust KPI framework. This framework should do the following:

- **Define success**: Clarify what success looks like for the organization. This could be improved customer satisfaction, faster response times, reduced operational costs, or more innovative services.

- **Map KPIs to objectives**: Ensure that each KPI directly supports one or more business objectives. For instance, if the objective is to reduce IT costs, KPIs might focus on cost savings from automating tasks or building internal apps.

- **Set benchmarks**: Establish baseline metrics for each KPI so that progress can be tracked over time. For example, organizations might measure app usage today and compare it with usage six months after a major Power Platform initiative.

- **Use real-time data**: Leverage tools such as Power BI to gather real-time data and provide continuous insights into Power Platform adoption. This ensures that decision-makers have timely information to adjust strategies and initiatives as needed.

- **Review and refine**: Periodically review KPIs to ensure they remain relevant as the organization's needs and goals evolve. As Power Platform capabilities expand, new KPIs may be necessary to measure emerging areas of value, such as artificial intelligence or machine learning adoption.

The role of leadership in driving KPI success

Leadership plays a crucial role in the success of any Power Platform initiative, especially when it comes to identifying and measuring KPIs. Leaders must do the following:

- **Champion the adoption of Power Platform**: Actively encourage the use of Power Platform across departments, ensuring that all teams understand the value of the platform and its alignment with business objectives
- **Align teams with KPIs**: Ensure that all stakeholders, from IT to business units, are aware of the KPIs and understand how their contributions impact the overall success of the platform
- **Foster a data-driven culture**: Emphasize the importance of data-driven decision-making, ensuring that teams use KPIs to assess progress and make continuous improvements

Leveraging financial metrics

Financial KPIs, such as ROI, **total cost of ownership** (**TCO**), and payback period, are vital in measuring the financial success of your Power Platform initiatives. These metrics help quantify the economic value generated by the solutions. For instance, calculate the ROI by comparing the cost savings or revenue generated by a Power Platform solution against the initial investment.

Qualitative benefits

In addition to quantitative KPIs, consider qualitative benefits such as improved employee satisfaction, increased agility, and enhanced collaboration. These factors, while not easily measurable in numbers, significantly contribute to the overall success of Power Platform adoption. Collecting user feedback and testimonials can provide insights into these qualitative improvements.

Communicating success

Effectively communicating the success of Power Platform adoption is crucial for maintaining stakeholder support. Regularly present KPI results to leadership, highlighting both the quantitative and qualitative benefits. This ongoing communication ensures that the value of Power Platform initiatives is recognized and that there is continued investment in the platform.

By acquiring and applying these skills to identify and align KPIs, your organization can effectively measure the success of Power Platform adoption. These KPIs will guide you in tracking progress, demonstrating value, and making informed decisions about future initiatives. As we move forward, the next section will explore securing data transmission and API access in Power Platform deployments, a key component in ensuring the security and reliability of your solutions.

Figure 13.2 presents a detailed diagram illustrating the continuous cycle of KPI definition and refinement.

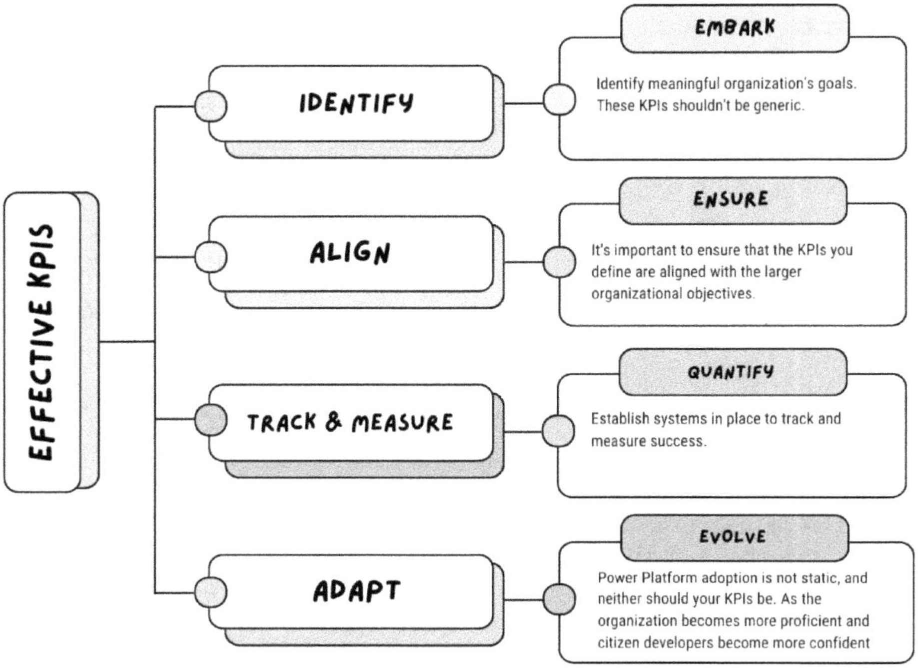

Figure 13.2 – Overview of KPI definition

This cycle emphasizes the importance of an iterative approach, where each step is paired with a specific action aimed at enhancing the overall process of KPI identification, measurement, and improvement. Starting with the initial establishment of KPIs, the cycle moves through stages of data collection, analysis, and feedback, ensuring that KPIs remain relevant and aligned with organizational goals. Regular refinement helps organizations adapt to evolving business needs, uncover new insights, and optimize performance across various departments.

By understanding how to set, monitor, and refine KPIs, organizations can ensure their Power Platform initiatives align with broader business goals and deliver tangible results. Through practical examples and insights, the next section will guide you in defining SMART goals and KPI benchmarks, helping you continuously improve and refine your Power Platform adoption journey.

SMART goals and KPI benchmarks

Setting clear, actionable goals is essential for the success of any business initiative, including Power Platform adoption. In this section, we will explore how to develop proficiency in setting SMART goals and establishing KPI benchmarks that align with your organization's strategic objectives.

We'll also provide practical examples tailored to IT leaders and C-level executives, showing how SMART goals and KPIs can drive measurable results and ensure the success of Power Platform projects.

Understanding SMART goals

SMART goals provide a structured framework that enables organizations to set clear, actionable objectives that can be tracked and measured. Each element of a SMART goal plays a critical role in ensuring that the goal is realistic and aligned with broader business objectives:

- **Specific**: Clearly define the goal, leaving no room for ambiguity. It should answer "who, what, where, when, and why."

- **Measurable**: Identify how success will be quantified. KPIs play a critical role here, as they provide the metrics used to evaluate progress.

- **Achievable**: The goal should be realistic and attainable within the given resources, skills, and timeframe.

- **Relevant**: Align the goal with broader business objectives to ensure it supports the overall organizational strategy.

- **Time-bound**: Set a clear deadline or timeframe to keep the goal on track and accountable.

By applying the SMART framework, IT leaders and C-level professionals can ensure that their Power Platform initiatives are not only strategically aligned but also measurable and actionable.

Establishing KPI benchmarks

KPIs provide the metrics necessary to track progress toward achieving SMART goals. When setting KPI benchmarks, it's important to do the following:

- Define baseline metrics for current performance
- Set realistic target values for each KPI
- Ensure KPIs are closely tied to business objectives, reflecting both quantitative and qualitative outcomes

For example, if the goal is to reduce the IT backlog by enabling citizen developers to create apps, KPIs might include the following:

- Number of apps built by citizen developers
- Reduction in the IT backlog as a percentage over a set period
- Time saved by automating manual tasks through Power Platform solutions

The power of SMART goals and KPI benchmarks for Power Platform initiatives

In the context of Power Platform adoption, setting SMART goals and KPI benchmarks ensures that digital transformation initiatives stay on course and deliver measurable results. The following examples illustrate how IT leaders and C-level executives can apply this framework to achieve success.

Example 1 – reducing IT backlog with citizen developers

The SMART goal is to empower citizen developers to reduce the IT backlog by 30% within 12 months by building custom apps using Power Apps:

- **Specific**: Focus on empowering citizen developers to reduce the IT backlog
- **Measurable**: Set a 30% reduction in the backlog as the target
- **Achievable**: Equip business users with training and support to build apps
- **Relevant**: Aligns with the goal of increasing agility and reducing IT dependency
- **Time-bound**: 12-month period for the goal to be achieved

The following are the KPI benchmarks:

- **Baseline**: 10 apps built by the IT team per month
- **Target**: 25% of the total app development is handled by citizen developers
- **Measure**: Reduction in requests for app development from business units, tracked through the IT ticketing system

Practical example: A healthcare organization struggling with IT backlogs implemented Power Platform to enable business users in non-technical departments to create apps that automate administrative tasks such as patient intake or data management. By setting a SMART goal to reduce IT backlog by 30% and establishing clear KPIs, they were able to track progress and showcase measurable improvements in operational efficiency.

Example 2 – improving operational efficiency through automation

The SMART goal is to automate 40% of manual processes in the HR department within nine months using Power Automate, reducing processing time by 25%:

- **Specific**: Automate manual HR processes
- **Measurable**: Target 40% of processes and aim for a 25% reduction in processing time
- **Achievable**: Leverage existing Power Automate capabilities and training
- **Relevant**: Reduces operational overhead and improves service delivery
- **Time-bound**: Nine-month deadline to complete automation

The following are the KPI benchmarks:

- **Baseline**: Time spent on manual HR processes, such as onboarding or payroll
- **Target**: Reduction in processing time by 25%
- **Measure**: The number of automated workflows implemented by HR, tracked through workflow logs and employee feedback on efficiency

Practical example: A financial services company struggling with manual HR processes—such as paper-based onboarding – set a SMART goal to automate 40% of these processes. Using Power Automate, the company integrated digital workflows that cut processing times by 25%, streamlining HR operations. This not only improved efficiency but also allowed the HR team to focus on more strategic tasks.

Example 3 – enhancing customer experience through digital solutions

The SMART goal is to launch a new customer self-service portal using Power Apps within six months, increasing customer satisfaction by 20%:

- **Specific**: Build and launch a customer self-service portal
- **Measurable**: Increase customer satisfaction by 20%
- **Achievable**: Leverage existing Power Apps expertise within the IT team
- **Relevant**: Aligns with the goal of improving customer experience
- **Time-bound**: Six-month timeframe to launch the portal

The following are the KPI benchmarks:

- **Baseline**: Current customer satisfaction score from feedback surveys
- **Target**: 20% improvement in satisfaction, measured by post-launch customer feedback
- **Measure**: Usage statistics for the portal (e.g., number of daily logins) and customer satisfaction ratings tracked through surveys

Practical example: A retail company aimed to reduce the volume of customer support inquiries by building a self-service portal using Power Apps. The goal was to improve the customer experience and reduce support costs. By setting clear KPIs around portal usage and satisfaction rates, the company successfully launched the portal, achieving a 20% increase in customer satisfaction within six months.

Example 4 – fostering a culture of innovation by nurturing citizen developers

The SMART goal is to nurture and empower 50 new citizen developers within the next 12 months by providing training, resources, and mentorship, resulting in at least 15 new apps built that solve specific departmental challenges:

- **Specific**: Focus on nurturing 50 new citizen developers and empowering them to create 15 new apps that address department-specific problems
- **Measurable**: Track the number of new developers trained and the number of apps developed
- **Achievable**: Provide comprehensive training programs, mentorship, and resources to encourage participation
- **Relevant**: Aligns with the broader goal of fostering innovation and reducing reliance on IT by encouraging citizen development
- **Time-bound**: Achieve the goal within a 12-month period

The following are the KPI benchmarks:

- **Baseline**: Number of current active citizen developers in the organization
- **Target**: 50 new citizen developers by the end of 12 months
- **Measure**: Number of apps successfully developed and deployed by new developers, tracked through Power Platform's governance dashboard

Practical example: A manufacturing company aiming to foster innovation set a SMART goal to nurture 50 new citizen developers within a year. Through targeted training sessions, regular workshops, and assigning department mentors, they empowered non-technical employees to build apps that addressed operational inefficiencies, such as inventory management and employee scheduling. By the end of the year, 20 new apps were successfully deployed, streamlining internal processes and reducing the workload of the IT department, showcasing how nurturing citizen developers drive innovation and self-sufficiency across the organization.

Setting and achieving SMART goals for citizen development is not only a strategic necessity but also a catalyst for fostering innovation and operational efficiency within an organization. By establishing clear benchmarks, providing necessary resources, and tracking progress meticulously, companies can transform non-technical employees into empowered developers, driving substantial business value. This structured approach ensures that the adoption of Power Platform aligns with broader organizational objectives and paves the way for sustainable growth and self-sufficiency.

Summary

In this chapter, we took a deep dive into the critical components necessary for defining, tracking, and measuring the success of Power Platform adoption. The chapter provided a comprehensive framework for establishing a strategic roadmap, setting SMART goals, and aligning KPIs with organizational objectives. These steps are essential to ensure that Power Platform initiatives not only drive measurable outcomes but also contribute to long-term business transformation.

Throughout this journey, we emphasized the importance of leveraging tools such as the CoE Starter Kit. This toolkit plays a key role in helping organizations assess their current maturity level, monitor their progress, and provide the necessary governance to scale Power Platform adoption across the enterprise.

In this next chapter, we will explore how to track progress beyond the initial milestones and delve deeper into maintaining momentum. You will learn how to sustain the value of Power Platform initiatives through careful monitoring, periodic adjustments, and ensuring that goals remain relevant as your organization continues its digital transformation journey.

In essence, the next chapter will empower you to go beyond setting metrics by showing you how to **track**, **evaluate**, and **sustain** your Power Platform success over time, ensuring it drives continuous value to your organization.

14

Tracking Success Measures: Monitoring Progress and Achieving Objectives

In this chapter, we'll focus on the importance of defining and tracking **key performance indicators** (KPIs) to measure progress and ensure your Power Platform initiatives reach their objectives. Implementing new technologies such as Power Platform isn't just about deployment; it's about continuously monitoring adoption, gathering user feedback, and making informed decisions to optimize usage and results.

Tracking progress is an ongoing process that goes beyond hitting initial milestones. To truly understand the impact Power Platform has on your organization, it's important to set the right success measures and maintain regular monitoring. This begins by gathering baseline data on user knowledge and engagement with Power Platform when it is first introduced. From there, regular follow-up surveys and feedback will provide insights into how users are adapting, how the platform is being used, and where improvements might be necessary.

User adoption plays a critical role in the success of any technology rollout. In this chapter, you'll learn how to monitor user engagement with Power Platform through surveys and feedback channels to understand how the platform is contributing to both satisfaction and productivity. Conducting surveys – at the time of launch and periodically thereafter – will help you identify how well Power Platform is meeting user needs and whether additional training or resources are required.

In this chapter, you'll further your knowledge about KPIs in terms of how they're defined and tracked to establish success measures, monitor user adoption, and gather data on fusion team knowledge and satisfaction.

We will explore the following topics:

- Defining KPIs and tracking them
- Implementing Power Platform – success measures and adoption
- Tools to automate success measures
- Gathering maker feedback to assess rollout success
- Using CoE analytics to assess makers' knowledge and satisfaction
- Community engagement and collaboration
- Direct maker feedback loops

Defining KPIs and tracking them

In any Power Platform adoption journey, defining and tracking KPIs is vital to measuring progress and ensuring that objectives are achieved effectively. KPIs allow organizations to quantify their success, monitor performance against specific goals, and make data-driven adjustments to their strategy as needed. Establishing clear KPIs and tracking them systematically not only keeps projects aligned with business objectives but also fosters accountability, encourages continuous improvement, and ensures that resources are allocated effectively.

The importance of defining KPIs early in the journey

KPIs should be established from the outset – that is, when the organization first begins its Power Platform adoption. At this stage, KPIs help define the desired outcomes, providing a roadmap for success. Without defined KPIs, organizations risk losing focus on their broader strategic objectives and may struggle to measure the value of Power Platform initiatives.

According to Microsoft's adoption methodology, the first phase of Power Platform adoption should involve building a clear strategy and vision that aligns with business goals. This step requires identifying the challenges Power Platform aims to address, such as streamlining workflows, reducing manual processes, or empowering citizen developers. KPIs are instrumental in measuring the success of these strategic goals. They ensure that organizations remain focused on key outcomes throughout the adoption process.

KPIs should do the following:

- **Align with broader business objectives**: Each KPI must support a specific business outcome, such as increased productivity, cost savings, or enhanced customer satisfaction
- **Be measurable and actionable**: KPIs should be based on quantifiable data that can be tracked consistently

- **Drive continuous improvement**: By regularly reviewing KPIs, organizations can adapt their strategy to meet evolving needs

For example, KPIs may measure the number of applications that have been built by citizen developers, the percentage of manual processes that have been automated, or the increase in overall process efficiency.

Tracking KPIs to ensure progress

Once KPIs have been established, tracking them over time is essential. The Power Platform *Adoption Strategy Best Practices guide* (`https://learn.microsoft.com/en-us/power-platform/guidance/adoption/methodology`) emphasizes the importance of regularly reviewing performance data and progress against established goals. KPIs should be monitored using real-time dashboards and reports, such as those available in the **Center of Excellence** (**CoE**) Starter Kit. This allows organizations to measure ongoing adoption, identify gaps, and course-correct if necessary.

The following are some of the key benefits of tracking KPIs:

- **Gain visibility into adoption and usage trends**: Tracking the number of active users, application creation rates, and the usage of automation tools provides a clear picture of how Power Platform is being adopted across the organization

- **The ability to identify success and challenges**: Monitoring KPIs helps teams understand where Power Platform initiatives are excelling and where additional support or training may be required

- **Data-driven decision-making**: By continuously reviewing performance metrics, organizations can make informed decisions about where to invest resources, how to improve user experience, and what areas to prioritize for further development

The admin best practices for Power Platform highlight how key metrics, such as application usage or flow execution, can be tracked and analyzed through the CoE Starter Kit, which provides centralized visibility into all Power Platform activities. This level of oversight is crucial to understanding how well the platform is integrated into day-to-day operations and identifying areas for improvement.

Practical steps for defining and tracking KPIs

To define and track KPIs effectively, organizations can follow these practical steps:

1. **Identify key business objectives**: Begin by understanding the broader business goals that Power Platform will support. This could include improving operational efficiency, reducing costs, or enhancing customer service. For example, a KPI might be the time saved by automating manual workflows.

2. **Set measurable targets**: For each objective, establish measurable targets. KPIs should have a clear baseline (for example, the current state of operations) and a target value (for example, reducing the IT backlog by 30% within 6 months). These targets should be realistic and achievable but also ambitious enough to drive progress.

3. **Use the CoE Starter Kit for tracking**: Implement the CoE Starter Kit, which provides pre-built dashboards for tracking KPIs related to application usage, maker activity, and adoption rates. The Starter Kit allows organizations to view progress in real time and adjust strategies based on performance data.

4. **Monitor KPIs regularly**: Establish a cadence for reviewing KPIs – this could be weekly, monthly, or quarterly, depending on the project phase. Regular monitoring ensures that organizations can spot trends, address issues promptly, and celebrate successes along the way.

5. **Adapt KPIs as needed**: As the organization matures in its Power Platform adoption, it may be necessary to adjust KPIs to reflect new priorities. For example, in the early stages, KPIs might focus on adoption and training, while later KPIs could measure innovation or the financial impact of Power Platform solutions. The maturity model for Power Platform provides a helpful framework for adjusting KPIs as organizations move through different stages of adoption.

Key areas to measure with KPIs

When defining KPIs, it's important to measure across different areas to get a comprehensive view of progress. The *Nurture Best Practices guide* (`https://learn.microsoft.com/en-us/power-platform/guidance/adoption/nurture-best-practices`) emphasizes nurturing users and makers to ensure continued engagement with the platform. Here are some examples of key areas that should be tracked with KPIs:

*   **User adoption**: Track the number of active users and the frequency of application creation to measure how engaged employees are with Power Platform

*   **Solution impact**: Measure the business outcomes of solutions built using Power Platform, such as the time saved from automation or the reduction in manual errors

*   **Innovation**: Monitor the rate at which new apps and automations are being created by different teams, as well as how effectively Power Platform is enabling innovation within the organization.

*   **Governance and compliance**: Ensure that governance policies are being followed by tracking the number of compliant applications, security incidents, and adherence to data protection rules

Defining and tracking KPIs is crucial for measuring progress and ensuring that Power Platform initiatives are aligned with business objectives. By establishing clear metrics, organizations can continuously monitor adoption and usage, assess their success, and make data-driven decisions that lead to sustained growth and improvement. Tools such as the CoE Starter Kit provide valuable insights into performance and help organizations stay on course to achieve their Power Platform goals. Through effective KPI tracking, organizations can ensure they aren't just adopting Power Platform but using it to drive real business value.

In summary, implementing and leveraging Power Platform effectively necessitates setting clear KPIs and success measures, such as tracking user adoption, solution impact, and governance compliance. Tools such as the CoE Starter Kit help visualize these metrics in real time, allowing organizations to make informed, data-driven decisions that align with their business goals and foster continued engagement and innovation.

Implementing Power Platform – success measures and adoption

Implementing Power Platform successfully requires more than just deploying the tools – it involves establishing clear success measures and continuously monitoring user adoption to ensure that the platform is delivering the intended outcomes. Success measures provide a roadmap for evaluating how well Power Platform is supporting business objectives, whereas monitoring user adoption ensures that the platform is being used effectively across the organization.

Defining success measures

Defining success measures is the first step in ensuring that your Power Platform implementation aligns with organizational goals. These measures should be closely tied to business objectives, such as improving productivity, reducing operational costs, enhancing customer satisfaction, or enabling innovation through citizen development.

When defining success measures, consider these key aspects:

- **Business alignment**: Identify the core business challenges Power Platform is expected to address. For example, if the goal is to reduce manual processes, a success measure might be the percentage of workflows automated using Power Automate.

- **User engagement**: Consider how success will be measured in terms of user adoption. For example, you can track the number of active users, applications created, and flows deployed to understand how employees are engaging with Power Platform.

- **Operational efficiency**: Establish clear goals for efficiency gains. A success measure could be the reduction in processing time for critical business tasks by using Power Apps or Power Automate to automate previously manual workflows.

- **Innovation and scalability**: If the goal is to foster innovation, you can measure the number of solutions that have been developed by citizen developers or the rate at which new features (such as AI Builder or Custom Copilots) are adopted.

Quantifying success measures

Once success measures have been defined, it's crucial to establish ways to quantify them. This involves setting measurable, data-driven goals that can be tracked over time to assess progress. Here's how you can quantify common success measures:

- **User adoption**: Track metrics such as the number of active users per week or month, the number of applications that have been created by non-IT staff (citizen developers), and the frequency of application usage. Adoption rates can also be measured by user engagement levels in training sessions and the number of makers contributing to new solutions.

- **Process efficiency**: Calculate the time saved by automating processes. For example, measure the reduction in manual data entry hours or the improvement in processing times for specific tasks after workflows are automated using Power Automate.

- **Cost reduction**: If one of the goals is to reduce costs, quantify the savings by comparing the cost of developing solutions in-house using Power Platform versus purchasing third-party software or custom development services.

- **Innovation**: Measure innovation by tracking the number of new solutions that have been deployed using Power Platform, the departments involved in application development, and the introduction of new services or capabilities powered by the platform.

These measures should be aligned with the **SMART** framework – **Specific**, **Measurable**, **Achievable**, **Relevant**, and **Time-bound** – to ensure that they provide meaningful insights into the success of your Power Platform initiatives.

Monitoring user adoption

Monitoring user adoption is crucial for understanding how well Power Platform is being embraced across your organization. Adoption monitoring allows you to identify which departments or teams are utilizing the platform effectively and where there may be barriers to usage.

Several metrics can be used to monitor user adoption:

- **Number of active users**: Track how many employees are actively using Power Apps, Power Automate, and Power BI regularly

- **App creation and usage**: Measure how many applications are being created and how often they're being used by different teams

- **Citizen developer participation**: Monitor the number of non-IT users (citizen developers) who are creating solutions; this indicates the democratization of application development within the organization

- **Training and support engagement**: Track attendance at training sessions, the completion of online learning modules, and the number of support tickets related to Power Platform

Tools to automate success measures

Power Platform offers several built-in tools and components that can be used to automate the process of tracking success measures and monitoring user adoption. Let's take a look at the key tools available within the platform.

The CoE Starter Kit

The **CoE Starter Kit** is an essential tool for organizations looking to monitor and govern their Power Platform usage. It provides pre-built solutions that help administrators track user adoption, maker activity, application usage, and overall platform performance.

The CoE Starter Kit includes **Power BI Dashboards**, which offer insights into the number of applications being created, the frequency of application usage, and the departments contributing to new solutions. These dashboards are fully customizable and allow for real-time monitoring of user adoption metrics.

Additionally, the Starter Kit provides governance and compliance tracking, ensuring that applications are following the organization's policies and that data security measures are in place.

Power BI for custom dashboards

Power BI is a powerful tool within Power Platform that can be used to create custom dashboards and reports to track success measures. By integrating data from Power Apps, Power Automate, and Power BI itself, organizations can monitor user adoption, application performance, and other key metrics.

Power BI allows you to visualize adoption trends, such as how quickly different departments are adopting Power Platform or how much time has been saved through automation.

You can also set up automated alerts in Power BI to notify stakeholders when specific adoption milestones are reached or when KPIs fall below target levels.

Power Automate for process automation

Power Automate can be used to automate the process of tracking certain success measures. For example, workflows can be set up to notify administrators when a certain number of applications have been created or when a specific user adoption threshold has been met.

It can also be used to automate the process of gathering user feedback via surveys. For example, a workflow could automatically send out satisfaction surveys to users after a new application is deployed, helping to measure user satisfaction and application success.

Microsoft Dataverse for data centralization

Microsoft Dataverse serves as the underlying data platform for Power Platform, allowing organizations to store and manage their data in one centralized location. By using Dataverse, organizations can collect and store data on application usage, user engagement, and maker activity, which can then be analyzed and reported on through Power BI or other tools.

This centralized approach to data management ensures that all success measures are tracked consistently across the organization, providing a single source of truth for decision-makers.

Power Apps Usage Analytics

Power Apps Usage Analytics allows administrators to monitor detailed application usage patterns, including which users are accessing which applications, how often applications are being used, and which applications are driving the most value.

This tool provides valuable insights into application performance, helping organizations identify high-value applications and prioritize resources accordingly.

Defining success measures and monitoring user adoption are critical components of any successful Power Platform implementation. By setting clear, quantifiable goals that are aligned with business objectives, organizations can measure the effectiveness of their Power Platform initiatives and make informed decisions to drive continuous improvement. With tools such as the CoE Starter Kit, Power BI, Power Automate, and Dataverse, organizations can automate much of the tracking and reporting process, ensuring that they stay on track to achieve their objectives and maximize the value of their Power Platform investments.

Gathering maker feedback to assess rollout success

A successful Power Platform implementation hinges not only on the deployment of tools but also on how well the platform is adopted and utilized by its makers – those who build applications, workflows, and other solutions. To assess the effectiveness of the rollout, organizations must gather data on their makers' knowledge, engagement, and satisfaction. Using multiple channels to collect this information provides a more comprehensive understanding of how the platform is being adopted, helping organizations identify areas of success and those requiring further support or improvement.

This section will explore several channels that organizations can use to gather critical data on their makers' experiences and satisfaction levels with Power Platform. These channels range from surveys and usage analytics to community engagement and feedback loops, offering diverse insights into both technical and user-focused aspects of the platform's rollout.

Surveys and feedback forms

One of the most direct and effective ways to gather data on makers' knowledge and satisfaction is through **surveys and feedback forms**. These tools allow organizations to collect qualitative and quantitative data on how makers are engaging with Power Platform, where they face challenges, and how satisfied they are with the tools provided:

- **Initial knowledge surveys**: At the beginning of the Power Platform rollout, organizations can conduct surveys to assess baseline knowledge among makers. This helps identify how familiar makers are with the platform's tools (Power Apps, Power Automate, and Power BI) and what specific training or resources might be needed to improve their proficiency. For example, a survey might ask makers about their experience with low-code/no-code tools and their understanding of automation or data integration.

- **Post-training feedback**: After delivering training programs, organizations can distribute feedback forms to gauge how effective the training was in boosting makers' confidence and competence with Power Platform. Questions might include ratings on the quality of the training, whether the content was relevant, and how likely makers are to apply what they've learned in real-world scenarios.

- **Satisfaction surveys**: Periodically, organizations should send out satisfaction surveys to gauge makers' ongoing experience with the platform. These surveys can measure satisfaction with application-building tools, the ease of automation, and the overall experience of using Power Platform to meet business needs. Satisfaction surveys help identify areas for improvement in terms of the platform's features, usability, and support services.

Sample survey for gathering data on maker knowledge and satisfaction

To assess Power Platform rollout success effectively, organizations should implement surveys and feedback forms that target key aspects of maker knowledge and satisfaction. These forms provide insights into how users engage with Power Platform, the challenges they face, and their overall satisfaction with the platform's tools and support. Here's a summary of the key sections and questions that should be included in a comprehensive survey:

- **Basic information**: Collect maker details such as name, department, role, and experience with Power Platform. This helps categorize feedback based on different user groups.

- **Knowledge and training**: Assess makers' current understanding of Power Platform tools (Power Apps, Power Automate, Power BI, and so on) and their confidence in using the platform to create solutions. Questions can gauge the effectiveness of any formal training that's been received and identify additional training needs.

- **Usage and adoption**: Gather data on how frequently makers use the platform, what types of applications or workflows they have built, and their satisfaction with the platform's features and capabilities. This section helps measure user engagement and the practical application of Power Platform within the organization.

- **Support and satisfaction**: Evaluate the quality of support provided to makers and their awareness of internal resources, such as user communities or forums. Questions in this section can also capture recommendations for improving support services.

- **Overall experience and feedback**: Open-ended questions allow makers to share what they like most about Power Platform, suggest improvements, and rate how likely they are to recommend the platform to others.

By gathering data through these surveys, organizations can measure progress over time, identify gaps in knowledge or satisfaction, and adapt their training and support strategies accordingly. Surveys are especially useful because they offer a direct line of communication between makers and administrators, ensuring that user feedback is heard and acted upon.

Usage analytics

Another crucial channel for gathering data on makers' knowledge and engagement is usage analytics. Power Platform provides built-in tools to track and monitor how makers are using the platform, offering insight into usage patterns, application-building frequency, and adoption trends across the organization:

- **Active makers and application creation rates**: By analyzing data on the number of active makers – those who are consistently building applications or automating processes – organizations can assess how well Power Platform is being adopted. High maker activity suggests that employees are confident in their abilities and are integrating the platform into their workflows.

- **Application usage and deployment metrics**: Tracking how many applications are created and how frequently they're deployed helps determine the value and impact of Power Platform within the organization. For example, a low number of deployed applications might indicate that makers are struggling to turn their ideas into functional solutions, while high deployment rates suggest successful adoption and practical application.

- **Process automation analytics**: Monitoring the usage of automation workflows in Power Automate provides insight into how effectively makers are using the platform to streamline processes. Metrics such as the number of workflows that have been created, executed, and maintained help evaluate whether makers are embracing automation as part of their day-to-day operations.

The CoE Starter Kit is a powerful tool for collecting and analyzing usage data across Power Platform. It provides pre-built dashboards that track active makers, application usage, and overall platform adoption. By leveraging these insights, organizations can make informed decisions about where to focus further training, support, or governance.

By leveraging these comprehensive usage and adoption metrics, organizations can gain a deeper understanding of how effectively their teams are utilizing Power Platform. This data-driven approach not only highlights areas of success but also uncovers opportunities for targeted interventions.

Using CoE analytics to assess makers' knowledge and satisfaction

The CoE Starter Kit offers a variety of analytics tools and dashboards to help organizations gather data on maker activity and satisfaction, providing valuable insights to assess the success of Power Platform rollouts. Let's consider some real-life examples of how organizations can leverage these tools to gather and analyze data, ensuring that they're not only measuring adoption but also identifying areas for improvement.

Monitoring active makers and application usage

Scenario: A large retail organization rolled out Power Platform to improve operational efficiency by empowering employees to create applications that automate manual processes. The CoE Starter Kit allowed them to track how many employees were actively using the platform to create applications and workflows:

- **Action**: Using the **Makers Dashboard** within the CoE, the IT department monitored metrics such as the **number of active makers** and **total applications created**. The dashboard provided insights into which departments were adopting the platform and how engaged users were in building solutions.

- **Result**: The data showed that while some departments had high maker activity, others were lagging. The organization used this insight to target additional training sessions in underperforming departments and increase overall adoption. After 3 months, the number of active makers grew by 25%, indicating a successful increase in platform engagement.

Tracking application performance and user satisfaction

Scenario: A financial services company wanted to evaluate how Power Apps was being used to improve internal processes, such as customer data management and reporting. They needed a way to track application performance and gather user feedback to ensure that the applications were delivering the expected value:

- **Action**: The CoE Starter Kit provided **App Analytics**, which tracked application usage, execution times, and user feedback. The organization set up custom forms that prompted users to provide feedback after interacting with the applications. This feedback was automatically logged in the CoE's database.

- **Result**: By combining application performance metrics with user satisfaction data, the company identified two underperforming applications with poor satisfaction ratings. They were able to troubleshoot the issues, make updates to improve user experience, and track the impact of these changes. After these improvements, satisfaction scores rose by 30%, and application usage increased by 15%.

Measuring the adoption of citizen development

Scenario: A healthcare provider implemented Power Platform to reduce its reliance on the IT department for small, day-to-day application development needs. The goal was to foster a culture of **citizen development** by encouraging non-technical staff to build simple applications:

- **Action**: The IT team used the **CoE's Adoption Metrics Dashboard** to track the number of citizen developers and their contribution to application development. The dashboard provided insights into how many non-technical staff were using Power Apps and Power Automate to create solutions for their teams.

- **Result**: Initially, the data showed that only 10% of citizen developers were actively building applications. To address this, the organization launched a dedicated training program and provided additional support. Over the next 6 months, the number of active citizen developers doubled, and more than 40% of applications in production were built by non-IT employees.

Gathering insights into user training and support needs

Scenario: A manufacturing company introduced Power Automate to streamline production workflows and wanted to ensure that employees were well-supported during the transition. They needed data on how many employees were using Power Automate and where additional training was required:

- **Action**: The CoE Starter Kit's **Training Dashboard** allowed the company to track training participation and feedback. It also tracked which users were struggling with specific workflows by monitoring failed automation runs and the number of support tickets related to Power Automate.

- **Result**: The data revealed that a particular department was facing high failure rates with their automation workflows, which also correlated with low training attendance. The organization scheduled targeted follow-up training and created support materials for that department. As a result, workflow failures dropped by 40%, and employee satisfaction with Power Automate improved.

Identifying usage patterns and customizing support

Scenario: A global consulting firm deployed Power BI, Power Apps, and Power Automate across various locations and wanted to understand usage patterns to ensure that each tool was being adopted effectively.

They also wanted to know whether employees were satisfied with the platform or encountering difficulties:

- **Action**: Using the CoE's **Usage Analytics**, the firm monitored the frequency of tool usage, identifying which teams were adopting Power Platform tools and which teams weren't as engaged. They also distributed periodic satisfaction surveys, integrated with Power BI, to gather insights on user experience and the effectiveness of the tools.

- **Result**: The analytics results showed that while Power BI adoption was strong, Power Automate was underutilized in certain regions. Feedback from the satisfaction surveys revealed that employees in those regions found Power Automate confusing and needed more localized training. By customizing the support that was provided and providing region-specific workshops, Power Automate adoption increased by 35% in those locations.

Leveraging the analytics and data visualization tools within the CoE Starter Kit provides organizations with a clear view of how Power Platform is being adopted, where makers are succeeding, and where challenges exist. By using components such as the Makers Dashboard, App Analytics, Adoption Metrics, and Training Dashboards, organizations can gather critical data on user engagement and satisfaction. This real-time feedback helps tailor support strategies, foster citizen development, and ensure that Power Platform rollouts deliver sustained value across the organization.

The insights and data that are gathered from these tools not only help in customizing training and support but also play a crucial role in enhancing community engagement within the organization.

Community engagement and collaboration

Creating a **community of practice** for Power Platform users within the organization is another effective channel for gathering feedback and assessing maker satisfaction. By fostering collaboration and knowledge-sharing, organizations can provide makers with a space to ask questions, share best practices, and offer feedback on their experiences with Power Platform:

- **Internal forums or discussion boards**: Setting up internal forums where makers can discuss their Power Platform projects, ask for advice, and troubleshoot challenges encourages collaboration. Administrators can monitor these discussions to identify common pain points or knowledge gaps, as well as areas where makers excel. Active engagement in these forums indicates a thriving user community, while frequent questions or complaints can signal the need for additional resources or training.

- **Workshops and office hours**: Hosting regular Power Platform workshops or office hours provides makers with direct access to platform experts who can answer their questions, offer tips, and guide them through complex challenges. Feedback gathered during these sessions offers valuable insights into makers' learning needs and satisfaction levels.

- **User groups and hackathons**: Organizing user groups or hackathons where makers can collaborate on Power Platform projects not only fosters innovation but also serves as a channel to gather real-time feedback on the platform's tools and features. Observing how makers work together to solve problems using Power Platform can reveal both strengths and areas for improvement in the platform's user experience.

Community engagement provides qualitative data that goes beyond numbers and statistics, offering deeper insights into how makers feel about their experiences, what motivates them, and how they interact with Power Platform in their daily tasks.

Real-life examples of Power Platform community engagement and collaboration

In this section, we will consider some real-life examples of Power Platform community engagement.

Power Platform user groups and knowledge sharing

Scenario: A global insurance company wanted to promote collaboration and encourage employees to share best practices for building Power Apps and automating workflows. To achieve this, they established an **internal Power Platform user group** where employees from different departments could come together to discuss their projects, ask questions, and offer advice to their peers:

- **Action**: The company set up regular **monthly virtual meetups** where makers could present their application-building experiences and share solutions they had developed using Power Apps and Power Automate. They also created a dedicated **internal forum** on Microsoft Teams where employees could post questions, share documentation, and collaborate on application development challenges.

- **Result**: By fostering this community of practice, the company saw a significant increase in application creation across departments since makers began learning from one another and sharing solutions that could be replicated or adapted by other teams. User satisfaction also improved as employees felt supported by their peers and had a space to learn from others' experiences. This collaborative approach helped democratize development, leading to a 40% increase in applications created by non-IT staff.

Hackathons to drive innovation and collaboration

Scenario: A healthcare organization looking to improve operational efficiency through innovation decided to host an annual **Power Platform hackathon**. The goal was to bring together makers from various departments so that they could collaborate on developing new solutions using Power Apps, Power Automate, and Power BI:

- **Action**: The organization invited employees with varying levels of experience, including beginners, to form cross-functional teams. Each team was tasked with identifying a business challenge and building a prototype application or workflow to address it.

Mentors from the IT department and Power Platform champions provided guidance throughout the event.

- **Result**: The hackathon not only produced several viable solutions that were later adopted within the organization but also boosted maker engagement by encouraging collaboration across different departments. The event fostered a strong sense of community and excitement around using Power Platform to solve real-world problems. After the hackathon, participants reported higher confidence in using Power Platform tools and felt more motivated to continue building solutions for their teams.

Power Platform CoE office hours and expert support

Scenario: A large retail company implemented Power Platform to streamline business processes but noticed that some employees were hesitant to use the platform due to limited technical knowledge. To address this, the company's CoE introduced a series of *office hours* where employees could drop in virtually and receive expert guidance on Power Platform-related questions or challenges:

- **Action**: During these weekly office hours, Power Platform experts and experienced makers from the CoE made themselves available to answer technical questions, review application designs, and provide troubleshooting support. These office hours were also an opportunity for makers to share their project ideas and receive feedback from peers in a collaborative setting.

- **Result**: These sessions helped to build a sense of community and foster collaboration among employees who were using Power Platform. As a result, employees were more willing to experiment with the platform and create applications, knowing they had access to expert help and peer support when needed. This initiative led to increased maker confidence and greater adoption of Power Platform, particularly in departments that had previously been slow to adopt the tools.

Building a strong community of practice for Power Platform users within an organization through user groups, hackathons, and office hours fosters collaboration and engagement. These initiatives not only provide makers with a space to learn and share best practices but also help identify and resolve challenges, leading to a more successful and widespread adoption of Power Platform across the organization. By investing in community-building activities, organizations can drive innovation and ensure makers feel supported and empowered to create impactful solutions.

These sessions not only build community but also lay the groundwork for more structured feedback mechanisms. Next, we'll explore how direct maker feedback loops can further enhance innovation and align solutions with user needs.

Direct maker feedback loops

Finally, organizations should implement **feedback loops** that allow makers to provide continuous input on their experience with Power Platform. These can be automated mechanisms within the platform itself, as well as informal check-ins conducted by platform administrators:

- **In-tool feedback forms**: Integrating feedback forms directly into Power Platform's interface allows makers to submit feedback while using the platform. This can be done through prompts that ask makers to rate their experience with a specific feature or suggest improvements. These forms provide real-time feedback and can help identify issues as they arise, ensuring a proactive approach to problem-solving.

- **One-on-one check-ins**: Administrators and platform champions can schedule regular one-on-one or group check-ins with makers to discuss their ongoing experiences with Power Platform. These check-ins offer makers a chance to voice concerns, share success stories, and provide insights into how they're leveraging the platform.

- **Feedback on feature updates**: When new features are rolled out within Power Platform, it's important to gather feedback on how makers are responding to these updates. Are the new features intuitive? Do they improve the maker's workflow? This feedback can guide future development and ensure that the platform continues to meet user needs.

Summary

This chapter emphasized the importance of defining and tracking KPIs to measure the success of Power Platform initiatives. Effective KPI tracking ensures that Power Platform adoption aligns with business objectives, enabling organizations to optimize their strategies and monitor progress. This includes gathering baseline data on user engagement, using regular surveys to gauge satisfaction, and applying tools such as the CoE Starter Kit for real-time monitoring.

Practical steps were provided for setting and tracking KPIs, along with examples of how organizations can leverage tools such as Power BI, Power Automate, and Dataverse to automate and streamline the process. Additionally, this chapter highlighted the value of community engagement and diverse data channels, including maker feedback loops, to continuously refine the implementation and drive sustained success across the organization.

In the next chapter, we'll explore how AI-driven copilots are transforming the way organizations approach digital transformation. These AI copilots, integrated into platforms such as Power Platform, are designed to assist users in building, optimizing, and scaling solutions with greater efficiency. By examining the role of AI and how it enhances user capabilities, the next chapter will provide insights into the future landscape of digital transformation, where intelligent automation and machine learning drive innovation and operational excellence.

15

Embracing AI-Powered Copilots and Agents in Digital Transformation

Artificial intelligence (AI) is revolutionizing digital transformation, with AI-powered copilots at the forefront of this change. These intelligent assistants leverage advanced machine learning algorithms and natural language processing to interpret user inputs, provide context-aware recommendations, and automate complex workflows. By integrating seamlessly into a variety of platforms, AI copilots enhance user capabilities, making advanced technology accessible to both technical and non-technical users. This democratization of AI tools empowers organizations to optimize operations, reduce manual effort, and accelerate innovation.

In this chapter, we explore how AI-powered copilots are reshaping digital transformation strategies. These assistants are not merely tools for automation; they function as collaborative partners, assisting users in drafting content, analyzing data, generating insights, and managing projects with greater efficiency. Their integration into platforms such as Microsoft 365 demonstrates how AI can enhance productivity in everyday tasks, such as writing documents, creating presentations, and managing email communications. Beyond individual productivity, AI copilots have a transformative impact on organizational efficiency by fostering collaboration, enabling data-driven decision-making, and streamlining workflows across teams.

The following topics will be covered:

- From automation to generative intelligence with copilots
- Copilots within Power Platform
- Solution planning with Power Apps Plan Designer
- What are AI Agents
- Microsoft's answer to AI Agents

From automation to generative intelligence with copilots

AI-powered copilots are advanced assistants that leverage large language models (LLMs) to understand context, generate content, and provide actionable insights. These copilots represent a significant evolution in AI capabilities, shifting from rule-based systems to highly adaptive tools capable of interpreting natural language inputs. Unlike traditional automation tools, which require explicit programming, copilots make interactions more intuitive and user-friendly. By assisting in tasks such as drafting documents, analyzing data, generating reports, and automating workflows, they enhance productivity, support data-driven decision-making, and democratize access to technology for a broader audience.

The development of LLMs has propelled AI to unprecedented levels of sophistication. LLMs such as OpenAI's GPT series are trained on vast datasets, allowing them to generate human-like text, answer complex questions, and adapt to a variety of tasks. Generative AI, a subset of LLM applications, introduced a new paradigm where AI systems could not only analyze and respond but also create—be it drafting text, generating code, or even composing music. This ability to produce coherent, contextually relevant outputs revolutionized user expectations and applications of AI.

OpenAI, a pioneer in this domain, accelerated the adoption of AI through products such as ChatGPT. The release of ChatGPT highlighted the power of conversational AI, offering users an approachable and effective way to interact with AI systems. Its user-friendly design and remarkable versatility sparked widespread interest, quickly amassing millions of users, and driving the global adoption of generative AI technologies. OpenAI's success demonstrated the potential of LLMs not only in professional and academic settings but also in everyday tasks, from learning new concepts to streamlining work processes.

The growth of LLM usage has been exponential, fueled by advancements in computational power, the availability of massive datasets, and improved training techniques. AI copilots, a direct beneficiary of these developments, have become indispensable in platforms such as Microsoft 365, where they assist users in drafting emails, summarizing content, analyzing trends, and automating routine activities. Their integration into enterprise ecosystems bridges the gap between technical capabilities and user needs, making advanced technology accessible to professionals, students, and citizen developers alike.

Generative AI, powered by LLMs, has shifted the role of AI from a passive tool to an active collaborator. By understanding context, providing recommendations, and automating complex workflows, AI copilots amplify human potential and enable individuals to focus on creative and strategic endeavors. This transformation is not just about doing tasks faster but about redefining the nature of work, empowering users to achieve more with greater ease and efficiency.

AI-powered copilots are advanced assistants that use LLMs to improve user interactions and support tasks such as drafting and data analysis, enhancing productivity and accessibility. This evolution began with early AI efforts, progressing through machine learning to sophisticated LLMs. OpenAI's ChatGPT highlights this shift, highlighting the potential of conversational AI. These copilots turn AI into an active collaborator, allowing users to focus on creative tasks and reshaping the nature of work.

Integration into Microsoft 365

Microsoft 365 Copilot is a prime example of how AI-powered assistants can transform the way individuals and organizations approach their daily work. Seamlessly embedded into core applications such as Word, Excel, PowerPoint, Outlook, and Teams, Copilot enhances productivity and streamlines workflows by leveraging advanced AI capabilities directly within the tools users already know and trust. This integration eliminates the need to switch between applications or learn entirely new interfaces, enabling users to maximize efficiency without disrupting their established routines. Let's take a look at some of the Microsoft tools that have been infused with Copilot functionality:

- In Microsoft Word, Copilot revolutionizes the writing process by generating content from simple user prompts. Whether drafting a proposal, summarizing a lengthy report, or creating a formal letter, Copilot interprets the user's intent and provides a starting point, saving valuable time. Users can refine and adapt the suggestions, making the process both collaborative and intuitive. In *Figure 15.1*, you can see Copilot in Microsoft Word being used to generate content in a document.

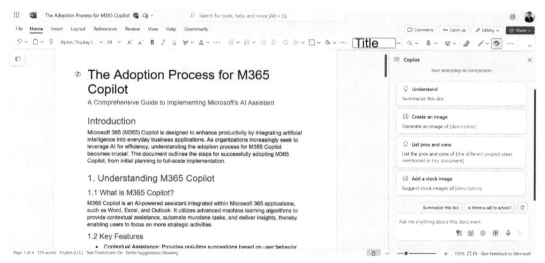

Figure 15.1: Copilot being used in Microsoft Word to generate content

- In Excel, Copilot acts as a data analyst, helping users uncover trends and insights with minimal effort. By interpreting queries in natural language, it simplifies tasks such as creating complex formulas, generating pivot tables, and visualizing data patterns. This functionality democratizes data analysis, empowering users with varying levels of technical expertise to extract actionable insights.

- PowerPoint users benefit from Copilot's ability to transform outlines or documents into polished presentations. By recommending slide layouts, adding visuals, and ensuring consistency in design, Copilot accelerates the creation of professional-grade slides. For users who may find presentation design daunting, Copilot provides a guiding hand, ensuring the focus remains on content and storytelling.

- In Outlook, Copilot reduces the burden of email management by drafting responses, summarizing lengthy threads, and prioritizing messages. This capability helps users maintain focus on high-priority tasks without getting bogged down by routine communication. Copilot also assists in scheduling and meeting preparation, providing summaries of previous discussions to ensure continuity and clarity.

- Microsoft Teams integrates Copilot to enhance collaboration and streamline meeting workflows. Copilot can prepare agendas, capture action items in real time, and generate meeting summaries that ensure alignment across team members. By acting as a virtual assistant, it reduces administrative overhead and keeps teams focused on achieving their objectives. In *Figure 15.2*, we can see Copilot being used in Microsoft Teams to generate a meeting agenda.

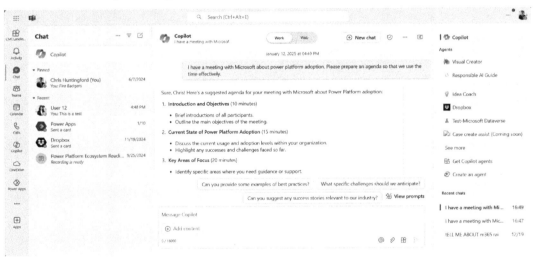

Figure 15.2: Copilot being used in Microsoft Teams

Beyond individual applications, Copilot's integration across the Microsoft 365 ecosystem allows for interconnected functionality. For instance, data analyzed in Excel can be seamlessly incorporated into a Word document or PowerPoint presentation, with Copilot providing context-aware recommendations throughout the process. This interconnectedness fosters a cohesive and efficient work environment, where AI not only enhances individual productivity but also drives team collaboration and organizational efficiency.

Microsoft 365 Copilot's design prioritizes accessibility and ease of use. By understanding natural language commands, it reduces the learning curve for unpracticed users while empowering seasoned professionals to work faster and smarter. The seamless integration of Copilot into Microsoft 365 reflects a broader vision of AI as a partner in productivity, enabling users to focus on strategic and creative endeavors while routine tasks are managed effortlessly.

Microsoft 365 Copilot exemplifies the transformative impact of AI-powered assistants on daily work for individuals and organizations. Integrated into familiar applications such as Word, Excel, PowerPoint, Outlook, and Teams, Copilot enhances productivity by streamlining workflows, allowing users to generate content, analyze data, create presentations, and manage emails with ease. This seamless functionality fosters collaboration and organizational efficiency, as users can leverage AI capabilities without needing to switch applications or learn new interfaces. By interpreting natural language commands, Copilot makes these tools accessible to all skill levels, prioritizing user experience and enabling professionals to focus on strategic tasks while routine functions are automated. In the next section, we will examine the copilot functionality available in several of the Power Platform tools.

Copilots within Power Platform

AI-powered copilots are revolutionizing the Power Platform ecosystem by enabling users to build, automate, and manage solutions with unprecedented ease and efficiency. These copilots leverage advanced AI models to interpret user inputs, provide intelligent suggestions, and automate complex tasks, making the development process more accessible for both technical and non-technical users. The integration of copilots across components such as Dataverse, Power Apps, Power Automate, and Power Pages demonstrates the Power Platform's commitment to democratizing technology and empowering makers at all skill levels. These copilots perform more tasks than makers would ordinarily do manually, making the build time a lot shorter. In fact, copilots are so prevalent in the Power Platform maker experience that as soon as the user opens the maker portal, they are presented with the opportunity to leverage a copilot. This is evident in *Figure 15.3*.

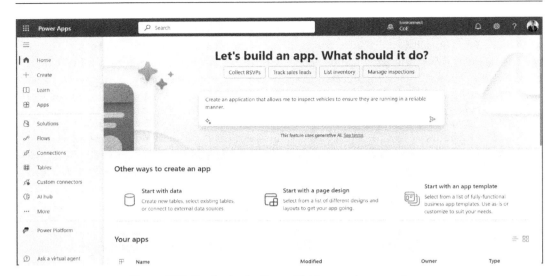

Figure 15.3: Copilot in the Power Platform maker experience

Dataverse model creation

Dataverse is the foundational data platform for Power Platform, and its integration with AI copilots simplifies the process of creating and managing data models. Traditionally, designing a relational data model required significant technical expertise, from defining entities/tables to establishing relationships and implementing data validations. Copilots in Dataverse reduce this complexity by automating much of the groundwork.

Using natural language, users can describe the type of application they want to build or the data they need to manage, and the copilot translates these descriptions into a structured data model. For example, a user might prompt the copilot with, "Create a data model for tracking customer interactions and support tickets", and the copilot will generate relevant tables, relationships, and attributes, including suggestions for data types and field validations. In *Figure 15.4*, natural language has been used to request the creation of a facilities management data model.

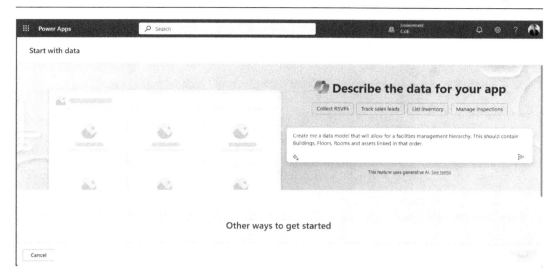

Figure 15.4: Using natural language to set up the start of a facilities management data model

Once the model is created, it can then be refined in the maker's experience. In *Figure 15.5*, the result of the prompt used in *Figure 15.4* can be seen. There are four tables that have been created with some base columns. These tables have been linked together to form the data model.

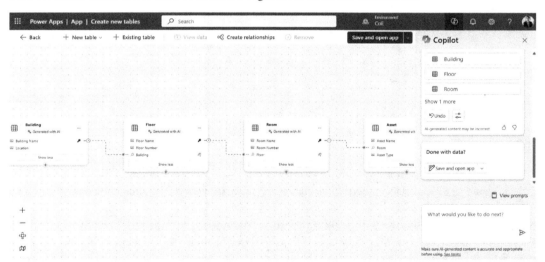

Figure 15.5: The data model that has been created because of the facilities management prompt

The copilot also assists in refining and optimizing models by analyzing data patterns and usage trends. It can recommend improvements, such as adding indexes to frequently queried fields or normalizing data structures for better performance. This capability allows makers to focus on higher-level design considerations while ensuring that the underlying data platform is robust and efficient.

Canvas apps

Canvas apps are a cornerstone of the Power Platform, offering a highly visual, drag-and-drop interface for building applications. Copilots in canvas apps make the app-building process even more intuitive by guiding users in creating app layouts, adding functionality, and optimizing the user experience.

For instance, a user can describe the purpose of the app, such as "I need an app to manage employee timesheets," and the copilot will generate a preliminary layout with screens for time entry, approval workflows, and reporting. The copilot also provides intelligent suggestions for controls, such as date pickers, drop-down menus, or file upload fields, based on the app's intended functionality. In *Figure 15.6*, canvas apps can be extended and configured by using the embedded copilot functionality.

Figure 15.6: Copilot leveraged within canvas apps to assist with the creation of the app

Copilots in canvas apps assist with formula creation, reducing the complexity of Power FX, the platform's low-code programming language. Users can describe their requirements in plain language – such as "Calculate the total hours worked this week for each employee" – and the copilot generates the corresponding Power FX formula. This significantly lowers the learning curve for new makers while enhancing the productivity of experienced developers.

Power Automate

Power Automate copilots streamline the creation of workflows by enabling users to design automations through conversational inputs. Instead of manually selecting triggers and actions, users can describe their process in natural language, and the copilot builds a flow accordingly. For example, a user might say, "Set up a flow that sends an email to my manager whenever a new sales lead is added to Dataverse," and the copilot will generate the corresponding automation.

The copilot also provides recommendations for optimizing workflows, such as suggesting error-handling mechanisms or identifying opportunities to consolidate redundant steps. Additionally, it analyzes workflow performance and offers insights to improve efficiency, such as using batch processing for large datasets or adjusting triggers to reduce unnecessary executions. In *Figure 15.7*, the copilot functionality is being leveraged to understand what this flow does.

Figure 15.7: Copilot being leveraged in Power Automate as a
mechanism to understand what this cloud flow does

Power Automate copilots enhance accessibility by integrating with a wide range of connectors, enabling users to automate processes that span multiple systems. By simplifying flow creation and optimization, copilots empower makers to automate complex tasks with confidence and precision.

Power Pages

Power Pages copilots bring the power of AI to website creation and management, enabling users to design, build, and customize web portals with minimal effort. Users can start by describing their website requirements in natural language, such as "Create a customer portal for submitting and tracking support tickets." The copilot generates a starter template with relevant pages, navigation, and forms pre-configured.

Beyond layout generation, the copilot assists in content creation by drafting page copy, suggesting SEO keywords, and optimizing accessibility features. It also helps users configure backend integrations, such as connecting forms to Dataverse for data storage or setting up role-based access controls to secure sensitive information. In *Figure 15.8*, Copilot is being used to help with the site design and navigation.

Figure 15.8: Copilot functionality in Microsoft Power Pages

For developers, the copilot simplifies the customization process by providing code snippets or configurations for advanced functionalities, such as adding custom APIs or embedding Power BI dashboards. This allows users to tailor their web portals to specific business needs while maintaining an elevated level of usability and design consistency.

We are seeing the addition of copilot to more and more Power Platform products and the capability is being hugely enhanced. In writing this book we are aware of many pieces of copilot-related functionality in public preview, such as the utilization of copilot to generate model-driven apps. We expect this functionality to become more widespread and commonplace as the technology advances.

A key point to make here is that copilots help makers build solutions and enhance the creation experience greatly, however, we have not gone into depth about the ability for users to use copilots within the solutions that have been created. This is currently available in Power Apps and Power Pages and allows users to interact with the user experience and data using natural language in the copilot panel.

AI-powered copilots are revolutionizing the Power Platform by simplifying solution development and management for users of all skill levels. They automate complex tasks through natural language processing, allowing users to create data models in Dataverse, build apps in canvas apps, model-driven apps, design workflows in Power Automate, and develop websites in Power Pages with ease. By providing intelligent suggestions and optimizing processes, these copilots enhance productivity and promote accessibility, empowering makers to focus on higher-level design while efficiently leveraging technology. In the next section, we will explore how Power Apps Plan Designer uses AI to help you start your Power Platform projects.

Solution planning with Power Apps Plan Designer

The PowerApps Plan Designer is a groundbreaking tool that leverages AI to guide makers through the initial stages of designing user-focused, intelligent solutions. Recognizing that planning is a critical but often challenging step in app development, Microsoft introduced Plan Designer to streamline and optimize this process. By integrating AI capabilities, it enables makers to craft effective solutions tailored to their unique business needs with minimal effort.

How Plan Designer works

Plan Designer simplifies the planning process by combining natural language inputs with contextual AI recommendations. Makers begin by describing their business problems, goals, and expected outcomes. For example, a user might input, "I need an app to track and manage the facilities and assets within my organization." Plan Designer uses this information to generate a comprehensive starting point for the app. In *Figure 15.9*, Plan Designer is being used to facilitate the creation of a facilities management solution.

Figure 15.9: Plan Designer being leveraged to facilitate the creation of a facilities management solution

The Plan Designer allows us to create these incredible, documented, bundles solutions that provide a great start to a useful solution. This is one of the most innovative sets of functionality we have seen come out in the Power Platform tool set and we believe that it hugely accelerates the gap to getting started with a strong solution.

The future of solution planning with AI

Power Apps Plan Designer represents a shift toward intelligent, user-focused app development. By leveraging AI, it transforms a traditionally complex phase into an intuitive and efficient process. As the Power Platform continues to evolve, Plan Designer will integrate even more advanced capabilities, such as predictive analytics and deeper automation suggestions, further empowering makers to build impactful solutions with ease.

Plan Designer exemplifies how AI can enhance every stage of the app development lifecycle, making it an indispensable tool for organizations aiming to innovate quickly and effectively.

Key functionalities

The following are some of the key functionalities of Plan Designer:

- **Contextual analysis**: The AI analyzes the provided input, business context, and any attached process diagrams or data models to understand the requirements fully

- **Role identification**: It identifies and recommends user roles, such as HR managers, trainers, and new employees, based on the described solution

- **Data model recommendations**: Plan Designer proposes relevant data tables, fields, and relationships for use in Dataverse, ensuring the data structure aligns with the app's purpose

- **Automation suggestions**: It suggests Power Automate workflows that could enhance the solution, such as triggering email notifications for training completion or onboarding progress tracking

By automating these initial steps, Plan Designer reduces the cognitive load on makers, allowing them to focus on refining and personalizing their solutions.

Advantages

Now, let's explore some of the benefits of using Plan Designer:

- **Streamlined planning**: By automating complex tasks such as data modeling and workflow design, Plan Designer eliminates much of the guesswork in solution planning

- **User-centric approach**: Its ability to recommend user roles ensures that the app design aligns with the needs of its intended audience, fostering better adoption and usability

- **Consistency and best practices**: The AI incorporates established best practices into its recommendations, ensuring that the resulting solution is efficient and scalable

- **Accelerated development**: By providing a sturdy foundation, Plan Designer shortens the development cycle, allowing makers to move quickly from concept to implementation

In conclusion, Power Apps Plan Designer transforms the app development process by using AI to streamline planning and enhance efficiency. By enabling creators to easily articulate their business needs, it ensures the design of user-centric solutions. As it continues to evolve, this tool will play a crucial role in helping organizations innovate quickly and effectively. Using this tool allows makers to truly leverage the power of AI in the power Platform to help make project planning and execution successful. In the next section, we will take a look at another form of Power-Platform-related AI infused into Copilot Studio in the form of AI Agents.

What are AI Agents?

We are now in the era of the "AI Agent." Agents are AI-driven systems designed to perform specific tasks or functions with precision and efficiency. They operate based on pre-programmed rules, sophisticated learning algorithms, or advanced autonomous decision-making capabilities. These AI Agents serve as the cornerstone of AI integration, bridging the gap between human intent and actionable outcomes seamlessly.

AI Agents can be categorized into several types, each offering unique functionalities and levels of autonomy. These range from simple rule-based Agents that follow strict guidelines to complex fully autonomous Agents capable of making independent decisions and adapting to new situations. By leveraging the strengths of different AI Agents, organizations can enhance operational efficiency, improve customer service, and drive innovation in industries such as healthcare, logistics, and finance.

The versatility of AI Agents allows them to be deployed in diverse applications, from automating routine tasks to providing personalized recommendations and insights. As technology continues to evolve, the potential for AI Agents to transform various sectors and create new opportunities is boundless.

Types of AI Agents

Let's look into the following types of AI Agents.

Rule-based Agents

These Agents operate strictly according to predefined rules and instructions, which makes them highly predictable and dependable for specific tasks. They do not possess the capability to learn from past experiences or adapt to new situations. Ideal applications for rule-based Agents include simple, repetitive tasks such as filtering spam emails, regulating thermostats, and managing inventory levels. Due to their limited scope, they are best suited for environments where the conditions and requirements remain stable and do not require complex decision-making.

Semi-autonomous Agents

These Agents combine programmed rules with learning capabilities. They can analyze data and adapt their actions based on past experiences, although they still require human oversight. Semi-autonomous Agents are often found in applications such as **robotic process automation** (**RPA**), where they automate repetitive tasks while being able to adjust operations based on new data. Additionally, these Agents are used in autonomous vehicles, which can navigate and make driving decisions by learning from real-time traffic data and historical patterns. By blending rule-based actions with adaptive learning, semi-autonomous Agents offer a balanced approach to handling tasks that need both consistency and flexibility.

Fully autonomous Agents

Fully autonomous Agents operate independently, making decisions and improving their actions over time without human intervention. These Agents leverage advanced machine learning algorithms and deep neural networks to analyze vast amounts of data, recognize patterns, and make informed decisions. Their ability to learn from experience and adapt to new situations makes them highly versatile and valuable in dynamic environments.

In *Figure 15.10*, we can see a breakdown of the three Agent types and a simple summary of when to select each type.

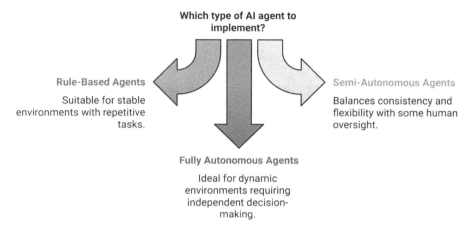

Figure 15.10: A summary of the various Agent types with a simple breakdown of when to choose each one

In healthcare, fully autonomous Agents can be used for continuous patient monitoring, real-time diagnosis, and personalized treatment recommendations. In logistics, these Agents optimize supply chain operations, manage inventory levels, and enhance delivery efficiencies. Additionally, they are being explored in fields such as autonomous driving, where they can navigate complex traffic scenarios, make split-second decisions, and improve overall road safety.

While still emerging, these Agents represent the future of AI, with the potential to revolutionize industries and create unprecedented levels of efficiency and innovation.

Practical uses of AI Agents

Let's find out about some of the practical uses of AI Agents:

- **Customer service**: Chatbots and virtual assistants streamline customer interactions by providing instant, accurate responses

- **Healthcare**: AI Agents assist in diagnostics, personalized treatment plans, and remote monitoring of patients

- **Finance**: Fraud detection systems and automated trading Agents optimize security and efficiency

- **Education**: Intelligent tutoring systems deliver customized learning experiences based on student performance and needs

- **Home automation**: Smart devices such as thermostats and security cameras use AI Agents to enhance comfort and safety

- **Manufacturing**: AI Agents optimize production processes, predict maintenance needs, and ensure quality control

- **Retail**: Personalized shopping experiences and inventory management are enhanced by AI Agents analyzing customer behavior

- **Energy management**: AI Agents improve energy efficiency by controlling power usage and predicting energy demands

- **Transportation**: Route optimization and predictive maintenance for public transit systems are managed by AI Agents

- **Agriculture**: AI Agents aid in precision farming by monitoring crop health, predicting yields, and optimizing resource use

- **Entertainment**: AI Agents create personalized content recommendations and enhance user experiences in gaming and streaming services

Figure 15.11 summarizes the various industry examples in a more cohesive way, showing agentic AI as the center of process optimization and transformation.

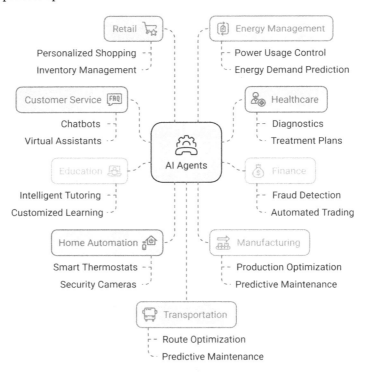

Figure 15.11: A summary of various industry examples with agentic AI in the center

AI Agents are advanced, AI-driven systems designed to perform specific tasks efficiently, utilizing pre-programmed rules, learning algorithms, or autonomous decision-making. They vary in complexity from simple rule-based Agents to fully autonomous Agents that can learn and adapt independently. These Agents enhance operational efficiency and innovation across numerous industries, including healthcare, logistics, finance, and customer service, with practical applications such as chatbots, personalized medicine, and automated trading. As technology progresses, the versatility and potential of AI Agents to revolutionize various sectors continue to expand. In the next section, we will look at Microsoft's answer to AI-infused Agents.

Microsoft's answer to Agents

Microsoft has made incredible strides in the development and integration of AI Agents through the Power Platform. The Power Platform enables organizations to build, analyze, automate, and chat with customized AI-driven solutions, thereby enhancing productivity and efficiency across various industries.

Copilot Studio – creating AI-powered AI Agents

Copilot Studio is a tool that allows users to create intelligent Agents without the need for extensive coding knowledge. These Agents can engage with customers, answer queries, and perform tasks based on predefined rules and AI capabilities. For example, a retail company might deploy an Agent to assist customers with product recommendations, order tracking, and returns processing. The Agent can leverage AI to understand natural language queries and provide personalized responses based on customer history and preferences. Another example is a healthcare provider using an Agent to schedule appointments, provide medication reminders, and answer common health-related questions, improving patient engagement and satisfaction.

It is important to understand that agentic behavior is not simply an AI-infused chatbot or copilot; it is far more than that. agentic solutions contain elevated levels of automation that assist in the flow of information and processes in a highly intelligent manner.

Consider a scenario in the customer support industry where a company is grappling with high volumes of customer inquiries, leading to long wait times and decreased customer satisfaction. By deploying Agents created using Microsoft's Copilot Studio, the company can significantly enhance its customer service operations.

These intelligent Agents can handle a wide array of customer interactions, from answering frequently asked questions to processing returns and tracking orders. By understanding natural language queries, these Agents can provide instant, accurate responses tailored to each customer's needs. For instance, an Agent could assist customers in troubleshooting technical issues by guiding them through step-by-step solutions, thereby reducing the need for human intervention and speeding up resolution times.

These Agents can learn from past interactions to continuously improve their performance. They can analyze patterns in customer inquiries to identify common issues and proactively address them, further enhancing the customer experience. This level of automation not only alleviates the workload on human support staff but also ensures that customers receive timely and efficient service, leading to higher satisfaction and loyalty.

The key point to make here is that these Agents learn and get better over time, which promotes a whole new level of intelligent automation that hugely helps organizations evolve in the way they view process automation and productivity.

Creating Agents

Makers can easily create Agents within the Power Platform. There are two primary methods for doing this depending on the current tools you have available to you in your ecosystem. Agents can be created directly through the Copilot Studio maker portal. This can be seen in *Figure 15.12* where the simple conversational user experience is used to create an Agent.

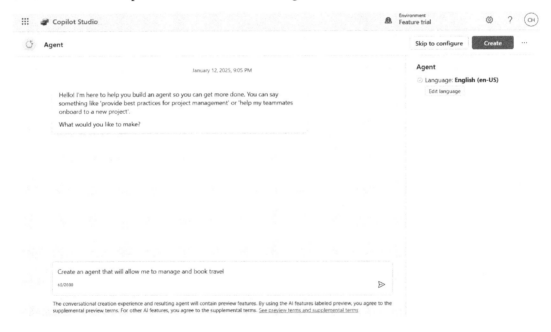

Figure 15.12: Creating an Agent in the Copilot Studio maker portal

As you progress through the process, you will have the chance to add more content, such as further instructions, which act as an initial prompt to help set context and some guardrails, knowledge sources, deterministic topics, and actions. This is visible in *Figure 15.13* where the Agent is being further refined and configured.

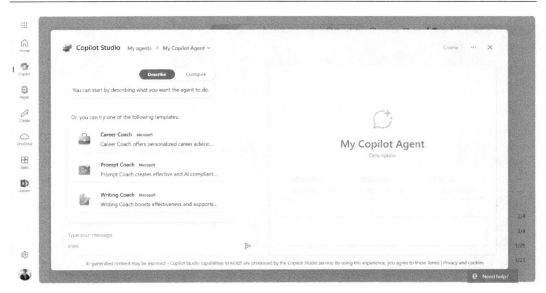

Figure 15.13: Configuring an Agent in Copilot Studio

The new Agent designer is embedded directly within the Microsoft 365 Copilot user interface where makers can create Agents within this experience. These Agents can then be initiated directly through the Microsoft 365 Copilot experience. *Figure 15.14* shows that these Agents can be built with relative ease by makers.

Figure 15.14: Creating an Agent directly from the Microsoft 365 Copilot user experience

Some of the key points to consider when creating these Agents, and what makes these copilots truly agentic are the following:

- What data is this Agent grounded in? It is important to ensure that the Agent has the correct knowledge sources associated with it so that it is grounded in reliable data. The better and more refined the data, the better the responses will be.

- Actions and automations! A standard copilot may generate content but not actually undertake or perform actions. Agents will perform actions leveraging automation. In copilot studio, one of the primary methods for performing these actions is by leveraging Power Automate. As shown in *Figure 15.15*, leveraging Power Automate is a fantastic way to create Copilot Studio actions.

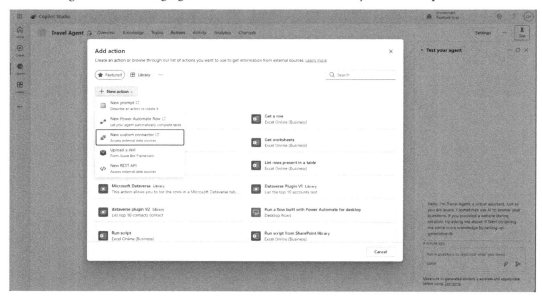

Figure 15.15: Creating actions within Copilot Studio Agents

Ultimately, Copilot Studio Agents are extremely powerful and allow makers to leverage their current Power Platform skills to create AI Agents. Understanding Copilot Studio, connectors, Power Automate, plugins, and Dataverse is extremely valuable in this process and the skills Power Platform users have learned in the past are extremely valuable right now. To learn more about creating Agents using Copilot Studio, go and take a look at Microsoft Learn for more information: `https://learn.microsoft.com/en-us/training/modules/power-virtual-agents-bots/`. There are some fantastic learning paths available.

Microsoft's advancements in AI Agents through Power Platform represent a significant leap for organizations looking to enhance productivity. The Copilot Studio tools empower users, regardless of their coding experience, to develop intelligent Agents that can interact with customers, answer questions, and automate various tasks. We believe these Agents have the potential to greatly improve many areas of organizations, such as customer service, by efficiently managing inquiries, delivering personalized responses, and learning from previous interactions to boost their performance. The creation process is user-friendly, thanks to the integrated Agent designer in Microsoft 365 Copilot, which ensures that these Agents are based on reliable data and can execute actions through Power Automate. This approach is transforming how organizations manage automation and drive efficiency.

Responsible AI

When developing AI-infused solutions, it is crucial to consider Microsoft's Responsible AI principles, which are designed to ensure that AI technologies are developed and implemented in a manner that is ethical, transparent, and accountable. These principles include fairness, reliability and safety, privacy and security, inclusiveness, transparency, and accountability.

Fairness ensures that AI systems treat all individuals and groups equitably, preventing discrimination and bias. Reliability and safety focus on creating robust and secure AI systems that perform consistently and safely under a variety of conditions. Privacy and security emphasize safeguarding personal data and respecting user privacy, ensuring that AI solutions comply with data protection regulations.

Inclusiveness highlights the importance of designing AI systems that are accessible and beneficial to all, including marginalized and underrepresented groups. Transparency involves making AI systems understandable and explainable to users, allowing them to trust and effectively interact with these technologies. Finally, accountability ensures that individuals and organizations developing and deploying AI systems are responsible for their impact and outcomes.

By adhering to these principles, developers and organizations can build AI-infused solutions that are not only innovative and efficient but also ethical and trustworthy, fostering greater acceptance and a positive impact on society.

Summary

The evolution of Agents within the Power Platform signifies a monumental shift in intelligent automation, empowering organizations to enhance productivity and streamline processes. This journey began with the introduction of the Copilot Studio maker portal and the Microsoft 365 Copilot user experience – tools that provide makers with the ability to effortlessly create and configure Agents. These Agents are meticulously grounded in reliable data, ensuring accuracy and efficiency, and can execute complex actions through Power Automate, thereby transforming routine tasks into automated processes.

One of the most remarkable features of these Agents is their ability to learn and improve over time through machine learning algorithms and continuous data inputs, allowing them to adapt to new scenarios and optimize performance. This capability transforms intelligent automation and alters how organizations view process automation. Knowledge of existing Power Platform skills is invaluable for creators to build AI Agents that enhance customer service and operational efficiency by accurately handling queries, seamlessly managing workflows, and providing unprecedented insights. However, the development of these AI-infused solutions must align with Microsoft's Responsible AI principles, which emphasize fairness, reliability, safety, privacy, security, inclusiveness, transparency, and accountability. These principles guide ethical AI development, ensuring that technologies are equitable, secure, and beneficial to all segments of society while fostering trust through clear and accountable operations.

The journey of creating intelligent Agents within the Power Platform is a testament to the transformative power of AI. It promises a future where automation and efficiency are harmoniously integrated with ethical principles, ensuring that technological advancements contribute positively to societal progress. As organizations continue to innovate and build upon these foundations, the potential for AI to revolutionize industries and improve lives becomes increasingly evident.

As we wrap up these 15 chapters and think about what is possible for ourselves as well as our organizations, we must always keep in mind that humans are the most important when it comes to change and adoption. Technology is simply a catalyst that can be physically seen to promote change, but the people are the ones who really matter. As we move into this era of AI, it is important to remember that the Power Platform has taught us some amazing fundamentals about how to create a safe space for people to both use and build AI-infused solutions. Everything you have learned in this book today can be re-applied when driving digital transformation programs for your business across many types of technology.

Victor and I thank you for spending your time reading this book.

Get This Book's PDF Version and Exclusive Extras

UNLOCK NOW

Scan the QR code (or go to `packtpub.com/unlock`). Search for this book by name, confirm the edition, and then follow the steps on the page.

Note: Keep your invoice handy. Purchases made directly from Packt don't require one.

16
Unlock Your Exclusive Benefits

Your copy of this book includes the following exclusive benefit:

- ☁ Next-gen Packt Reader
- 📄 DRM-free PDF/ePub downloads

Follow the guide below to unlock them. The process takes only a few minutes and needs to be completed once.

Unlock this Book's Free Benefits in 3 Easy Steps

Step 1

Keep your purchase invoice ready for *Step 3*. If you have a physical copy, scan it using your phone and save it as a PDF, JPG, or PNG.

For more help on finding your invoice, visit `https://www.packtpub.com/unlock-benefits/help`.

> **Note**
>
> If you bought this book directly from Packt, no invoice is required. After *Step 2*, you can access your exclusive content right away.

Step 2

Scan the QR code or go to `packtpub.com/unlock`.

On the page that opens (similar to *Figure 16.1* on desktop), search for this book by name and select the correct edition.

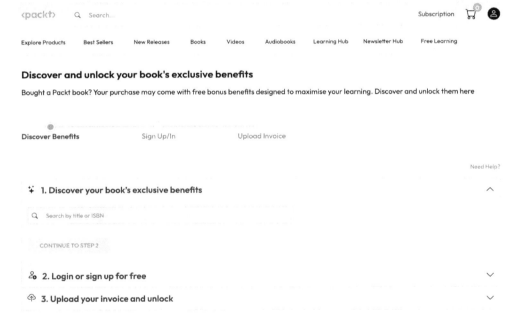

Figure 16.1: Packt unlock landing page on desktop

Step 3

After selecting your book, sign in to your Packt account or create one for free. Then upload your invoice (PDF, PNG, or JPG, up to 10 MB). Follow the on-screen instructions to finish the process.

Need help?

If you get stuck and need help, visit
`https://www.packtpub.com/unlock-benefits/help`
for a detailed FAQ on how to find your invoices and more. This QR
code will take you to the help page.

> **Note**
>
> If you are still facing issues, reach out to `customercare@packt.com`.

Index

packtpub.com

Subscribe to our online digital library for full access to over 7,000 books and videos, as well as industry leading tools to help you plan your personal development and advance your career. For more information, please visit our website.

Why subscribe?

- Spend less time learning and more time coding with practical eBooks and Videos from over 4,000 industry professionals

- Improve your learning with Skill Plans built especially for you

- Get a free eBook or video every month

- Fully searchable for easy access to vital information

- Copy and paste, print, and bookmark content

Did you know that Packt offers eBook versions of every book published, with PDF and ePub files available? You can upgrade to the eBook version at packtpub.com and as a print book customer, you are entitled to a discount on the eBook copy. Get in touch with us at customercare@packtpub.com for more details.

At www.packtpub.com, you can also read a collection of free technical articles, sign up for a range of free newsletters, and receive exclusive discounts and offers on Packt books and eBooks.

Other Books You May Enjoy

If you enjoyed this book, you may be interested in these other books by Packt:

Microsoft Power Apps Cookbook – Third Edition

Eickhel Mendoza

ISBN: 978-1-83546-515-8

- Develop responsive apps with Canvas and Model-Driven frameworks
- Leverage AI-powered Copilot to accelerate your app development
- Automate business processes with Power Automate cloud flows
- Build custom UI components with the Power Apps Component Framework
- Implement data integration strategies using Dataverse
- Optimize your app for performance and smooth user experiences
- Integrate Robotic Process Automation (RPA) and Desktop flows
- Build secure, scalable, external-facing websites using Microsoft Power Pages

Learn Microsoft Power Apps – Second Edition

Matthew Weston, Elisa Bárcena Martín

ISBN: 978-1-80107-064-5

- Understand the Power Apps ecosystem and licensing
- Take your first steps building canvas apps
- Develop apps using intermediate techniques such as the barcode scanner and GPS controls
- Explore new connectors to integrate tools across the Power Platform
- Store data in Dataverse using model-driven apps
- Discover the best practices for building apps cleanly and effectively
- Use AI for app development with AI Builder and Copilot

Packt is searching for authors like you

If you're interested in becoming an author for Packt, please visit `authors.packtpub.com` and apply today. We have worked with thousands of developers and tech professionals, just like you, to help them share their insight with the global tech community. You can make a general application, apply for a specific hot topic that we are recruiting an author for, or submit your own idea.

Share Your Thoughts

Now you've finished *The Power Platform Playbook for Digital Transformation*, we'd love to hear your thoughts! Scan the QR code below to go straight to the Amazon review page for this book and share your feedback or leave a review on the site that you purchased it from.

`https://packt.link/r/1-805-12139-1`

Your review is important to us and the tech community and will help us make sure we're delivering excellent quality content.

www.ingramcontent.com/pod-product-compliance
Lightning Source LLC
LaVergne TN
LVHW081514050326
832903LV00025B/1488